ADOBE® CREATIVE SUITE® 5
DESIGN PREMIUM
HOW-TOs
100 ESSENTIAL TECHNIQUES

SCOTT CITRON AND MICHAEL MURPHY

Adobe

Adobe Creative Suite 5 Design Premium How-Tos
100 Essential Techniques

Scott Citron and Michael Murphy

This Adobe Press book is published by Peachpit.

Peachpit
1249 Eighth Street
Berkeley, CA 94710
510/524-2178
510/524-2221 (fax)

Peachpit is a division of Pearson Education.

For the latest on Adobe Press books, go to www.adobepress.com.

To report errors, please send a note to errata@peachpit.com.

Editor: Rebecca Gulick
Production Editor: Hilal Sala
Development and Copy Editor: Kim Saccio-Kent
Copyeditor: Patricia Pane
Proofreader: Liz Merfeld
Cover and Interior Designer: Mimi Heft
Indexer: Valerie Haynes Perry
Technical Reviewer: Pierre Granier
Compositor: codeMantra

ISBN-13: 978-0-321-71985-0
ISBN-10:   0-321-71985-9

9 8 7 6 5 4 3 2 1

Printed and bound in the United States of America

Dedications

from Scott
I dedicate this book to my father, Al, the youngest old guy I know; and to Jennie P., for everything else.

from Michael
To Lee Ann, for hanging in there with me while the boys were baking and the world was imploding.

Acknowledgements

What began as a quick two-month writing job turned into a formidable six-month challenge.

On the surface, tackling this book seemed deceptively simple: come up with 100 tips, split the writing with a friend, cash the check. Little did we know the amount of work, research, testing, and learning it would actually require.

On that note, our thanks go out to the many smart folks we called upon when checking our facts and scratching our heads. Among them, Bob Levine (our go-to Windows guy), Mordy Golding (Illustrator savant), and most notably our web life-saver Chris Converse, who steered us through the turbulent waters of Dreamweaver and Flash bruised but intact, and a wee bit smarter.

We also thank Rebecca Gulick and Victor Gavenda at Peachpit and Adobe Press for making this project happen. To Kim Saccio-Kent, our Developmental Editor, for pushing us to go deeper and do better. To our Technical Editor, Pierre Granier, for making sure what we wrote actually worked, and to Hilal Sala for turning this all into a real book.

Misery loves—and needs—company. Because of that, we each thank our respective bright, witty, and devastatingly good-looking co-author (Why, thank you! No... thank you!).

And last, another round of applause for our friend Noha Edell of Adobe Systems, whose continued support we cherish.

Contents

CHAPTER ONE

Getting Started

Every new version of the Adobe Creative Suite brings with it an array of powerful new features. Creative Suite 5 (CS5) is no exception—from Photoshop's Content-Aware Fill and Puppet Warp to Illustrator's Perspective Drawing and Variable-width Strokes to InDesign's Grid-ified tools and rich-media document capabilities to Dreamweaver's CMS framework integration and HTML5 support to Flash Professional's new Text Layout Framework and under-the-hood physics engine.

Along with the updates to veteran applications, newcomers like Flash Catalyst and the CS Live suite of online services make the CS5 Design Premium edition an unprecedented set of creative, productivity, and publishing tools capable of transforming your visual communication across the ever-changing media landscape, from print, to the Web, to mobile devices.

Beyond the specific features, though, a new version of CS5 brings with it a fresh start—a chance to explore new creative possibilities, improve existing workflows, and learn new skills. Once you've peeled off the shrinkwrap and installed the new software, use this book to help you fast-track that process.

So let's get started.

#1 Synchronizing Suite Color Settings

Color Management in a Nutshell

Color management refers to accurate transmission of color information between a source (a Photoshop image, Illustrator drawing, or InDesign layout) and a destination (a monitor or printer).

The source contains information relating to its color. For example, a photo taken with a digital camera includes information about how the camera recorded color in that image file. A monitor is a destination for that image, and it requires information about how to display that color. Another destination, an inkjet printer, also requires information about how to reproduce that color. The color information stored within a source is referred to as a profile. An RGB display using three colors of light and a CMYK inkjet printer using ink each reproduce color in profoundly different ways, but each uses the source's profile to understand how to best render the desired color within its available color space.

(continued on next page)

Maintaining color consistency is a challenge that designers have been dealing with since the beginning of the digital design age. Precision color output ultimately relies on understanding the destination device (inkjet printer, offset printing press, RGB display, etc.) of your design and effectively communicating a project's color information to that device. For print projects, talking with your printer (the person, not the device) is highly recommended. Many printers will gladly provide you with well-tested settings files calibrated to their devices.

On a more general level, however, there are a few basic settings in CS5 that will get you off on a good foot toward reliable color outcome in most situations. The settings that we discuss in this tip apply to Photoshop, Illustrator, InDesign, and Acrobat only. Flash Professional, Flash Catalyst, and Dreamweaver do not include color-management tools.

Before diving into your next project, make sure to synchronize your color settings so that Photoshop, Illustrator, InDesign, and Acrobat are all on the same page. You can do this simultaneously (for all but Acrobat) from Adobe Bridge by choosing Edit > Creative Suite Color Settings. If you've ever modified one application's color settings separately, the dialog box may indicate that your settings are unsynchronized (**Figure 1a**).

Figure 1a Bridge CS5's Suite Color Settings dialog box indicating that the various suite applications are not using consistent color settings.

To synchronize Photoshop, Illustrator, and InDesign, click the Apply button, and the color setting selected in the dialog box will be applied to all applications. The default setting in the U.S. English version of CS5 is North America General Purpose 2, which includes specific settings for RGB and CMYK working spaces, color-management policies, and conversion options.

If you want to deviate from this default, you can modify the color settings in any of those applications (the Color Settings dialog boxes in each are nearly identical), then save your custom settings and apply them suite-wide from Bridge.

One change you might want to make is to the RGB working space. sRGB is the default, but sRGB is a relatively small color space. By changing that to Adobe RGB (1998) you broaden your working color space to the much wider dynamic range that CS5 applications are capable of. When picking a CMYK working space, it's best to choose the profile that your printer (the person, not the device) provides so that your translation between RGB images and CMYK printers is accurate and the best possible conversion for the specific printing destination occurs. With your settings changed to suit your needs, save them as a color-settings file (.csf). By default, they'll be stored in the same Settings folder where all other color-settings files are saved for CS5.

If a source and a destination know everything they can about one another, the information from the source's profile can be effectively "translated" by the destination device for the best possible color output.

Acrobat's Separate Synchronization

Historically, Bridge has synchronized everything but Acrobat, which had to be synchronized separately from within that application. However, since Acrobat is on a separate release cycle from the rest of the suite, Acrobat 9 synchronizes only with CS4 (which you may still have installed if you upgraded from CS4). The Color Management settings in the Acrobat 9 Preferences dialog box will always show up as "unsynchronized" because Acrobat 9 does not communicate color information with the applications in CS5 if an installation of CS4 still exists on your computer. If you've saved a custom color setting, you can simply choose it for Acrobat 9 separately.

(continued on next page)

4

(continued)

If you didn't save your settings, you'll have to make
sure that each option in
Acrobat matches what you
established for the other
CS5 applications. Once that's
done, Acrobat 9 (techni-
cally a CS4 application) will
be using the same settings
as Photoshop, Illustrator,
InDesign, and Bridge CS5.
However, Acrobat 9 will still
indicate that it is unsynchronized if CS4 is present on
your computer.

Once you've customized and saved your settings, then applied them
suite-wide from Bridge, you'll see the settings reflected in Photoshop,
Illustrator, and InDesign as well as an icon indicating that your suite settings are synchronized (**Figure 1b**). From that point on, each application is using the same color profiles and color-management policies to
ensure consistent color.

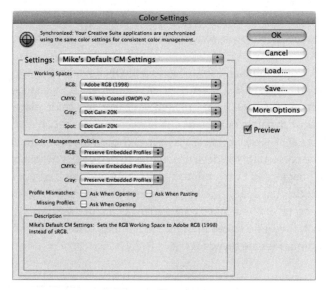

Figure 1b Photoshop's Color Settings dialog (Edit > Color Settings…)
indicating that those Creative Suite applications that can be
synchronized have been, using a custom color-settings file.

#2 Setting Preferences

Every application in CS5 has its own preferences. Command-K (Ctrl-K) is the keyboard shortcut for accessing Illustrator, InDesign, and Photoshop preferences. Dreamweaver uses Command-U (Ctrl-U); Flash Catalyst uses Command-comma (Ctrl-comma); and Flash Professional has no default keyboard shortcut.

The behavior of preference settings is uniform across CS5. If you want to change a preference for all future documents you create in a given application, make your preference changes while no documents are open. If you want to change preferences for a specific document only, make your preference changes while that document is open. All other documents will continue to honor the application's defaults.

Before you dive right in and start using CS5, get off to the right start by paying attention to a few preferences in certain applications that we think should be set differently. This is all subjective, of course, but after many years of working with these applications, there are some things we've become accustomed to setting up differently than Adobe thinks we should.

Photoshop Recommendations

Photoshop CS5's user interface was modified slightly to add a drop shadow around the image canvas in Standard and Full Screen modes. This is a bit distracting. We prefer not to have any visual clutter when we work, so we turn off this default right from the start (**Figure 2a**).

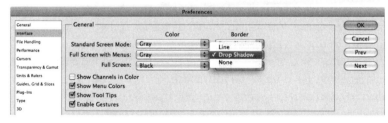

Figure 2a In the canvas border options in Photoshop's interface preferences, you can replace the drop shadow border (added to the canvas as a default in CS5) with either a line or no border at all.

Navigating Preferences by Keyboard

InDesign and Photoshop have the same Preferences dialog user interface: a pane on the left lists the separate groups of settings, and the main area of the dialog is where you modify those settings. You can use your keyboard to jump to any of the first ten choices in the left pane. For example, pressing Command-4 (Ctrl-4) when the InDesign Preferences dialog box is open jumps you to the Advanced Type settings, which is the fourth item in the list. In Photoshop, that same key combination jumps you to the Performance options, which is the fourth item in Photoshop's dialog. Command-0 jumps you to the tenth item in either list. There are no shortcuts for anything past the first ten options in either dialog.

6

Setting Up Scratch Disks

Photoshop files can get quite large, as can Illustrator artwork—especially if you take advantage of the new advanced CS5 features. When either application maxes out your system's available RAM, it looks for "scratch" disk space to use as temporary memory. Basically, what the application does is write information to available hard drive space. By default your primary hard drive is used, but this can severely compromise the performance of Photoshop, Illustrator, and possibly your entire operating system. If you regularly keep an external drive with ample space connected to your computer, you can designate that to be the primary scratch disk instead of your hard drive.

Photoshop allows you to specify many scratch disks, in any order you desire, in its Performance preferences. Illustrator allows only a primary and a secondary scratch disk, which you can select from its Plug-ins & Scratch Disks preferences.

Photoshop is holding up beautifully after 20 years, but some of us using it might find that our eyes aren't. If the text in the application's interface is causing you to squint, you can modify the UI font sizes (Preferences > Interface) from their default (Small) to either Medium or Large (**Figure 2b**). Most UI preference changes like this in the CS5 applications don't become active until you've restarted the application.

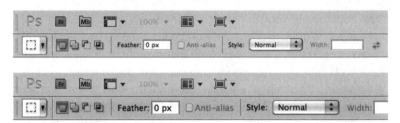

Figure 2b Photoshop's default "Small" UI fonts (top) compared to the new "Large" setting available in the Interface preference options (bottom).

Illustrator Recommendations

Illustrator CS5 finally adds functionality that many InDesign users are already used to: using Command-Click (Ctrl-click) to select an object that's behind another object. This is the new default setting, and we recommend letting it stand. (If you prefer things the old way, you can turn it off in the Selection & Anchor Display preferences, but this is a new default we like a lot.)

Scale Strokes & Effects has been off by default for more versions that we can remember. Not scaling should be the exception, not the rule, so turn Scale Strokes & Effects on in Illustrator's General preferences.

Illustrator's Smart Guides feature has Object Highlighting on by default so everything "lights up" when you mouse over it. This is another needless visual distraction. Many people turn off Smart Guides altogether. Unfortunately, when they do so, they lose all the other great functionality like dynamic alignment guides and measurement data. Instead of taking an all-or-nothing approach, turn off just Object Highlighting in the Smart Guides area of Illustrator's preferences (**Figure 2c**).

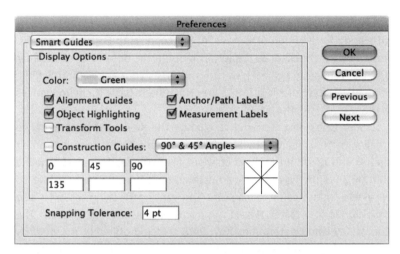

Figure 2c Use the Smart Guides preferences to turn off Illustrator's intrusive Object Highlighting, but retain the other useful Smart Guides features.

The Appearance of Black preferences (see **Figure 2d**) are set to "Display All Blacks as Rich Black." This is a big mistake for print design. When we look at our print jobs, we want to see what they're really going to look like. The difference between a swatch at 100 percent Black and Rich Black (a black made up of 100 percent black, plus percentages of cyan, magenta, and yellow) is quite pronounced. You may want your large, bold headlines in Rich Black, but not your body copy. It's important to see your blacks on screen as people will see them in print. To do that, change this preference to "Display All Blacks Accurately." This is also a preference in InDesign, and we recommend the same setting in that application, too.

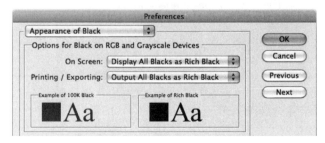

Figure 2d The preference for displaying and outputting all blacks as Rich Black in Illustrator's default Appearance of Black settings can produce misleading screen appearances and lead to unwanted results in print.

InDesign Recommendations

InDesign's Type preferences have "Apply Leading to Entire Paragraphs" turned off (unchecked) by default. This opens the door to inconsistency, especially in larger projects, so turn this on as your application default. You can always turn it off on a per-document basis if circumstances warrant it.

Under Units and Increments, change the Keyboard Increments to smaller, more useful values, like those in **Figure 2e**. By default, tapping the up and down arrow keys changes font size, leading, and baseline shift by 2 points. Typographic adjustments are typically more subtle, so we like to set this value to 0.5 point. The Kerning/Tracking setting is also a bit high for our tastes. We set this from 20/1000 em to 5/1000 em. The Cursor Key value determines how far a selected object is "nudged" by the arrow keys. This value can be as low as 0.1 point, but we prefer to keep it to the lowest round number: 1 point. Many of these preference settings are available in Illustrator, too, so to get the default behavior you like in both applications, make the same changes in Illustrator's Type preferences.

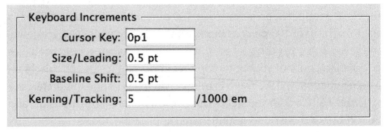

Figure 2e Our preferred settings for keyboard increments in both InDesign and Illustrator.

Dreamweaver Recommendations

We're amazed that Dreamweaver's Code view still defaults to a very small and nearly unreadable font after many versions. Do your eyes a favor and switch Dreamweaver's Code View font to something larger and more legible (**Figure 2f**). Personally, we like Verdana in the 10- to 12-point range.

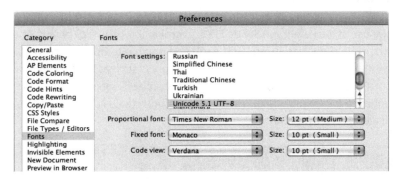

Figure 2f Dreamweaver's font preferences.

#3 Setting Up Workspaces

CS5 is made up of multiple separate applications that you use for distinct purposes—InDesign for page layout, Dreamweaver for Web-site design and management, Photoshop for image editing, and so on. However, the applications are so feature-rich that, within each, you may frequently find yourself concentrating on a specific kind of task that uses only a small subset of its features.

When designing a print brochure in InDesign, you may make extensive use of the Paragraph Styles, Effects, Stroke, and Text Wrap panels. But when the client has approved the job and it's time to go to press, you'll be making greater use of output-related panels such as Links, Preflight, and Flattener Preview. Using prebuilt or customized workspaces, you can optimize InDesign's working environment for distinctly different phases of a project (**Figure 3a**).

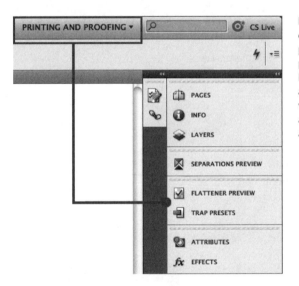

Figure 3a A set of prepress-specific panels given prominence when InDesign's Printing and Proofing workspace is made active from the application bar.

The same is true for Photoshop, Illustrator, Flash Professional, Dreamweaver, Flash Catalyst, and Bridge. Each application ships with a set of useful workspaces defined for sets of related tasks (**Figure 3b**). Photoshop comes preconfigured with workspaces optimized for painting, photography, and 3D; Illustrator includes workspaces that mimic the basic setup of InDesign, Photoshop, and even Freehand; and Flash Professional ships with workspaces specifically geared toward animators, developers, or designers.

Dreamweaver: Odd Man Out

All applications in the CS5 Design Premium suite—except for Dreamweaver—put the workspace button/menu in the far right of the Application Bar (Window > Application Bar), next to the Help search field (if there is one) and the CS Live button. For some reason, Dreamweaver's workspace button is on the left of the Application Bar.

Use Workspaces to Find What's New in CS5

Most applications in CS5 (Dreamweaver and Illustrator are the exceptions) contain a "New in CS5" workspace that exposes all of the panels used by features unique to the new version, and highlights menu items for features that are new or dramatically improved from the previous version.

(continued on next page)

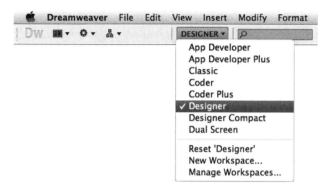

Figure 3b Dreamweaver CS5's workspace menu optimizes the application environment for different working modes, including one for a dual-screen setup.

You can also set up your own optimized arrangement of panels, menu items, and menu-item highlighting and save that as a custom workspace. The process is the same across all applications in the suite. Simply open and arrange the panels you want to have available, and close those you don't. Once everything is arranged to your liking, save your workspace for future use. In most CS5 applications, you go to Window > Workspace > New Workspace and, in the New Workspace dialog box (**Figure 3c**), give your new workspace a name and click OK (or Save). There are some subtle differences to this otherwise consistent feature, however. In Illustrator, it's Window > Workspace > Save Workspace, and in Dreamweaver, it's Window > Workspace Layout > New Layout.

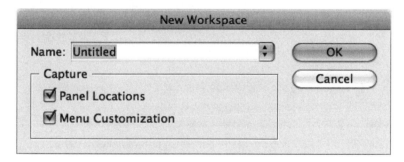

Figure 3c The New Workspace dialog box allows you to save customized workspaces. Photoshop and InDesign allow you to save individual panel locations and any menu customization you may have done.

If you've heard about a great new CS5 feature and can't find it, activate the appropriate application's New in CS5 workspace and start exploring the active panels and highlighted menu items.

Customize Your Menus

Photoshop and InDesign allow you to customize their menus to selectively hide or show options and apply color coding to menu items to make them stand out. From either application, choose Edit > Menus to access the customization options. If you don't want to see the InCopy menu options in InDesign because you don't own InCopy, for example, you can simply turn off those options by clicking the visibility (eye) icon next to the InCopy menu item to hide it and all submenus within it. Unfortunately, the other applications in CS5 do not include this functionality.

#4 Extending the Power of CS5

When you purchase CS5, you get more than just what's included in the box (or the downloaded installers). There are numerous online resources that can dramatically extend the power of the applications in the suite.

Adobe Exchange

The Adobe Marketplace & Exchange (www.adobe.com/go/exchange) offers downloadable artwork, brushes, and scripts, as well as thousands of plug-ins and extensions from Adobe and third-party developers. The plug-ins and extensions can help you automate tasks, customize workflows, create specialized professional effects, and more. Each application in CS5 Design Premium has its own Exchange (**Figure 4a**).

Figure 4a The Illustrator Exchange site includes templates, brushes, vector artwork, and other free or paid resources specific to Illustrator.

Each application-specific Exchange offers specialized plug-ins and other tools:

- InDesign users can download a wizard to automatically generate a calendar layout, a script that automates the placement of multipage PDFs, and more.

- Illustrator users can download free extensions, vector artwork, custom brushes, and templates.

- Photoshop users can download custom Actions and brushes, backgrounds, button art, and gradients.

- Dreamweaver users can find custom widgets, jQuery and Spry navigational elements, CSS-based menus, video players, and page-layout templates.

- Flash developers can download components, players, preloaders, and more.

The Exchanges offer a mix of both free and paid resources. For example, widgets on the Dreamweaver Exchange (See Chapter 6, Tip #55, "Using the Widget Browser") are often free, but many of the other items are paid products with commercial-use licenses.

Adobe Labs

Feeling cutting edge? Adobe Labs (labs.adobe.com) is your source for public beta software that Adobe has yet to release as ready-for-prime-time products. This is where Lightroom, BrowserLab, and Flash CS5 Professional's new Text Layout Framework, among other game-changing technologies, started out. Recently, exciting new extensions to Creative Suite products like the Adobe Illustrator CS5 HTML5 Pack have been made available here in an effort to keep applications aligned with the rapid pace of change in the photography, design, print, Web, and application development fields.

Adobe Configurator

The engineers at Adobe seem to really like adding customization options for Photoshop and InDesign. In addition to menu customization, an Adobe AIR application called Adobe Configurator (available on Adobe Labs) allows you to create custom panels in either application. These panels can either combine existing panel features into a custom panel tailored to your needs, or allow you to add brand-new functionality into each application. For example, you can add a panel to either Photoshop or InDesign that displays a Web page directly in the panel.

Kuler

Kuler is an extension that installs with InDesign, Photoshop, Illustrator, Flash Professional, and Flash Catalyst to give you access to color combinations created by and shared among the Adobe community. In any of these applications, go to Window > Extensions > Kuler to open the Kuler panel (**Figure 4b**).

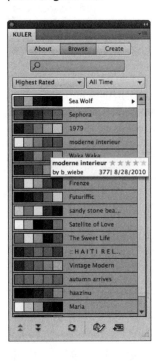

Figure 4b The Kuler panel in Photoshop with swatch sets filtered by the highest ratings. The tool tip indicates the set's creator, its average rating, and upload date.

You must be online to use Kuler, in which case you'll see swatch sets containing combinations of colors, called *themes*. Themes are organized and sortable by categories like highest rated, most popular, newest, and so on, and you can filter what's displayed in the Kuler panel by category and date range.

Illustrator has the best support for Kuler themes. When you find a theme you'd like to add, select it in Illustrator's Kuler panel and click the Add Selected Theme to Swatches button at the bottom of the panel. The swatches are added as a theme in the Swatches panel, and named identically to the original Kuler theme.

In Photoshop, it's a bit more involved. There, you'd choose Preset Manager from the Swatches panel. In the resulting dialog, select all swatches, hit the Delete key then exit the dialog. The Swatches panel should contain no swatches at all.

Next, select the theme you want in Photoshop's Kuler panel and click the Add Selected Theme to Swatches button. The Swatches panel will be populated with the swatches in that theme.

Finally, from the Swatches panel menu, select Save Swatches, which saves the theme using an ".aco" extension. It should be saved in the default location for swatch settings (on the Mac: youruserfolder/Library/Application Support/Adobe/Adobe Photoshop CS5/Presets/Color Swatches; on Windows: youruserfolder\AppData\Roaming\Adobe\Adobe Photoshop CS5\Presets\Color Swatches\Sets). You'll have to quit and relaunch Photoshop to see the custom swatch set as an option in the Swatches panel menu, but it will appear near the bottom of the menu, grouped with other custom swatch sets (**Figure 4c**).

Figure 4c A custom Kuler color theme saved as a Photoshop Swatch set.

You can then get Photoshop's default swatches back by choosing Reset Swatches from the Swatches panel menu. This will not delete any custom Kuler themes you've added.

Kuler themes added to Flash Professional are saved as Flash Color Set (.clr) files and should be saved in youruserfolder/Library/Application Support/Adobe/Flash CS5/en_US/Configuration/Color Sets (on the Mac) or youruserfolder\AppData\Local\Adobe\Flash CS5\en_US\Configuration\Color (on Windows).

When you add a Kuler theme in InDesign, the swatches are added to the current document (or to the entire application if no documents are open) at the bottom of the Swatches panel. InDesign does not support organization of swatches by themes or swatch sets, so the new Kuler swatches will appear in the panel with all other document swatches.

Kuler support for Dreamweaver is available only via a free, third-party plug-in, available at www.webassist.com/free-downloads/dreamweaver-extensions/palettepicker.

#5 Setting Up an Adobe ID

With your purchase of CS5 Design Premium edition comes one year's free access to a number of online services collectively known as CS Live (See Chapter 11, "Using the CS Live Services"). These services include:

- **Acrobat.com**—an online service for document sharing, Web-based meetings, and video conferencing.

- **Buzzword**—a collaborative online word-processing application built into Acrobat.com.

- **Adobe CS Review**—a collaborative review and commenting service for shared online project reviews that's integrated into Photoshop, InDesign, and Illustrator.

- **SiteCatalyst NetAverages**—a Web analytics service.

- **BrowserLab**—a Web-based service that tests your Web pages in a number of different browsers on different platforms.

- **Adobe Story**—a script-writing application integrated into Adobe's video applications in the Production Premium edition of CS5.

During this free-access period, using any of these services requires only one thing: an Adobe ID.

An Adobe ID is simply the user name and password you create to access these and other Adobe services online.

More Reasons to Create an Adobe ID

While the CS Live services may not remain free after one year, having an Adobe ID is entirely free, and is necessary for accessing Adobe services that aren't part of CS Live. For example, using Dreamweaver's Widget Browser (See Chapter 6, Tip #55, "Using the Widget Browser") requires signing in with an Adobe ID, as does posting comments on the user-to-user forums, downloading trial versions of Adobe software, reading informative white papers, and accessing other services like Photoshop.com.

Use Your E-mail Address

You're not required to use your e-mail address as your Adobe ID, but we recommend it. Besides the fact that it's easy to remember, some parts of the Adobe site are fussier about the type of ID you create than others. An e-mail address is the one thing that every part of Adobe.com accepts as an Adobe ID.

To create your Adobe ID, go to adobe.com and click the Your Account link at the top of the home page. On the next page (**Figure 5a**), enter an ID (preferably your e-mail address) and a password. Once your account is set up, you have full access to all of the new CS Live services and many other resources available on Adobe.com.

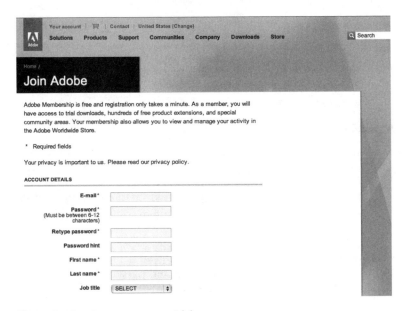

Figure 5a Creating an account on Adobe.com.

#6 Keeping CS5 Design Premium Up-to-Date

Remember waiting for disk-based software updates to come in the mail? Or hearing second-hand that an update or bug fix was available months after it had been released? Back in the day, it was up to you to seek out needed updates. Now, those updates are effortlessly pushed out via the Internet to all registered users. Receiving notifications, downloading, and installing interim updates to applications in CS5 is now a seamless process.

When you install CS5, the Adobe Application Manager installs a background application that periodically checks for updates online and notifies you with an icon in the Windows taskbar or Mac OS menu bar (**Figure 6a**). A numeral next to the icon indicates the number of applications for which there are updates.

Figure 6a The Adobe Application Manager's update icon in the Mac OS menu bar, indicating four available updates.

20

Keep Adobe Up-to-Date

If you find a problem with Adobe software that you think is a bug, don't assume that someone else has already reported it. They may not have. Also, the urgency and engineering resources applied to fixing a reported bug are related not just to the severity of the problem, but on how wide-spread it seems. That means that the more bug reports Adobe receives for a par-ticular problem, the more attention it will get. You can report bugs (and request features) at adobe.com/cfusion/mmform/index.cfm?name=wishform.

Choosing Open Updater from the update icon's menu launches the Adobe Application Manager, an AIR application that lists what updates are available for which applications (**Figure 6b**) and allows you to install all or just a few of the available updates. If you need to quit or restart applications, the Application Manager prompts you along the way.

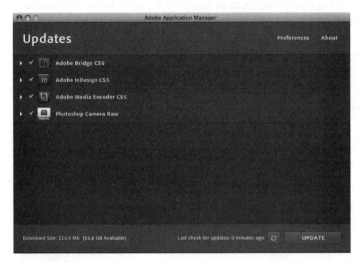

Figure 6b Available updates in the Adobe Application Manager.

If you tend to ignore these updates, you might want to rethink that behavior. In the first six months of CS5's release, the pace of change and updates to applications has been unprecedented. In addition to the usual patches and bug fixes, Adobe has added significant new features to some of its applications as updates (See Chapter 6, Tip #58, "Working with HTML5 and CSS3 in Dreamweaver") and all evidence indicates that it will continue to do so throughout the CS5 product life cycle.

CHAPTER TWO

Working with Bridge

When medals are handed out for Adobe's least sexy application, Bridge stands apart from the crowd. Based on the old File Browser in Photoshop 7.0, Bridge wins the Wally Cox award for dullest software at the cotillion.

But not every program can be Photoshop. Or Flash. Every suite of stars has to have its occasional worker bee, a role that Bridge plays with ease.

Aside from a general speed up overall, Bridge CS5 comes with a short list of improvements over its CS4 version. For a brief look at this list, we encourage you to read on.

#7 Using the Enhanced Batch File Renaming Options

One of Bridge's stronger features is its ability to batch rename multiple files. New options in CS5 offer improved flexibility over such renaming operations, allowing you to replace all or part of a string of characters in a filename. Adding to its power is its support for regular expressions to match patterns in filenames; preview the new names for all the files in the batch; and save frequently used naming schemes as presets.

You can rename files in a group, or *batch*. When you batch rename files, you can choose the same settings for all the selected files. For other batch-processing tasks, you can use scripts to run automated tasks.

Here's how to rename files in a batch:

1. Select the files that you want to rename.

2. Choose Tools > Batch Rename.

3. Set the options shown in **Figure 7a** and described here.

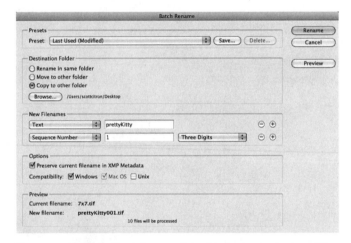

Figure 7a Inside the Batch Rename dialog box is a large selection of file renaming and relocating options.

Destination Folder: Place the renamed files in the same folder, move them to another folder, or place copies in another folder. If you choose to put the renamed files in a different folder, click Browse to select the folder.

New Filenames: Choose elements from the menus and enter text as appropriate to create new filenames. Click the Plus button (+) or Minus button (–) to add or delete elements.

Options: Select Preserve Current Filename In XMP Metadata to retain the original filename in the metadata. For Compatibility, select the operating systems with which you want renamed files to be compatible. The current operating system is selected by default.

Preview: One current and one new filename appear in the Preview area at the bottom of the Batch Rename dialog box. To see how all selected files will be renamed, click the Preview button.

Figure 7b Until you add your own custom renaming conventions, the Presets drop-down menu looks like this.

Using Batch Renaming Presets

Select a preset from the Presets menu to rename files with frequently used naming schemes. By default, the choices available are Last Used, Default, and String Substitution. To save new batch rename settings for later use, click Save (**Figure 7b**).

#8 Using Camera Raw on TIFFs and JPEGs

Even if you're not working with images in your camera's raw format, you don't have to miss out on the power and versatility of Adobe Camera Raw. This powerhouse plug-in supports both TIFFs and JPEGs. The secret is in knowing how to invoke Camera Raw when opening your file.

To process JPEG or TIFF images in Camera Raw, select one or more files in Bridge, and then choose File > Open In Camera Raw or press Command-R (Ctrl-R). When you finish making adjustments in the Camera Raw dialog box, click Done to accept changes and close the dialog box. In the JPEG and TIFF Handling section of the Camera Raw preferences, you can specify whether JPEG or TIFF images with Camera Raw settings are automatically opened in Camera Raw (**Figure 8a**).

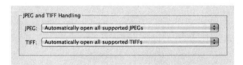

Figure 8a To set Photoshop to automatically open any TIFF and JPEG image in Adobe Camera Raw, configure your File Handling preferences like this.

To open raw images in Camera Raw, select one or more raw files in Bridge, and then choose File > Open In Camera Raw or press Command-R (Ctrl-R). When you finish making adjustments in the Camera Raw dialog box, click Done to accept the changes and close the dialog box. You can also click Open Image to open a copy of the adjusted image in Photoshop. Hold Shift and the Open Image button changes to read Open Object. Click Open Object and your file opens in Photoshop as a Smart Object. To return to Adobe Camera Raw, double-click the tiny icon in the lower-right corner of the Layers thumbnail (**Figure 8b**).

Figure 8b Click this icon to reopen the file in Adobe Camera Raw for additional editing.

To open raw images in Photoshop, select one or more raw files in Bridge, and then choose File > Open. This will open your image in Camera Raw. When you finish making adjustments in the Camera Raw dialog box, click Open Image to accept changes and open the adjusted image in Photoshop. Press Option (Alt) while clicking Open Image to open a copy of the adjusted image and not save the adjustments to the original image's metadata. Press Shift while clicking Open Image to open the image as a Smart Object in Photoshop.

At any time, you can double-click the Smart Object layer that contains the raw file to adjust the Camera Raw settings.

More File Open Tricks

Shift-double-click a thumbnail in Adobe Bridge to open a camera raw image in Photoshop without opening the Camera Raw dialog box. Hold down Shift and choose File > Open to open multiple selected images.

#9 Taking Advantage of the New Export Presets

Exporting to Social Networking Sites

Keeping pace with the rise of interest in social networking, Bridge CS5 provides a simple mechanism to upload images to popular services. As of this writing, Bridge CS5 is compatible with Facebook, Flickr, and Photoshop.com (which offers public access, commenting, and sharing of photos).

A useful addition to Bridge CS5 is the inclusion of new export commands (File > Export to). Borrowing a page from Adobe Photoshop Lightroom 3, Bridge uses modules to export files to either a chosen location on your hard drive or a page on Facebook, Flickr, or Photoshop.com.

To begin using export services go to Window > Export Panel. The Export panel holds selected images in queues until you're ready to export your files (**Figure 9a**).

Figure 9a The Export panel lets you drag images from the Bridge Content window onto icons that represent Facebook, Flickr, Photoshop.com, or your hard drive. Once you've finished building your queue, clicking the small arrow to the far right of the service name exports the queued images. Selecting the file in the queue either lets you clear it from the queue or reveals the image thumbnail in Bridge.

To select which services to include, go to the Export panel menu and choose Manage Modules (**Figure 9b**). Here you can enable the services of your choice as well as check for updates or reinstall your modules (**Figure 9c**).

Figure 9b The Manage Modules feature, which can be found in the Export panel menu. Also available is an option to view Bridge's export progress.

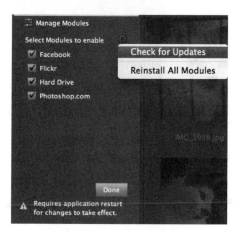

Figure 9c Choosing Manage Modules presents you with the panel seen here. From this menu you can decide to Check for Updates or Reinstall All Modules.

If exporting your files locally is of more interest, you can use the Export panel for this purpose too. First, build a queue by dragging and dropping from Bridge's Content window. Once the queue is built, click the diagonal arrow to invoke the Export dialog box.

The Export dialog is split into two tabs. The Destination tab is where you specify where your queue will be exported and how file naming will be handled (**Figure 9d**).

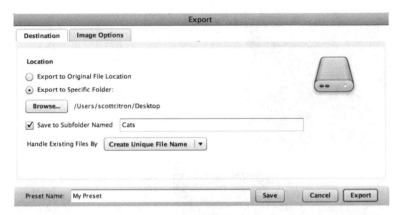

Figure 9d The Destination tab and various choices associated with where your queue is saved and how file naming is handled.

Click the Image Options tab (**Figure 9e**) to set image size and quality. In the bottom part of the window is the Metadata area where you can include original metadata, apply a metadata template, or add additional keywords. The very bottom of the window lets you name and save an Export preset.

Figure 9e The Image Options tab is divided into two sections. On the top are settings for image size, resampling method, and image quality. In the lower half, metadata settings control things like applying a metadata template or creating an export preset.

#10 Adding Watermarks to Multiple Images

Create a Custom Watermark in Photoshop

If a simple watermark is all you're after, Bridge's built-in Watermark function to the Output workspace does a yeoman's job. But if the watermark you're looking for includes any kind of layer effects like bevels, glows, or drop shadows you'll need to create your own in Photoshop.

Watermarks should be created with the same resolution as whatever it is you're watermarking. If you're making a 300 pixels per inch (ppi) contact sheet, the watermark that you create should also be 300 ppi.

To create a watermark in Photoshop, start by creating a New Document. The background should be Transparent, although solid colors or shades are okay, too. Create your mark using any color you prefer.

With the Adobe Bridge Output Module (Window > Workspace > Output) text or graphic watermarks can be easily added to PDF contact sheets for one or more images. Here's how:

1. Choose the images you want in your PDF and select Window > Workspace > Output. Click to choose the PDF button in the upper-left corner of the Output panel.

2. Choose a layout template from the Template drop-down menu.

3. Continue to customize the PDF by specifying from the Document, Layout, Overlays, Header, Footer, and Playback drawers.

4. Use Watermark drawer (**Figure 10a**) to add text or a graphic to each page or image. Text can be customized by font, size, and color. Graphic watermarks can be adjusted by scale, opacity, offset, and rotation.

Figure 10a The Watermark drawer in the PDF Output Module offers a variety of options. Watermarks can be either text or graphical of nearly any size, color, proportion, opacity, or rotation.

Add layer effects like bevels or drop shadows to taste. We like to use our email addresses as watermarks. Save your file as a PSD file to maintain your live text and allow changes to any drop shadows or bevels. Next, use Save As to save the file as a PNG to maintain the file's transparency.

The last step is to return to Bridge. There, go to the Watermark panel in the Output workspace and click Insert Image > Path. Navigate to your watermark.png file. Click Refresh Preview in the Output panel to redraw your PDF with your custom watermark.

#11 Using Mini Bridge in InDesign

Ever since the introduction of Bridge in CS2, users have battled with the essential usefulness of this file navigation and browsing add-on. For example, users had to leave their current application in order to take advantage of Bridge's many features.

In CS5, Adobe has largely eliminated this issue with introduction of Mini Bridge, an almost mirror image of Bridge that hides discreetly away in InDesign and Photoshop (**Figure 11a**).

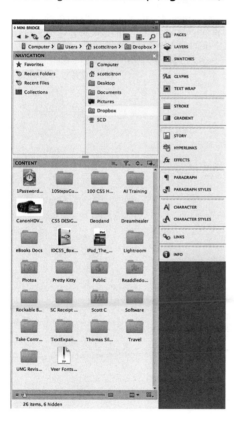

Figure 11a Although not an exact replica of Bridge, Mini Bridge acquits itself nicely by offering many of the most important tools found in its big brother.

32

Show Linked Files

A new and useful feature in Bridge and Mini Bridge is the ability to show linked files to any InDesign document. A document that contains linked files is indicated by a link icon in the upper-right corner of its thumbnail in the Content panel. To display linked files, Control-click (right-click) on the document icon and choose Show Linked Files in the Context menu.

Files can be dragged and dropped from the Mini Bridge panel into an InDesign layout. Files dragged from Mini Bridge are re-rendered into a multi-image Place cursor as if dragging directly from Bridge. New to CS5 is the ability to select any InDesign CS5 layout document (.Indd) and, via right-click, have it display all linked files (**Figure 11b**).

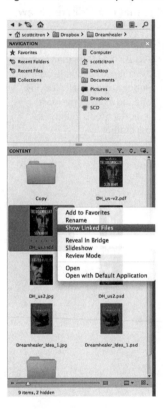

Figure 11b Right-clicking an icon in Mini Bridge with this Link badge in its upper-right corner, means that the software can display all files in the document, regardless of their location on your hard drive. Select Show Linked Files to invoke this feature.

CHAPTER TWO   Working with Bridge

#12 Using Mini Bridge in Photoshop

Along with InDesign, Photoshop is the other lucky recipient of the new Mini Bridge in CS5. Not a complete replacement for the full Bridge application, Mini Bridge acts as a useful extension of many of the standard operations you might otherwise turn to in Bridge.

Located by choosing Window > Extensions > Mini Bridge (**Figure 12a**), this new addition speeds Photoshop production by way of its quick access to standard Bridge features like file filtering, renaming, batch processing, merge to HDR, various preview modes, Photomerge, loading files into Photoshop layers, and more.

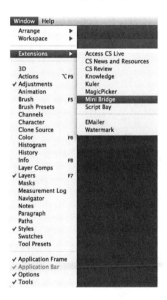

Figure 12a Search and ye shall find: Photoshop's Mini Bridge is buried a bit deeper than InDesign's, but well worth the hunt.

Open in Camera Raw

Just like in Bridge, Mini Bridge also allows users to open JPEG and TIFF files in Camera Raw. The process is simple.

1. Select your image in Mini Bridge.

2. Control-click (right-click) to invoke the Context menu.

3. Choose Open in Camera Raw.

4. Adjust your image to taste and choose either Done, to apply changes and close your image, or Open Image to apply changes and open the image in Photoshop.

As noted in Tip #8, Mini Bridge also gives users a quick way to open TIFFs and JPEGs in Camera Raw via its context menu (**Figure 12b**).

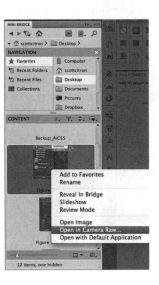

Figure 12b To open TIFFs and JPEGs in Camera Raw, Control-click (right-click) on any image in Mini Bridge.

CHAPTER THREE

Working with Photoshop

Credit the folks at Adobe Systems for not sitting on their laurels with the release of Photoshop CS5, which marks version 12 of this venerable giant. With more than 20 years as the de facto image-editing program, Adobe has continued pushing the world's reigning heavyweight leader. Timeless features like unsharp masking, the Clone Stamp tool, layers, and layer effects that might have become flabby and worn from lack of serious competition have improved steadily. Today, barely an image that appears in print or on screen can be found that hasn't been touched at some point in its life by Photoshop. Whether it's removing an unsavory color cast, restoring damaged photos, correcting perspective, or giving a model flawless skin, no other piece of software has become such an essential and ubiquitous part of society than Photoshop.

#13 Content-Aware Fill

Photoshop CS4 wowed the digital-imaging world with a remarkable feature called Content-Aware Scaling, which, for example, allows designers to stretch or shrink an image's background without distorting the happy family in the foreground. It's an impressive feature, albeit one we seldom use. That was in 2008, so when Photoshop CS5 introduced Content-Aware Fill, our initial response was ho-hum, but after using it for a while now, we've become quite impressed and use it often to almost magically remove items from images with little or no evidence they ever existed. And unlike other Photoshop features like Levels or Curves that can be found in other programs, Content-Aware Fill is a Photoshop exclusive.

Figure 13a shows a panorama of San Francisco stitched seamlessly together in Photoshop from three photographs using Photoshop's Photomerge and Auto-Blend features. An unfortunate by-product of this stitching process is the number of pixels that must be cropped out to produce a rectangular panorama (**Figure 13b**).

Figure 13a Three photos stitched together with Photomerge.

Figure 13b When the panorama is cropped to make a rectangular image, a lot of information is lost.

Rather than cut image data out, now you can use Content-Aware Fill to add missing data in.

1. Hold down Command (Ctrl), and click on the image thumbnail in the Layers panel. This will load the image as a selection.

2. From the Select menu choose Modify > Contract. Contract the selection by 10 pixels and click OK.

3. From the Select menu choose Inverse.

4. Choose Edit > Fill > to open the Fill dialog box.

(continued on next page)

5. In the Fill dialog box (**Figure 13c**) choose Contents > Use > Content-Aware. Click OK.

After a few minutes of churning and grinding, the image will be miraculously repaired (**Figure 13d**).

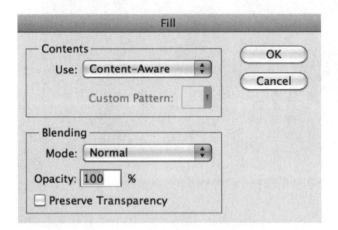

Figure 13c The Fill dialog now includes a Content-Aware option.

Figure 13d The finished panorama after applying Content-Aware Fill.

Tip
Try this easy shortcut to invoke the Fill dialog box. While holding the Shift key, tap the Delete or Backspace key.

Content-Aware Fill can also be used in conjunction with the Spot Healing Brush tool . **Figure 13e** shows a lovely scene that's unfortunately riddled with power lines and wires. With Content-Aware Fill and the Spot Healing Brush tool, we can salvage this image.

Figure 13e A mess of wires detracts from the subject of this photograph, an 18th-century Austrian church.

1. Add a new, blank layer by clicking on the Create a New Layer icon at the base of the Layers panel. Click to target the new layer on which you'll be working.

2. Select the Spot Healing Brush Tool from the Tools panel.

3. Choose Content-Aware and Sample All Layers in the Options Bar (**Figure 13f**).

Figure 13f Be sure to select Content-Aware and Sample All Layers.

4. Reduce the size of your brush to around 10–12 pixels and click once at one end of the wire you'd like to remove. Hold the Shift key and click once more at the opposite end of the same wire.

(continued on next page)

Clone Stamp to the Rescue

Although a godsend, Content-Aware Fill isn't always perfect; it may result in smearing and other imperfections. Fortunately, these problems can usually be fixed with the Clone Stamp tool.

In **Figure 13h**, we've made a loose selection around the bicyclist, whom we want to remove with Content-Aware Fill. **Figure 13i** shows the result of this operation to the image. Notice the slight misalignment in the fence and wall where the Content-Aware Fill was performed. But by using the Clone Stamp tool on a new, blank layer (with sample mode set to Current & Below), we can repair these minor problems **Figure 13j**.

5. Notice how the brush paints a straight line from end to end, before removing the wire.

6. Continue this through the image to remove all the unsightly wires.

Figure 13g With the wires removed, this photo of the church looks much better.

Figure 13h A rough selection made with the Lasso tool is all you need before applying Content-Aware Fill.

Figure 13i Depending on the weather or some other variable, you may get lucky after applying Content-Aware Fill. It is more likely, though, that your image will need a little touch-up, like here, where the fence planks fail to align horizontally.

Figure 13j In this figure, we see how the Clone Stamp tool rescued our fence image.

#14 Manipulating Images with Puppet Warp

Borrowing a cup or two of technology from Adobe After Effects, one of Photoshop CS5's more mind-bending new additions is Puppet Warp. By creating a mesh around a shape or area, Puppet Warp uses control points to isolate or distort parts of an image. Depending on your needs, Puppet Warp can subtly transform shapes like a woman's waist or hair, or radically distort one's arms or legs. Unlike the Liquify feature, Photoshop's other major pixel-pusher, Puppet Warp avoids a complicated interface of buttons and sliders in favor of an easier approach. Users simply click to place what are known as *pins* on the object to be warped.

Underlying the pins is a mesh that comes in three flavors: Fewer Points, Normal, and More Points (**Figure 14a**). These settings control the density of points that can be placed on an image. Controlling the elasticity of the mesh is a Mode menu whose choices include Rigid, Normal, and Distort.

Figure 14a Although Mode and Density are both set to Normal in this case, each drop-down menu allows two other choices.

While many of the Puppet Warp demos you'll see tend to showcase the silly side of warping images and objects, Puppet Warp also has a highly useful place, among more serious transforming and distorting tools. Here, we'll take a look at both.

We want to warp our purple cat but not its background, so we need to make a selection around the cat using the Quick Selection tool . Paint over the cat until you have a decent selection. If you go too far, hold down Option (Alt) and click to subtract from the selection (**Figure 14b**).

Figure 14b Our purple cat and selection, prior to removing its background.

Once you've refined your selection in Refine Edge or Quick Mask, press Command-J (Ctrl-J) to move the purple cat to its own layer. We no longer need the original background layer, so feel free to drag it to the Layer trash (**Figure 14c**).

Figure 14c The purple cat has now been extracted from its original background and is ready to be converted into a Smart Object.

Next, place a new background behind the cat, and drag the layer to the bottom of the layer stack. To allow changes to the warp afterward, we suggest converting the cat layer to a Smart Object. To do this, target the cat layer and choose Layer > Smart Object > Convert to Smart Object.

Click to target the layer with the purple cat and select Edit > Puppet Warp. Make sure to click the Show Mesh check box in the options bar to view the underlying grid. If you find the mesh annoying, you can always hide it later on. Click to place a range of pins similar to those in **Figure 14d**.

Figure 14d The purple cat with its mesh and new background behind it.

Each pin you place acts like an anchor to hold the image in position as well as a hinge around which other pixels can pivot or bend. Selected pins are indicated by a center black dot and can be moved, rotated, or deleted (**Figure 14e**). Hold Option (Alt) to move outside the dot and reveal a small circle. Dragging the circle clockwise or counterclockwise lets you rotate pixels around the center point. Deselected pins (those with no dot in the center) act as control points to nail or glue corresponding pixels in place, preventing them from moving.

Figure 14e To create the effect of the cat waving to the shadow, multiple pins were Shift-selected and then dragged upward.

Experiment with the purple cat until you're happy with the warp effect. Be careful, because too much warping with too few pins will give away the effect by stretching your pixels. When done, commit to the change by pressing Return (Enter) or clicking the Check icon in the options bar (**Figure 14f**).

Figure 14f The finished effect is enhanced by adding a drop shadow behind the cat.

Working with Pins

While in Puppet Warp mode, you'll see two icons in the options bar . These buttons control the depth of a pin and the pixels it controls. Let's say you want to put the purple cat's hand behind its head instead of in front. With a pin through the hand selected, you would simply click on the right-most icon to send the pin (and the puppet hand) behind. Sometimes multiple clicks are necessary, depending on the stacking order of things, but eventually the hand will appear as if it's behind the cat's head. To hide the pins temporarily, type H on your keyboard.

Fanciful though the cat image is, Puppet Warp is also a serious tool for fixing more conventional images. Take a look at the photo of St. Peter's Basilica in Rome (**Figure 14g**). Notice how the church is distorted, due to the lens of the point-and-shoot camera. By applying a few rows of strategically placed pins over the image, we're able to correct problems of perspective and parallax.

Figure 14g As seen here, photos taken with small point-and-shoot cameras tend to suffer from significant lens distortion, particularly at wide angles.

Using ruler guides helps to not only see the distortion, but also aid in correcting the problem. For this image, the Mode menu was set to Rigid, which helps prevent objects like the Basilica from flexing too much when warping, as in **Figure 14h**.

Figure 14h The improved and straightened image thanks to Puppet Warp.

#15 Making Better, Faster Selections and Masks

Refine Mask Is Back

If you were among those who shed a tear when Adobe removed the Extract tool from Photoshop CS4, your patience is now rewarded. Whereas the previous versions of Refine Mask were not to be taken lightly, the new Refine Mask tool takes the tool one or two steps further with the addition of new view settings, the Radius slider, the Refine Radius brush, and the ability to neutralize color fringing with the Decontaminate Color slider. If your job involves extracting images from their background, your life just got a whole lot easier.

In every new version of Photoshop there's always one or two features that alone justify the cost of upgrading. In Photoshop CS5 one of those features is the Refine Mask tool, which makes quick work out of creating masks and silhouettes. Although introduced with Photoshop CS3, it took until the CS5 version to fully prove its worth.

See **Figure 15a**. This photo of thriller author Shane Briant was taken on a hazy day in New York. We'll use Refine Edge to remove the photo's boring background and replace it with a beautiful landscape of the San Francisco Bay Area.

Figure 15a Replacing backgrounds is a common but unsavory task for most photographers and graphic artists because of the difficulty of doing it convincingly.

1. Use either the Magic Wand or the Quick Selection tool and select the sky. Choose Select > Inverse. Don't worry if the flyaway strands of hairs aren't included in the selection; you'll get those later.

2. Enter Quick Mask mode by pressing Q on your keyboard. This will give you a visual representation of your selection. Any areas, nooks, or crannies that aren't part of the selection can be added in by painting with White.

3. From the Select menu choose Refine Edge (or click the Refine Edge button that appears in the Options Bar when the Magic Wand or Quick Selection tool is selected).

Working with Photoshop

4. Spend a moment experimenting with the various sliders inside the Refine Edge dialog. Play with the View Mode menu to find the setting that provides the most useful background color for analyzing your mask.

5. Drag the Radius slider to around 60 pixels. Against a Black background this should give you a pretty good idea of the quality of your mask. Experiment by turning on and off the Smart Radius button. Does it help or not?

6. Switch the background to White (press W on the keyboard) and try applying the settings seen in **Figure 15b**. If your selection needs improvement, try painting just outside the hair with the Refine Radius tool . To see what you've done, take a look at **Figure 15c**, which shows the radius that Photoshop is examining for edge transitions and detail.

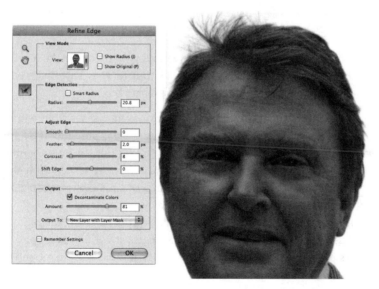

Figure 15b Select one of seven backgrounds available in the Refine Edge dialog that gives you the best view of your mask. Adjust the Radius slider (we used 20.8 pixels) so that Photoshop looks beyond our initial selection for other hard edges to include. Bump the Feather up to around 2 pixels, and increase Contrast to 8 percent. To reduce any haloing introduced by the Feather slider, enable Decontaminate Colors and set the percentage slider to around 81 percent.

(continued on next page)

#15: Making Better, Faster Selections and Masks

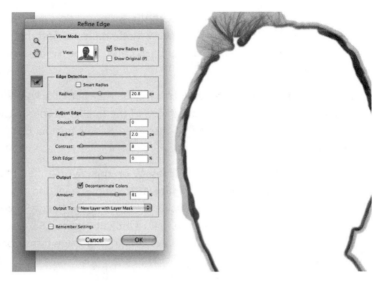

Figure 15c Clicking the Show Radius check box gives you a view like this, indicating how far outside the selection Photoshop is looking for edge transitions.

7. Tap the F key to cycle through the various view modes. Make sure that the Output section menu is set to Output To: New Layer with Layer Mask. Click OK to exit the Refine Edge dialog box.

How does your mask look? Are most of the hairs visible without a discernible halo around them? If any large areas are hidden by your layer mask (like the collar, for example), Option (Alt) click on the mask thumbnail to make it visible. From there, choose any standard brush of your choice and paint with white to reveal pixels in the photo, or black to conceal visible pixels.

When you're done, Option (Alt) click to hide the mask and take another look at your mask. If you're still not satisfied with your work, open the Masks panel and click the Mask Edge button (**Figure 15d**) to reopen the Refine Edge dialog.

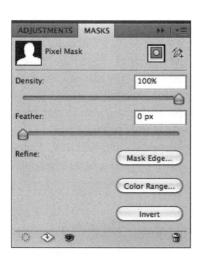

Figure 15d The Masks panel provides an easy way to return to the Refine Edge or Color Range dialogs.

To place a new background behind the silhouette, select File > Place, Copy/Paste, or drag and drop. Drag the image below the image you masked and take a look. If you're still not satisfied, click once on the layer mask thumbnail and choose the Mask Edge button in the Masks panel to return to the Refine Edge dialog. When you're done, your image should look like ours, **Figure 15e**.

Figure 15e Silhouetting, once the scourge of photographers and designers, is now actually fun thanks to Photoshop's Refine Edge feature.

#16 Simulating HDR Photography

High Dynamic Range Photography Explained

Recent years have seen an inexplicable and dramatic rise in popularity for High Dynamic Range (HDR) pho-tography. Dynamic range, or the difference between light and dark areas of an image, is greater than can be cap-tured by current technology. Although the human eye has little trouble equalizing such values in the real world, cameras (whether film or digital) are limited to a much narrower range.

To compensate for this limi-tation, HDR images are made from multiple shots of dif-fering exposures that, when combined in the digital dark-room, represent the world more as the human eye sees it. Like any trend or fad, HDR photography has also become the unfortunate *drop shadow* of photogra-phy and today is frequently overused by many just look-ing for an eye-catching effect.

In support of legitimate High Dynamic Range (HDR) photography, Photo-shop CS5 has made significant technical advances to aid photographers who want to work with such images. Its new HDR Pro features take a great leap forward compared to earlier releases of the software. As if this weren't enough, Photoshop CS5 also gives a sly wink to those who are interested in producing faux HDR images, rather than the true item itself, via the HDR Toning command (Image > Adjustments > HDR Toning).

In this tip we'll experiment with a few eye-catching faux HDR effects, plus explain how to use the HDR Toning feature to produce truly beautiful images.

Layer Limitations of HDR Toning

When working with Photoshop's HDR Toning command, be aware that the feature works on flattened images only. This means that using HDR Toning on a layered file or even a Smart Object will result in the file being flattened.

With your flattened image selected, choose Image > Adjustments > HDR Toning. Depending on the way you work and the expectations you have for your image, you can choose to work either by freely experi-menting with the presets, sliders, and curves, or taking some time to learn a bit first about how each control behaves. Although we don't discourage users from diving in and having fun, what follows is an annotated screen capture that includes callouts explaining the parts and menus that make up the HDR Toning dialog (**Figure 16a**).

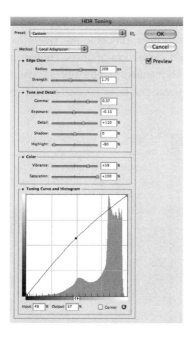

Figure 16a The HDR Toning dialog is the key to this powerful effect. Our recommendation is to freely experiment with the various sliders and drop-down menus, particularly the Preset menu, until you come up with a look you like.

Of course, one could easily stop here, after choosing a preset or following a few minutes of wild experimentation. However, by stacking your HDR toned image with its original, you can blend the two for an interesting effect. For example, **Figure 16b** is the result of a layered Photoshop file composited from the original tree silhouette image on the bottom and the version we created using HDR Toning on top. To align both images, select both layers and choose Edit > Auto-Align Layers.

Figure 16b
This image is a composite of the original image and the HDR toned image. Placed together in the same Photoshop file, a Luminosity blend mode was applied to the HDR image at the top of the stack.

Once the images are layered on top of each other (**Figure 16c**), experiment by applying varying blend modes to the topmost image (with the Move tool selected and the layer targeted, cycle through the list of blend modes by using the keyboard shortcut Shift+plus). Luminosity was used on the top layer. Remember to also play with the layer's opacity slider to further control the overall effect.

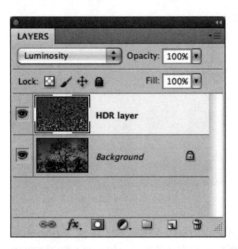

Figure 16c By stacking toned images into a single document, a range of interesting effects can be achieved by combining blending modes and opacities.

Using Effects Wisely

As with most effects, when used alone they tend to call unwanted attention to themselves. A better way is to combine those effects with the original image to produce a more pleasing overall result.

To do so, first make a copy of the layer to which you intend to apply your effects. Apply your chosen effect. Afterward, stack the affected layer above the original, unaffected layer. Use the Opacity slider on the affected layer to dial in or out the final amount of the effect.

#17 Painting with Bristle Brushes

Photoshop CS5 steps into the ring with Painter, Corel's longtime natural media champion, thanks to its new Bristle and Mixer brushes. Brush-tip properties such as shape, bristles, length, thickness, stiffness, angle, and spacing can all be controlled using simple sliders. If you have a drawing tablet like one of the many available from WACOM or other companies, you can now paint or draw in Photoshop CS5 more naturally than ever before.

The easiest way to learn your way around the Bristle brush tool is to start by adding paint to a simple pencil sketch or outline. In our case, we'll use the still life seen in **Figure 17a**, which was created in Adobe Illustrator. As we always recommend, don't paint on the original artwork. Instead, add a new, blank layer above the sketch on which to work. This way we preserve the original in case we want to go backward or move the sketch to the top of the layer stack for creative purposes. To add a new layer, choose Layer > New > Layer or click on the Create a New Layer icon at the base of the Layers panel.

Figure 17a This Illustrator line drawing will serve as the basis for our painting.

Tap the B key to access the brush tool (or click on it in the Tools panel), and then open the Brush panel to adjust your settings (**Figure 17b**). Although you can paint with any brush you choose in Photoshop, only the ten new Bristle brushes shown in **Figure 17c** can be controlled by the Shape menu and five sliders (bristles, length, thickness, stiffness, and angle) in the Brush dialog. Feel free to also experiment with the 11 other brush properties located in the dialog's far-left panel.

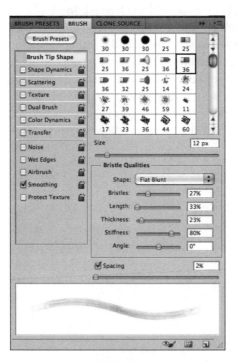

Figure 17b The command center for brushes in Photoshop is the Brush panel (F5).

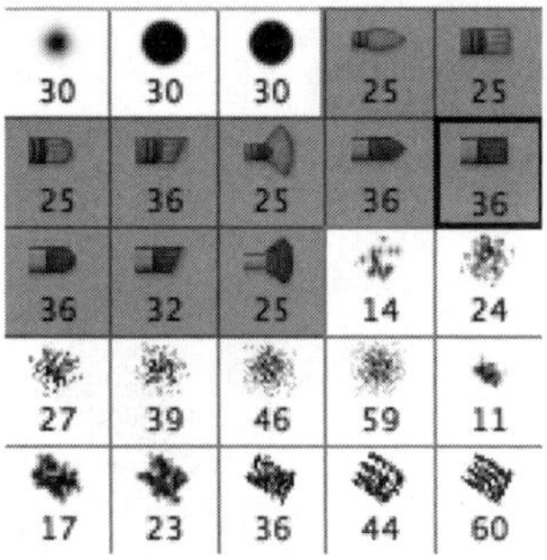

Figure 17c Only these ten new Bristle brushes are controlled by sliders labeled Bristles, Length, Thickness, Stiffness, and Angle.

For now, let's start by creating a brush based on the settings provided in **Figure 17d**. Save the brush as a preset called Fruit Brush 36 by choosing New Brush Preset from the fly-out menu in the upper corner of the Brush panel (**Figure 17e**).

Figure 17d We used these settings to create our new Fruit Brush.

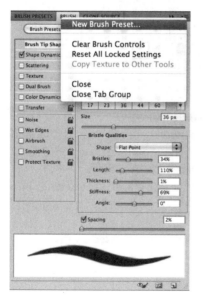

Figure 17e Save a new brush preset by clicking on this dialog from the Brush panel menu.

58

Slogging through the HUD

When you're working in the HUD Color Picker, it's easy to become frustrated when trying to figure out how to get from the Lightness and Saturation selector on the left to the Hue selector strip on the right. The secret is in using the Spacebar. Holding down the Spacebar temporarily freezes the color you've chosen while allowing you to slide your cursor over to the opposite side of the HUD. Admittedly awkward at first, after a few tries you'll find it easy to use.

Now we need some color. To pick up color, you have several options. Color can be added by clicking from the Swatches panel, the Color panel, the Adobe Color Picker at the base of the Tools panel, or now by invoking the heads-up-display, or HUD Color Picker (**Figure 17f**), by pressing Control-Option-Command/Command-Alt-Right click. Depending on your Preference settings, the HUD Color Picker can be displayed as either a strip or a wheel.

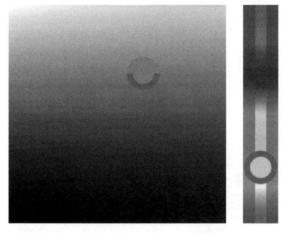

Figure 17f The new HUD Color Picker as seen in strip mode.

Start by choosing a green, red, or brown (Bosc, anyone?) for your pear color. Choose an opacity setting of 50 percent in the options bar and begin to paint with your Fruit Brush on the blank layer. Paint loosely, and don't worry about staying within the lines. If you're using a tablet instead of a mouse, notice how pressing lightly with the stylus translates into thinner strokes on your painting. Once you've established a thin ground cover of color, stop painting.

Add a new blank layer above the one you just worked on. Change the brush color by using the HUD Color Picker and feel free to change the size or hardness of your brush. Continue painting on the new layer and notice how the colors on the two layers interact with each other. Although not a requirement, we find that breaking out the painting into several layers gives us more control in the end (**Figure 17g**).

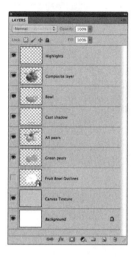

Figure 17g Here you can see how we broke apart the painting into individual layers. Although you can always paint using only one layer, working with a layered file gives you more options and control over the finished product.

New Brush Shortcuts

For our money, one of the best new Photoshop features is the ability to change brush sizes and hardness quickly and on the fly. With any painting tool selected, press Control + Option/Command + Alt and drag left or right to change brush size. Drag up or down to change brush hardness.

Add another blank layer and change color or brush attributes and paint again until your pears start to look well covered.

Choose a new color for the stems and create another blank layer. Pick a smaller brush or decrease the size of the tip you're using and paint the three short stems.

Create another blank layer and paint in the leaves.

Add two more blank layers. On one layer use a pale blue or green color to paint in the glass bowl. On the other layer choose a grayish light blue or green to paint in the cast shadow beneath the bowl.

60

At this point, you're basically done painting. Remember to hide the Fruit Bowl Outlines layer if you no longer want it visible. Experiment using various Photoshop filters, Layer Styles, Adjustment Layers, Graphic Styles, or Blending Modes to alter your painting or a layer or two. As long as you continue to work nondestructively (don't forget Smart Objects!), you'll never find yourself stuck in a creative corner.

Figure 17h A completely different look can be achieved with little effort. This rich painting is the result of a flowing hand, some quick brushstrokes, and creative Blending mode decisions in Photoshop CS5.

#**18** Mixer Brushes

To see how the Mixer Brush tool works, we'll start with the photo in **Figure 18a**. After opening the photo, select the Mixer Brush tool from the Tool panel ![icon]. Among the new options found in the Options Bar are menus to select from a variety of creative brush-blending options. Paint effects can range from dry to very wet, heavy mixes (**Figure 18b**). Although the Mixer Brush tool can be used to paint on a blank canvas, in this example we're going to treat the pixels in the image as if they are wet paint.

Figure 18a This photo will serve as the basis for our painting.

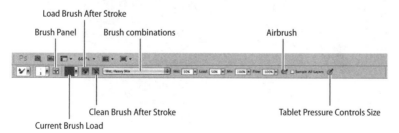

Figure 18b Photoshop's Options Bar when a Mixer Brush is chosen.

1. With the Mixer Brush tool selected, open the Brush panel and choose a Bristle tip, such as the Round Curve (25 pixels).

2. In the Layers panel, add a new blank layer on which to work. Make sure to also turn on Sample All Layers in the Options Bar.

(continued on next page)

Mixer Brushes Give Realistic Effects

If you like the new Bristle Brushes in Photoshop CS5 but yearn to combine paint in a more natural, organic way, then you'll love the Mixer Brush tool. Using the Mixer Brush, you can paint with multiple colors on one tip, blending and mixing them into existing colors from any photo or image. You can achieve precise control by choosing from a variety of paint characteristics ranging from very dry to very wet.

3. Begin painting. As you'll see, Photoshop will behave as if the pixels in the photo are wet inks or paint being pushed around by the brush.

4. Continue painting but feel free to experiment with differing tips, sizes, or combination presets. Don't limit your painting to only one layer. Create as many layers as are necessary to provide you with the degree of creative flexibility you'll need when done painting.

You can take advantage of Photoshop's many nondestructive tools, filters, blend modes, and styles to add to your basic painting. Just because you've covered your canvas with paint doesn't mean the creativity has to end there.

Figure 18c shows my finished version. Notice the dark yet sketchy outline that I applied afterward. This effect was the result of first running the Chalk & Charcoal filter (Filter > Filter Gallery;) on the original image. Afterward, I placed the filtered image at the top of my painting's Layer stack, setting its Blending Mode to Darker Color and Opacity to 58 percent.

Figure 18c By combining the original photo with Mixer Brush strokes layered above, the resulting image looks like a textured oil painting. Adding a top layer produced by the Chalk & Charcoal filter gives the painting another level of interest.

#**19** 3D Repoussé

One of the more amazing additions to Photoshop CS5 Extended is the new Repoussé feature (based on the French word meaning "to relieve or extrude"). The Repoussé feature converts 2D RGB objects into 3D. These objects can subsequently be extruded, inflated, and repositioned in space. When an image or illustration needs a burst of 3D realism, Repouseé is a wonderful tool for the job. Repoussé can be configured from within a single dashboard of menus and sliders controlling attributes like volume, angle, materials, and lighting of objects or text.

To get started with Repoussé, have a look at **Figure 19a**, which will act as the background for our project.

Figure 19a This cloud image will serve as the background for our 3D repoussé project.

1. Click anywhere inside the image with the Type tool and type "super dude," making sure to separate the words with a return. I suggest a bold font like Impact, which we set at around 105 points (**Figure 19b**).

(continued on next page)

Figure 19b Our background image with type added.

2. Adjust the type's leading and kerning to taste and then make a copy of the type layer (as a backup) using the keyboard shortcut Command-J (Ctrl-J). Afterward, hide the visibility of the copy by clicking on the eyeball icon in the left column of the Layers panel (**Figure 19c**).

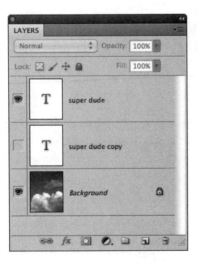

Figure 19c Hide the copy of the type layer as seen here.

3. With the original text layer targeted, choose 3D > Repoussé > Text Layer. Disregard the warning that the type must be rasterized (that's why we made a copy), and click Yes to continue.

4. With the Rotate the Mesh tool selected in the upper-left corner of the Repoussé dialog box (**Figure 19d**), use the tool to manipulate your text in 3D space. Of course, feel free to experiment with the other settings as well, paying special attention to the Extrude, Materials, and Internal Constraints settings. When you're satisfied with your effect, click OK.

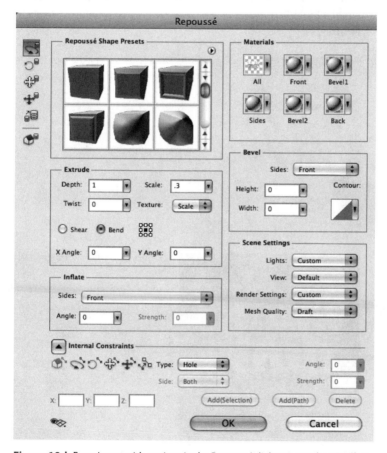

Figure 19d Experiment with settings in the Repoussé dialog to get the 3D effect you're looking for.

(continued on next page)

5. The only thing left for now is to fade the extrusion into the clouds. For this, we'll add a layer mask by clicking on the Add Layer Mask icon at the base of the Layers panel.

6. Click to target the layer mask and choose a large, soft-edge brush set to 30 percent opacity. With black as your foreground color, paint a few deft strokes at the base of the extrusion (**Figure 19e**). Stop painting when it looks like your type is disappearing into the fluffy clouds, as in **Figure 19f**.

Figure 19e Use a layer mask on the type layer to fade the extruded text into the clouds.

Figure 19f The finished composition.

With the ability to extrude selections, paths, or text, Repoussé is a powerful addition to Photoshop's existing 3D toolset, which in itself bears further experimentation and exploration.

#20 Applying Photoshop Filters to Video

With all the great video software already out there, the first time you heard about working with video in Photoshop you probably thought, "Why?" I know we did. But the deeper you dive into the subject, the more you realize just what a natural it is. If you're currently working with video in other applications, chances are good that Photoshop is already part of your workflow, and now Photoshop has tools you can use for video that can't be found in any other video-editing software, such as the Healing Brush tools, Content-Aware Fill, Adjustment Layers, Clone Stamp tool, Vanishing Point, and the Mixer Brush. While Photoshop isn't a replacement for Final Cut Pro or Premiere Pro, once you see what it can do, you'll never look at Photoshop in the same way.

To use Photoshop filters with video, start by opening a video file in Photoshop. You do that the same way you open a still image: choose File > Open (**Figure 20a**).

Figure 20a The first frame of a short video clip from a small digital camera.

The Application Frame

Photoshop's Application Frame is a hot-button topic for many. It's intended to isolate you from the file chaos of the Desktop, putting you in a gray cone of silence. For Windows users, who are forced to work in a hermetically sealed environment anyway, the Application Frame is no big deal, but this feature can make some Mac users bristle. Admittedly, we were churlish when first we tried the Application Frame, but if you put aside the "open wide and say ah!" Microsoft-ish side of using the Frame, you might eventually change your tune, as we have. And new to the Application Frame, you can double-click the frame's gray background as a shortcut for File > Open.

From the Window menu choose Animation. Make sure the Animation panel is displaying the Timeline, not Frames (**Figure 20b**). The thumbnail in the Layers panel indicates you're now working on a video layer instead of a normal image layer.

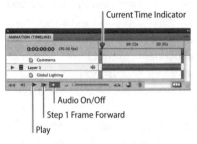

Current Time Indicator

Audio On/Off

Step 1 Frame Forward

Play

Figure 20b The Animation Timeline and controller.

With Layer 1 selected in the Layers panel, right-click or click the icon in the upper-right corner to reveal the panel menu. Choose Convert to Smart Object. Now duplicate Layer 1 by dragging it to the Create New Layer icon at the base of the Layers panel. Hide the Layer 1 copy, which we'll return to later.

Once the video is converted to a Smart Object, return to the Filter menu and apply the Watercolor filter (Filter > Artistic > Watercolor). We used Brush Detail = 9, Shadow Intensity = 0, Texture = 1. Click OK to apply. Now play the video by tapping the Spacebar or the Play button. You should see the filter effect applied to the entire 17-second clip.

If the filter effect flashes on and off, take a look at the green, stubble-like bars above the Comments layer in the Timeline. These lines indicate rendering progress. When the green line turns solid, it indicates that the effect is completely rendered. Playing the clip repeatedly should help to fill in any stubbly bars and fully render the watercolor effect.

Click on the eye icon to turn on visibility of the Layer 1 copy. Make sure you see the Smart Object icon in the lower-right corner. If not, go to the panel menu and choose Convert to Smart Object. With Layer 1 copy targeted, choose Filter > Stylize > Find Edges. Set Find Edges to taste and click OK.

Last, choose Filter > Texture > Texturizer to apply a canvas texture to the video (**Figure 20c**). Click OK to apply, and then play back your video. Try reducing the opacity of the Layer 1 copy to around 60 percent. This allows some of the watercolor effect on Layer 1 to come through.

Figure 20c Here we see the effect of applying the Texturizer filter's Canvas setting to the video.

The last step in this process is to save the document as a .psd file and then export the clip to be placed into another editing system (File > Export > Render Video). This process is known as final render and can be very slow, depending on the length of your clip and the speed of your computer. The beauty of this workflow is, should you decide later on to make a creative change to your clip, you can easily do so because of the nondestructive nature of the Smart Objects you created from the original video.

#21   What's So Smart About Smart Objects?

The concept of Smart Objects is similar to how files are handled in InDesign; placed files aren't actually embedded in InDesign but are instead represented by proxies or previews of the file. Any time we want to edit the original placed file, we have to step outside the InDesign layout and into another application to make our changes. Once the changes are made, we save and close the document and then return to InDesign, where our link is automatically updated.

Similarly, a Smart Object is a working preview of an image. With it we're free to transform, scale, mask, or filter the Smart Object, which is then regenerated through its link to its parent file. The only difference here is that the original isn't a traditional outside link, like in InDesign, but rather embedded into (and therefore portable with) the Photoshop document. Since the original can only be edited outside the document where it's placed, changes such as transforming, scaling, masking, and filtering are always un-doable and completely nondestructive. On the flip side, you can't perform operations that alter pixels directly such as burning, dodging, painting, or cloning.

Figure 21a is a photograph with drab colors, a flat and overexposed background, and a foreground that's dark and underexposed. Had this image been captured in a raw format, balancing dynamic range would be much easier. Here's how to use Smart Objects to make nondestructive changes to salvage this snapshot.

Figure 21a The underexposed foreground and flat background levels in this photo should be better balanced.

1. In Photoshop, select File > Open as Smart Object > and select the image you want to work on.

2. Double-click the Smart Object icon in the lower-right corner of the Layers panel thumbnail to launch the Adobe Camera Raw dialog box.

3. In the Basic panel, drag the Clarity and Vibrance sliders as shown in **Figure 21b** to punch up the background.

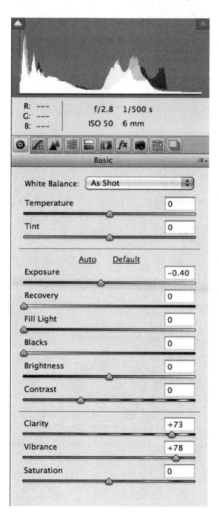

Figure 21b Increasing Clarity and Vibrance helps accentuate the otherwise flat colors in the background.

(continued on next page)

4. Switch to the Detail panel and drag the sliders as shown in **Figure 21c**. This will reduce the color noise you'll see in the sky. Click OK to exit the Camera Raw dialog.

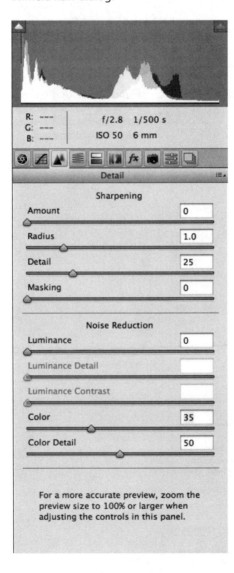

Figure 21c Camera Raw's Detail panel includes a set of sliders for reducing image noise.

5. From the Image menu, choose Adjustments > Shadows/Highlights. Drag the sliders as shown in **Figure 21d**. Pay particular attention to the Shadows > Amount slider. Increasing it and the Shadows > Radius slider will lighten up the figures in the foreground. Click OK to exit the dialog box.

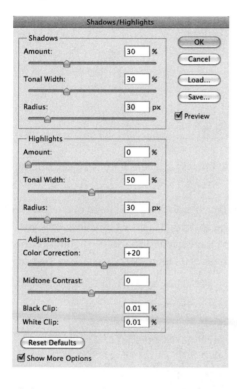

Figure 21d Applying the normally destructive Shadows/Highlights filter as a Smart Filter gives you infinite opportunities to tailor your results.

6. Click on Smart Filters Layer Mask. Take a 300-pixel brush and set its Hardness to around 6 percent. Paint on the Layer Mask with black set to a 25 percent Opacity (**Figure 21e**). This will return some of the darkness that was removed by the Shadows/Highlights filter.

(continued on next page)

Image Sharpening and Noise Reduction in Adobe Camera Raw

When working in the Detail panel to sharpen or control image noise, Adobe Camera Raw reminds you to always view your file at no less than 1:1, or 100 percent, magnification. This is because the effect of sharpening is hard to accurately discern at a lower magnification. This reminder can be seen at the base of the sliders and reads: "For a more accurate preview, zoom the preview size to 100% or larger when adjusting the controls in this panel."

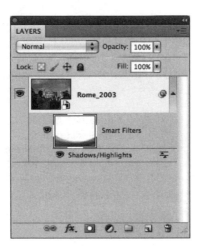

Figure 21e Painting with a large, soft brush on a layer mask helps bring back some of the darkness that was removed with Shadows/Highlights.

7. Click OK and Save your file as a layered Photoshop document (**Figure 21f**).

If you're wondering whether the above could have been done without first converting the image to a Smart Object, the answer is yes. But had we done that, we couldn't have applied Shadows/Highlights nondestructively and taken advantage of its Layer Mask to darken the bottom of the photo.

Figure 21f The end result of working nondestructively on this image.

Working with Photoshop

#22 Lens Correction Weight-Loss Clinic

Among the processes we routinely apply when retouching portraits is a healthy dose of the Lens Correction filter. Long buried in the Distort sub-filters list (Filters > Distort), now with Photoshop CS5 this useful gem has been promoted to a higher level of visibility (Filters > Lens Correction).

Among the more obvious uses for this filter, like fixing converging verticals of buildings, we often use Lens Correction to shave a few pounds off the faces we photograph. Maybe our subjects just aren't wan enough, but rarely do we see a portrait that won't benefit from a quick trip under the digital knife.

Open your image (we're using **Figure 22a**) and convert the background layer into a Smart Object (target the layer and choose Layer > Smart Objects > Convert to Smart Object). This allows you to revisit the filter settings at a later time and to check your work against the original.

Figure 22a A pleasant shot to begin with, no?

From the Filter menu choose Lens Correction. In the Lens Correction dialog, click the Custom tab. Adjust the settings as in **Figure 22b** or to taste. As you can see, we've dragged the Remove Distortion slider to +12 (i.e., more concave) and the Scale slider to 108 percent. The Scale slider is used to enlarge the image slightly to counter the decrease in overall dimensions resulting from the Remove Distortion change.

Use the Preview button to see a Before & After of the image.

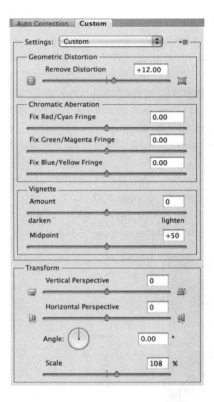

Working with Photoshop

Figure 22b Use these settings as a starting point for your own experimentation. Be careful not to go too far, otherwise you'll give away your handiwork.

When you're satisfied with the results, click OK to apply the settings and exit the filter dialog. Compare the final results shown in **Figure 22c** with its original in **Figure 22a**.

Figure 22c Introducing a subtle amount of concave distortion via the Lens Correction dialog is a simple way to improve most portraits.

#23 Using Adobe Camera Raw to Edit Raw Images

If you're among those who aren't sure why Photoshop's Camera Raw plug-in is important, allow us a quick moment of explanation. Say tomorrow is Mom's birthday, and you'd like to bring her a cake, for which you have two choices: buying a cake or baking a cake. They both taste good, but the store-bought cake is the product of someone else's decisions about how cake should look and taste. The cake you bake from scratch, though, reflects *your* choices and decisions about birthday cakes.

In the same way, JPEG and TIFF images begin life as raw cakes, but before you take a bite, the images are precooked and then baked to how the camera manufacturer thinks your images should look. Although this isn't necessarily bad, a prebaked image has much less latitude for creative expression as a raw image. Plus, software for processing raw images such as ACR 6.0 is much more sophisticated (think KitchenAid mixer and Viking stove) than the software inside your point-and-shoot camera (think Suzy Homemaker).

The other advantage of working with raw images is that all changes are the result of instructions being given to the image by the software. Not only does this method result in faster, almost instantaneous changes, but also all changes are nondestructive. Since pixels aren't pushed, pixels aren't harmed.

Let's start by having a look at **Figure 23a**. This is a deceptively simple photograph, one you might pass up after a cursory glance.

Adobe Camera Raw: A Brief History

Along with the release of Adobe Photoshop CS5 comes Adobe Camera Raw 6 (ACR). Adobe Camera Raw 6 marks a major upgrade in raw processing features unknown in previous versions. Rewritten from scratch using the same demosaicing algorithms found in Adobe Lightroom 3.0, ACR 6's processing engine produces sharper images with less noise than in the past. With the added bonus that JPEGs, TIFF and DNGs can also be opened in ACR 6, a brief stopover in Adobe Camera Raw should be on the itinerary of all photographers and digital artists.

Figure 23a Nothing much going on here at this stage of our photograph.

Yet by applying a number of features of ACR 6.0, this average photo turns into a dramatic and beautiful image. Begin by working from top to bottom in the Transform area of the panel. Adjust things like Distortion, Rotation, and Scale to counter the effects of the lens (**Figure 23b**). Use the Basic panel to control Exposure, Black values, Contrast, Clarity, and Vibrance (**Figure 23c**). Switch to the Detail panel to apply Sharpening and Noise Reduction, if needed (**Figure 23d**). Click on the HSL/Grayscale panel to adjust specific color Luminance or to convert your image to gray-scale (**Figure 23e**). The Effects panel is where you can now add film-like grain or post-crop vignetting (**Figure 23f**). Finally, the Camera Calibration panel provides menus to select a demosaicing process (2003 or the higher-quality 2010) and an appropriate Camera Profile (**Figure 23g**). To see the result of all these adjustments, have a look at **Figure 23h**.

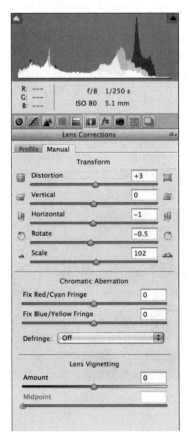

Figure 23b Use Manual Lens Corrections here to fix parallax distortion and a slight barrel distortion caused by the camera's wide-angle lens.

Working with Photoshop

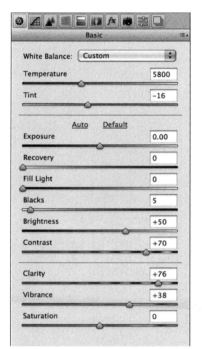

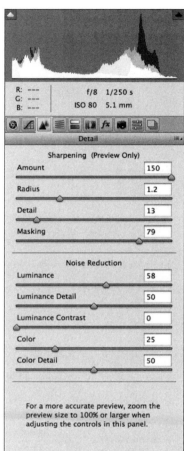

Figure 23c These settings in the Basic panel were used to mostly add Contrast, Brightness, Clarity, and Vibrance.

Figure 23d The Detail panel settings we used to apply Sharpening and Noise Reduction.

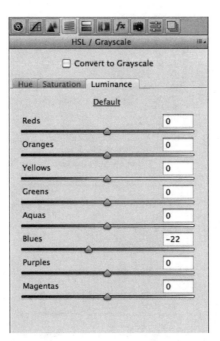

Figure 23e In the HSL/Grayscale panel we reduced the luminance of the blues.

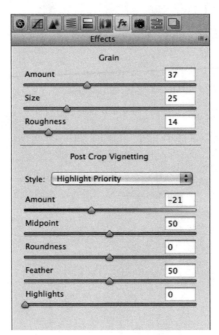

Figure 23f The Effects panel was helpful for adding Grain and Post Crop Vignetting.

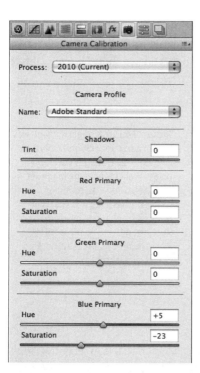

Figure 23g The Camera Calibration panel allowed us to make some final choices that affected the raw processing engine and the look of the blue primaries applied via the camera's profile.

Figure 23h The result of applying the above settings from inside of Adobe Camera Raw 6.0. Here we see either the final image, which could be the end of your processing, or the beginning of additional work in Photoshop.

#24 Using Vanishing Point to Create a 3D Mock-Up

Although Vanishing Point (Filter > Vanishing Point) is great for removing or cloning objects in perspective, one of its best uses is for producing mock-ups of packaging or products. In this tip, we show how easy it is to simulate a 3D book using finished 2D artwork.

1. We start by opening **Figure 24a**.

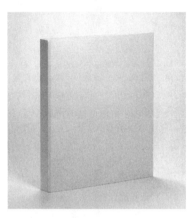

Figure 24a This original image was part of a free set of high-resolution, copyright-free, images we found on the Web. Each image in the set (tin cans, billboards, toothpaste tubes, bottles, etc.) was specially designed with white labels that were intended to be replaced by 2D artwork to realistically mock up common packaging or signage.

2. Also open the front-cover artwork you plan to use in its native application, be it Photoshop or Illustrator (**Figure 24b**). Select the cover artwork or image and copy to the clipboard (Edit > Copy).

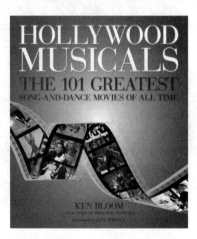

Figure 24b The 2D artwork to be used for the front panel of the book jacket.

3. Add a new blank layer to **Figure 24a**. Target the blank layer and choose Filter > Vanishing Point.

4. In the Vanishing Point dialog, choose the Plane Grid tool 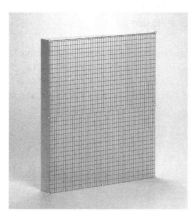 . Click with the tool on the upper-left corner of the front-cover area to place your first point of the perspective grid. Drag down and click to place another point on the lower-left corner. Continue dragging and clicking until your grid covers and aligns with the front area (holding the X key while clicking simultaneously invokes the zoom-in tool, which facilitates accurate point placement). Photoshop will warn you with a red or yellow grid if the grid you create doesn't align accurately with the verticals and horizontals of the image. When things are aligned properly, Photoshop signals this state by turning the grid blue (**Figure 24c**).

Figure 24c The book's front-jacket panel with perspective grid applied.

5. With the front grid selected, type Command/Control+V to paste the front artwork into the Vanishing Point dialog. Use Command/Control+plus or minus to zoom in or out. Chances are the artwork will be larger than necessary, so click on the Transform tool to scale the artwork smaller.

6. When you're done transforming and positioning the front-cover artwork, click OK to exit the dialog box (**Figure 24d**).

(continued on next page)

Controlling Squirrely Tools in Vanishing Point

As wonderful a tool as Vanishing Point is, often we find the behavior of positioning items to be erratic. Scaling with the Transform tool is one such tool. What tends to happen is that an object's transform handles become lost within the perspective grid, making rescaling or rotating impossible. To avoid this problem, start by scaling your object much smaller than the grid it's designed to cover. Next, loosely center the object on its grid and scale it slowly upward while holding the Shift key down to constrain proportions. If you hold the Option (Alt) key at the same time, the object will not only scale in proportion, but from its center as well. Once the object is properly scaled to size, release the mouse to commit the transform operation.

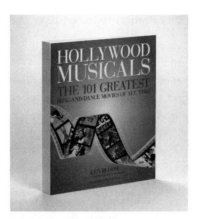

Figure 24d The mock-up with cover art in place.

From here you'll want to repeat steps 2–6 with the spine art, beginning by first copying it to the clipboard and then creating the spine's perspective grid in the Vanishing Point dialog (**Figure 24e**).

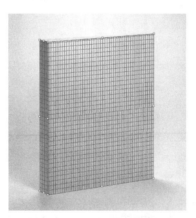

Figure 24e Back inside Vanishing Point, add a new perspective grid for the spine art. Provided you've copied the spine art to the computer's clipboard, you're now ready to choose Edit > Paste.

Remember to create another new, blank layer for the spine before invoking the Vanishing Point filter. With each object on its own layer, repositioning or tweaking the objects later will be much easier (**Figure 24f**).

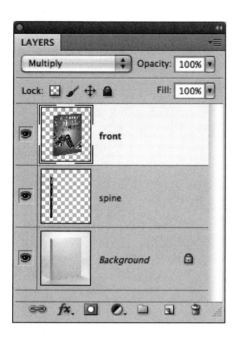

Figure 24f With each object on its own layer, making final adjustments will be easy.

The final important step to complete the 3D illusion is to select both spine and cover layers and change their blend mode from Normal to Multiply. **Figure 24g** shows the final composite mock-up.

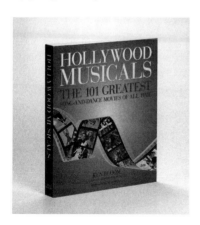

Figure 24g If done correctly, the mock-up can often look better than a photo of the actual book and real cover.

CHAPTER FOUR

Working with Illustrator

There's a classic *Saturday Night Live* commercial parody for a product called Shimmer, in which a husband (played by Dan Aykroyd) and wife (Gilda Radner) argue over whether the product is a floor wax or a dessert topping. As the debate escalates, a slick pitchman (Chevy Chase) breaks it up by stating that Shimmer is *both* a floor wax *and* a dessert topping.

Illustrator is a lot like Shimmer because it serves so many disparate needs. It's a print-based application that's also a Web graphics creation tool with a pixel grid. It's a vector-based object-creation model that supports transparency and Photoshop-like effects, and now creates naturalistic brush strokes. It's a two-dimensional tool that has rudimentary three-dimensional modeling and now allows you to draw in perspective.

Whatever task you throw at Illustrator, or whatever your particular artwork needs are, there are a multitude of features that help you explore creatively, work efficiently, and publish reliably.

#25 Understanding the Perspective Grid

Illustrator's new Perspective Drawing feature gives artists the ability to define a perspective grid, draw art on that grid, and add existing art to that grid in the appropriate perspective. This speeds up perspective-based drawing, but before you start drawing you need to understand the grid you're drawing on and its various settings and controls.

Every Illustrator document contains one perspective grid. By default, that grid is not shown. To reveal a document's perspective grid, go to View > Perspective Grid > Show Grid, or press Shift-Command-I (Shift-Ctrl-I). The default is a two-point perspective grid, but Illustrator has built-in grid presets for one-, two-, and three-point perspective drawing (**Figure 25a**) that you can also use as the basis for your drawing.

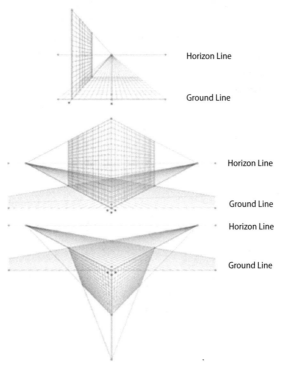

Figure 25a From top to bottom: Illustrator's one-point, two-point (the document default), and three-point perspective grid presets.

One-, Two-, and Three-point Perspective: What's the Difference?

To understand perspective, think about where the viewer is in physical space.

One-point perspective is what the viewer would see standing in the center of a long hallway, looking straight ahead. All planes (walls, ceiling, floor, etc.) converge to a single point—known as the vanishing point—on the horizon. The horizon line is always at eye level.

Two-point perspective is what the viewer would see standing in the center of a four-way intersection, looking directly at the corner of one block. To the left, the buildings down one street recede in one direction. To the right, the buildings recede in another direction toward a second vanishing point. Both points share the same horizon line.

(continued on next page)

You can make the grid visible simply by switching to the Perspective Grid tool 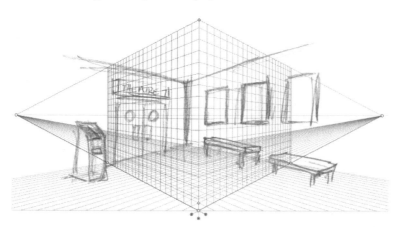 (Shift-P). This tool makes all of the grid's modification points active so you can reposition its horizon line or left and right planes, extend or redistribute its grid lines, and otherwise customize it to your needs. Any grid you customize can be saved as a preset to use in any other Illustrator document (View > Perspective Grid > Save Grid as Preset).

Customizing the Perspective Grid

Illustrator's perspective grid projects forward, so adjusting a grid to match a scanned sketch is pretty simple if the sketch's composition matches that default. However, not all perspective drawings are composed that way. The sketch in **Figure 25b**, for example, recedes toward its center.

Figure 25b Illustrator's default front-projecting grid does not match this composition.

(continued)

Three-point perspective is what you'd see flying in a helicopter looking down at that intersection. Buildings still recede off into the distance toward two vanishing points and one horizon line, but all the buildings' lines (from the rooftop to the street) also converge downward toward a third vanishing point.

The Grid Is Everywhere

Although the grid you see in your document appears to occupy a finite area defined by the grid lines for each plane, the perspective grid is, in fact, *everywhere* in the document. Moving objects in perspective beyond the visible edges of the grid doesn't remove them from its control. Instead, those objects appear farther above or below the grid's horizontal boundaries, or nearer to or farther back from its vertical boundaries, and they remain drawn in proper perspective.

Common Ground

Regardless of the type of perspective grid you choose, all grids share these basic components:

- a horizon line
- a left plane (two- and three-point perspective grids also contain a right plane)
- a ground plane

Station Point=Pivot Point

The station point of a two- or three-point perspective grid is the front-most corner of the cube formed by the grid. When you lock a grid's station point (View > Perspective Grid > Lock Station Point), your changes to the grid's vanishing points are inversely mirrored. In other words, moving the left plane's vanishing point inward moves the right plane's vanishing point outward by an equal amount, and vice versa. With the station point locked, the two planes effectively pivot from the point where they meet as you move either vanishing point.

Fortunately, grids can be customized. When the Perspective Grid tool is active, each grid plane has a control handle with which you can reposition that grid. If we move the handle for the right plane to the left, for example, the right grid plane can act as the grid for the left wall in the sketch (**Figure 25c**).

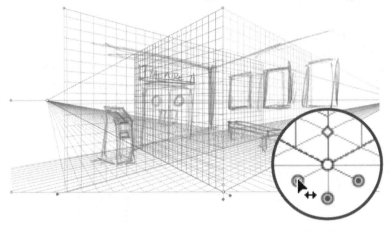

Figure 25c The right grid plane is moved to the left using its control handle (inset) to a position that matches the left wall of the sketch.

Once the grid plane is placed in the approximate position, its vanishing point can be moved to get the perspective angle as close to the sketch as possible (**Figure 25d**). With the plane positions transposed, their respective extents will overlap and create a very busy grid. This can be prevented by dragging the hollow diamond shapes (which control the grid extents) on the repositioned plane in toward where the two walls meet (**Figure 25e**).

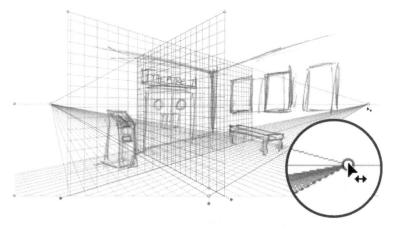

Figure 25d Moving the vanishing point (inset) sets an angle that better matches the original sketch.

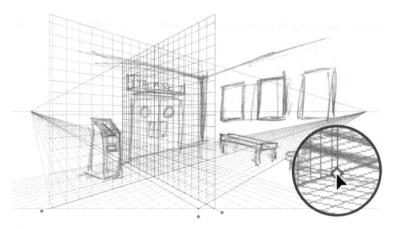

Figure 25e Pulling in the grid extents diamonds (inset) displays fewer grid lines and prevents the two grids from overlapping.

Tone Down Your Grid

As you add artwork, the perspective grid can become distracting. To minimize this, open the Define Perspective Grid dialog box (View > Perspective Grid > Define Grid) and change the grid's opacity from the default of 50 percent to something easier on the eyes, like 25 percent. Unfortunately, there's no application-wide way to change the default.

Grid Goodies, Part 1

When Illustrator's Smart Guides feature is turned on (which is the default) and you reposition the grid's horizon line, an "HH" value is displayed. This number indicates the horizon height, which is the distance between the horizon line and the ground line. If you're working on a drawing to scale, it can be helpful to put the grid's horizon line at a normal observer's height.

Grid Goodies, Part 2

The Define Perspective Grid dialog box (View > Perspective Grid > Define Grid) is your go-to place for all the perspective settings. From here, you can choose what type of grid to use (one-, two-, or three-point perspective), and select its measurement system, scale, gridline increments, viewing angle, horizon height, and the color of the left, right, and horizontal planes.

Similar position, vanishing point, and grid extent adjustments can be made to the left plane so that it can serve as the grid for the right wall in the sketch. Once that's done, the grid is completely customized for the perspective needs of this illustration (**Figure 25f**). Once the grid is established, the next step is mastering the appropriate drawing strategies to produce a finished perspective illustration (**Figure 25g**).

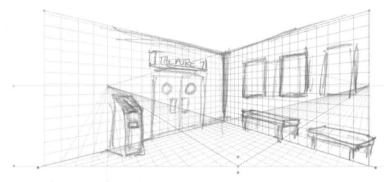

Figure 25f The customized perspective grid with its planes repositioned, horizon line adjusted, and grid extents pulled in to match the sketch.

Figure 25g A finished perspective drawing from the original sketch and the customized grid.

#26 Drawing in Perspective

As with any new feature, Perspective Drawing brings with it new tools, new behaviors, and new limitations that you need to become familiar with to work effectively.

One basic challenge is keeping track of which plane you're drawing on. Fortunately, Adobe added a hard-to-ignore element—the Active Plane Widget—at the top left of the document that appears whenever the perspective grid is visible (**Figure 26a**). The highlighted side of the cube shown in the widget indicates the currently active plane.

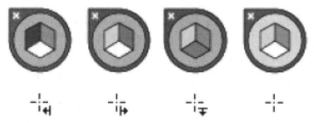

Figure 26a The Active Plane Widget in its various modes (top row, left to right): Left Grid, Right Grid, Horizontal Grid (or ground plane), and No Active Grid. Below each is the cursor's appearance when drawing objects on that grid.

All but one of Illustrator's object drawing tools work with the Perspective Drawing feature (**Figure 26b**): the Flare tool is not supported. With the perspective grid visible and the desired plane active, simply choose any other object drawing tool and start drawing. All shapes will be drawn in the perspective of the active plane.

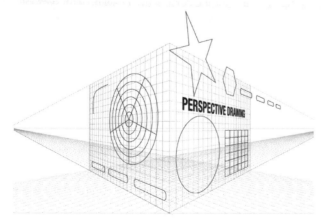

Figure 26b Rectangles, ellipses, polygons, stars, arcs, spirals, rectangular and polar grids, and live, editable type can all be drawn in perspective.

What the Perspective Drawing Feature Isn't

Illustrator is not a 3D modeling environment. Its Perspective Drawing feature provides no camera angle that can be changed, no surfaces to be mapped, and no means of controlling light or shadows. The perspective grid is basically a static framework on which you can draw and add shapes and text that will conform to that grid.

Once you set up your grid and start drawing on it, you're committed. You can't remove an object drawn on or added to the grid and return it to its "normal" state. Nor can you change the vanishing point or other aspects of the grid itself and have the artwork that's already on it adapt to those changes.

(continued on next page)

Plan out your perspective drawing before you get started and keep your expectations for the feature in…well, perspective. Knowing its limitation will help you take advantage of what it does well.

Fast Plane Switching

To switch quickly between different planes on the perspective grid, remember these shortcuts. Pressing the 1 key activates the left plane; 2 activates the horizontal (or ground) plane; 3 activates the right plane; and 4 exits Perspective Drawing, setting the widget to "no active grid."

These keyboard shortcuts also help you move selected objects from one plane to another. Hold down the mouse and select any perspective object, then tap a number key to move the object onto that plane. To copy an object to another plane, hold down the Option (Alt) key before pressing one of the shortcut numbers.

Holding down the 5 key while moving an object moves it perpendicular to its current plane.

Moving or modifying objects already in perspective requires switching to the new Perspective Selection tool 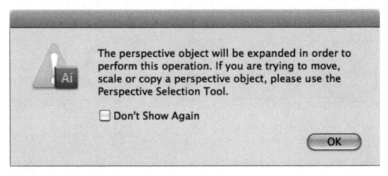 (Shift-V). Use this tool to scale objects in perspective, not the Scale tool. Using Illustrator's standard selection or transformation tools will break any object's connection to the grid and expand its appearance. Fortunately, Illustrator displays a prominent warning every time you run this risk (**Figure 26c**).

Figure 26c A useful warning dialog box prevents you from ruining your perspective drawing if you attempt to modify an object with the wrong tool.

Working Smarter in Perspective

Perspective Drawing is a great new feature that's actually easier to use and more flexible when it's combined with older Illustrator features. In the following example, we'll combine Perspective Drawing with symbols, clipping masks, and transparency to make the feature appear to do things it can't actually do.

Once an object is in perspective, it can't be removed from the grid and reverted to its flat state. Because of this it's important to work with symbols as much as possible (**Figure 26d**). Symbols used on the perspective grid are just placed instances, so you can modify the original symbol as flat artwork, then see all instances on the grid update in perspective.

Figure 26d These three symbols were used to build the finished illustration in Figure 26i.

A symbol is a single object, making it easier to select and position on a perspective grid. The stars-and-stripes pattern mapped to the left plane in **Figure 26e** is one symbol made up of multiple objects. Symbols can be easily contained within a clipping mask, as in **Figure 26f**.

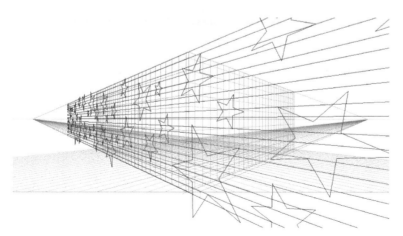

Figure 26e The stars and stripes symbol is placed into perspective on the left plane.

No Live Perspective for the Pen Tool

Perspective Drawing does not support one of Illustrator's most-used tools: the Pen tool. The easiest way to work around this is to draw your pen-based artwork *off* the perspective grid, then select it with the Perspective Selection tool and move it onto the active grid.

Type and Perspective

Live, editable text can be added to the perspective grid only after it's been typed. The text must be selected with the Perspective Selection tool and dragged onto the appropriate plane. To modify text that's already on the perspective grid, double-click it with the Perspective Selection tool to enter Isolation mode, where you can work exclusively on the text. Once you've modified your text and exited Isolation Mode, the text is re-rendered in perspective.

Do Your Rotating Off the Grid

You can't rotate shapes or symbols once they're on the perspective grid. If you want to rotate an object in perspective, you'll have to draw it off the grid, rotate it, switch to the Perspective Selection tool, and then move the rotated artwork onto the grid.

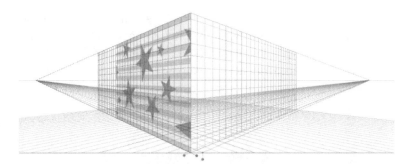

Figure 26f A rectangle drawn in perspective over the stars-and-stripes symbol and converted to a clipping path crops the pattern to create one side of the box.

By combining symbols and clipping masks, you can simulate art that wraps around an object, which is something the Perspective Drawing feature can't do (**Figure 26g**).

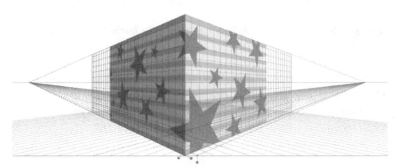

Figure 26g We copied the clipped symbol to the right plane, positioning it within the clipping mask to match up with the pattern on the left plane and create a wrap-around effect. We drew a black, semi-transparent rectangle with a multiply blend mode on the left plane to create a sense of depth.

Working with Illustrator

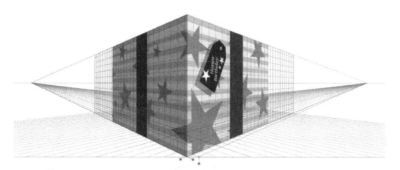

Figure 26h We added the gift tag and shadow symbols from Figure 26d to the right plane, and created the ribbon by drawing rectangles on both planes.

Figure 26i The finished perspective art. A gradient-filled rectangle drawn in perspective on the ground plane simulates a cast shadow. We added the bow at the top and the string on the tag off the perspective grid.

The Stroke Problem

Perspective drawing creates the illusion of 3D, but that illusion is shattered if your artwork contains strokes. Perspective drawing does not support strokes. If very thin strokes are used, it may not be a significant problem, but the heavier the stroke weight, and the farther back along the grid the stroked object appears, the worse the effect looks. To work around this shortcoming, convert the stroke to a shape (Object > Path > Outline Stroke) before putting the object in perspective.

#27 Creating Variable-width Strokes

The problem with Illustrator artwork is that it *looks* like Illustrator artwork. It tends to be a little too perfect and uniform unless you go to a lot of trouble, and sacrifice a lot of editability, to make it look otherwise. The fireplace illustration in **Figure 27a** should have a loose, casual feel, but that's undermined by the perfectly consistent line weight of every stroke.

Figure 27a A typical Illustrator line art drawing using normal strokes. The enlarged detail shows the uniformity of all strokes in the artwork.

The new Width tool 🖋 (Shift-W) lets you create variable-width strokes on a single path without adding anchor points or expanding the path. The Width tool adds a new kind of point—a width point—visible only when you hover over the path with the tool (**Figure 27b**).

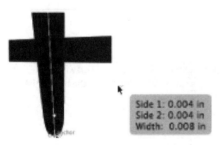

Figure 27b A width point selected with the Width tool and displaying Smart Guide data about the width of the stroke at that point.

To add a width point to any path, simply click somewhere on that path with the Width tool and drag either away from the path to widen the stroke, or toward the path to narrow it. To widen the stroke only on one side of the path, select the point, hold down the Option (Alt) key, and drag one of the width point's handles to the desired width on that side of the path (**Figure 27c**).

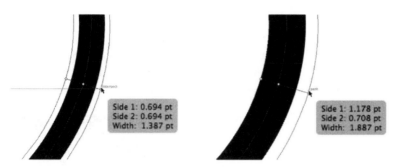

Figure 27c Widening a stroke equally on both sides of a path (left), and on only one side (right), with the Option (Alt) key.

Pin-point Width Point Precision

For greater control over your width points, double-click the point to open up the Width Point Edit dialog box. From there, you can put in specific widths for each side of the path. If you already have separate widths on either side of the path, changing the total width will add (or reduce) the width of each side proportionally.

To relocate a width point, select it with the Width tool and drag it to the desired position along the path. To "pull along" any other width points on that path and redistribute the changes in weight, hold down the Shift key while moving the selected width point. To delete a path, select it with the Width tool and press Delete.

Once you've modified a stroke's width, you can save the stroke as a Width Profile in either the Control panel or the Stroke panel (**Figure 27d**). That saved profile can be applied to any other stroke in your artwork, or used in any other Illustrator file.

Keep It Smooth

When you change the width of one width point that's on a path with other width points, holding down the Shift key will also modify those other width points to distribute the weight evenly along the path and avoid unwanted "bumps" in the stroke.

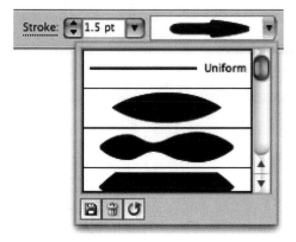

Figure 27d The Width Profile pull-down in the Control panel, with icon options for saving, deleting, or resetting profiles.

Why's My Stroke So Skinny?

The stroke weight values shown in the Stroke panel and Control panel refer to the thickest part of a variable-width path. If you apply a width profile to an existing path and don't see the result you expected, you may need to increase its stroke weight to get the desired appearance.

It's Not Just for Strokes

The Width tool also works with brushes applied to a path. Even Pattern brushes and Banner brushes can be transformed into variable-width brush strokes using the same steps described here. Only the new Bristle brush lacks support for the Width tool.

To make the most of your saved width profiles, you can flip them along the path using the Flip Along or Flip Across icons in the Stroke panel (**Figure 27e**). Flip Along flips the width profile from the start of the path to its end. Flip Across is only active for strokes with different weights on either side of the path, and flips them across that path.

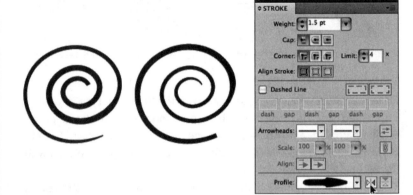

Figure 27e Both paths are identical, and use the same width profile, but the right path was flipped across the path length using the Stroke panel.

In the final fireplace illustration in **Figure 27f,** a single width profile was used for all elements of the fireplace frame, but made to look more varied by flipping the profile on select paths and subtly adjusting stroke weights. A second width profile was applied to the bricks and two others to the flames.

Figure 27f The finished illustration uses four custom width profiles.

#**28** Creating Better Dashed Strokes

For as long as Illustrator has been on the market, designers have been plagued by the behavior—or rather, the bad behavior—of its Dashed Strokes feature. In all versions before CS5, dash lengths and gaps were absolute values, so when a dashed stroke was applied to even simple rectangles and ellipses, the results were unpredictable. Complex shapes were an even bigger problem (**Figure 28a**).

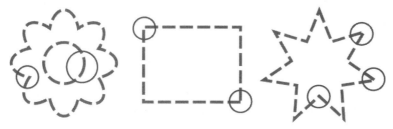

Figure 28a Illustrator's dashed strokes "the old way."

Illustrator CS5 fixes this problem with two new icons in the Stroke panel (**Figure 28b**). The first—Preserve Exact Gap and Dash Length—does exactly what Illustrator has always done. The second—Align Dashes to Corners and Path Ends, Adjusting Length to Fit—does what Illustrator users have been waiting many versions for: it makes the necessary calculations to position and adjust all dashes for a much more pleasing result (**Figure 28c**).

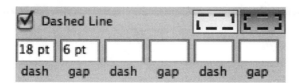

Figure 28b The Align/Adjust dash option selected in the Stroke panel.

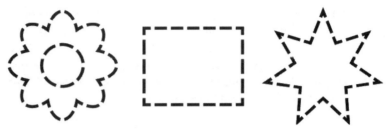

Figure 28c Adjusted—and much better-looking—dashed strokes in Illustrator CS5.

Illustrator allows for three different dash/gap value combinations for any dashed stroke, and the new adjusted strokes work just as well for those more complex dashed strokes (**Figure 28d**). All dash and gap settings between corner points are adjusted accordingly.

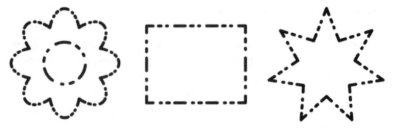

Figure 28d Complex dash combinations also benefit from new Align/Adjust behavior.

#29 Adding Arrowheads to Strokes

Arrowheads, which were previously effects added to strokes, have been moved to a logical home within the revamped Stroke panel. In addition to having a new location, arrowheads are now an attribute of the stroke, not an effect in a separate dialog box. They're easier to apply and and modify.

With a path selected, and the Stroke panel open in expanded view (**Figure 29a**), you can select any starting or ending arrowhead from the two respective pop-up menus. Each end of the path can have a different arrowhead setting. A new "swap" icon in the panel switches the choices made for the starting and ending arrowheads, in case the path was drawn in a way that Illustrator considers its end point to be what visually looks like its start point. In previous versions, you'd have to change each point's arrowhead type in the Add Arrowheads dialog box to accomplish this same task.

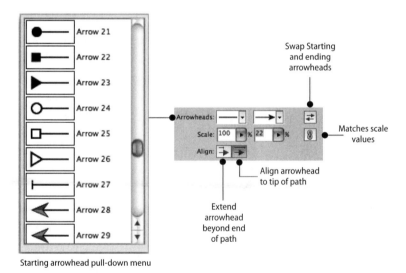

Starting arrowhead pull-down menu

Figure 29a Arrowhead options in the Stroke panel.

The default size of any arrowhead may not be appropriate for your stroke, depending on its length and width, so each arrowhead has independent Scale options. Previous versions only allowed a single scale value for both arrowheads. If you want to preserve that behavior, click the lock icon 🔒 next to those Scale value fields. That will match the value of both fields to what you enter in either one of them.

Historically, arrowheads extended out past the end points of the path. If you wanted your arrowhead tips to be exactly where the path ended, you'd have to "cheat" your path back a bit to achieve the proper alignment. That's no longer necessary in Illustrator CS5: the new default is for arrowhead tips to align to the start or end point of the path; see **Figure 29b.** If you want your arrowhead tips to extend beyond the end points of the path, you can select an optional setting in the Stroke dialog box (**Figure 29c**).

Figure 29b A path (left) with a normal stroke and 80 percent arrowhead (center) and with a variable-width stroke and a 22 percent arrowhead (right). The arrowhead is aligned to the end of the path in each instance.

Figure 29c The same path and stroke options as Figure 29b, but with the arrowheads set to extend beyond the end of the path.

All of these enhancements make arrowheads much easier to control, align, stylize, and modify without ever leaving the Stroke panel.

#30 Drawing with the Shape Builder Tool

Illustrator CS5's new Shape Builder tool 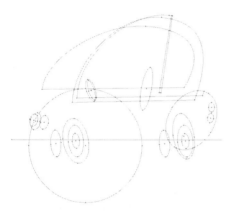 is like a dynamic version of the Pathfinder's Unite and Minus Front options, combined with Live Paint's shape-sensing, click-and-color functionality. **Figure 30a** shows an illustration at its very early stages, using only primitive shapes as the basis for a drawing of a car. No fill or stroke has been applied. Using only the Shape Builder tool, we can quickly and easily refine this collection of shapes to form the car and simultaneously fill it with appropriate colors.

Figure 30a An arrangement of drawn shapes created as the foundation for an illustration of a car. The single horizontal line defines areas where the shapes it intersects can be divided.

The Shape Builder shares a few behaviors with Illustrator's Live Paint feature, including Gap Detection and a Cursor Swatch Preview option that applies color as shapes are combined. Double-clicking the Shape Builder tool icon in the Tools panel accesses all of these options (**Figure 30b**).

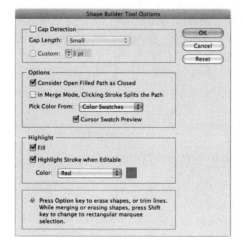

Figure 30b The Shape Builder Tool Options share several features with Illustrator's Live Paint.

Shape Builder vs. Pathfinder, Round 1

Pathfinder's Minus Front function acts on full shapes only, subtracting the foreground shape from the background shape. However, Shape Builder can "minus" any area created by the intersection of paths, whether or not they're complete shapes. This means drawing fewer exact shapes to get the same results.

Shape Builder vs. Pathfinder, Round 2

On speed alone, Shape Builder beats Pathfinder hands down. To subtract a shape with Pathfinder, you must select two objects, be sure the appropriate subtraction shape is stacked in front of the artwork you want to keep, then use the Minus Front option. Depending on the number of shapes you start out with, you might need to repeat that many times, often making copies of certain shapes to re-use them in subsequent Pathfinder operations.

To form a car from the collection of shapes in Figure 30a, we start by removing parts of any shape that won't be included in the final illustration. With all the shapes selected and the Shape Tool (Shift-M) active, you need only drag over selected shapes while holding down the Option (Alt) key to remove any portion of an object up to the point where it intersects with another shape (**Figure 30c**). Portions of the shapes "sensed" by the Shape Builder tool are highlighted as you move over them.

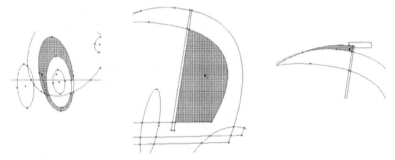

Figure 30c Three ways to remove portions of shapes with the Shape Builder tool: Option-click (Alt-click) and drag through continuous areas (left), Option-click (Alt-click) a single area (center), or Shift-Option-click (Shift-Alt-click) and draw a marquee over multiple areas (right).

Once the unwanted areas are removed, we can start combining those parts we want to keep. With the Cursor Swatch Preview active (**Figure 30d**), you can cycle through document swatches and choose a color to fill the remaining shapes with as the Shape Builder combines them (**Figures 30e and 30f**). As with deleting shapes, holding down Shift creates a marquee selection, and simply clicking and dragging creates a linear selection of continuous shapes.

Figure 30d The Shape Builder tool with Cursor Swatch Preview active.

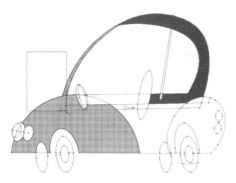

Figure 30e Combining shape areas by Shift-dragging to create a marquee selection.

Figure 30f Adding colors to different areas of the artwork as they're combined with the Shape Builder tool.

While much of what the Shape Builder tool does is inherited from the Pathfinder and Live Paint features, it works more quickly and more intuitively than either of those tools, producing finished illustrations (**Figure 30g**) from basic forms in very little time.

Figure 30g The finished illustration completed entirely with the Shape Builder tool.

Shape Builder vs. Pathfinder, Round 3

By default, you can use Shape Builder to achieve the same results as Pathfinder's Unite, Minus Front, Minus Back, Intersect, Exclude, and Merge functions. But you can also mimic Pathfinder's Divide, Trim, Merge, and Crop features by turning on Cursor Swatch Preview in the Shape Builder Tool Options dialog box and applying different colors to intersecting areas as you work with the tool. The colors applied define each area as a separate shape.

Shape Builder vs. Pathfinder, Round 4

Except for the Divide and Outline functions, Pathfinder works with shapes only, not open paths. Shape Builder works more like Live Paint when artwork contains a mix of shapes and paths. The Shape Builder tool uses a path's intersection of a shape to slice away a portion of that shape. Option-clicking (Alt-clicking) a segment of a path will "trim" that path back to the nearest inter-section point with another shape or path.

#31 Drawing Behind and Drawing Inside

Illustrator has a stacking order in each document where, by default, new art is created above existing art. To speed up the drawing process, reduce the need to re-stack artwork, and eliminate many of the steps involved in creating clipping masks, Illustrator CS5 introduces two new drawing modes: Draw Behind and Draw Inside. You can cycle through these modes by pressing Shift-D, or you can select any of them from a new icon at the bottom of the Tools panel (**Figure 31a**).

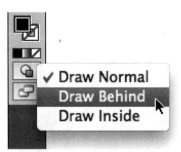

Figure 31a New drawing mode options at the bottom of the Tools panel.

Draw Behind effectively reverses Illustrator's default behavior by creating new artwork beneath the existing objects. As you draw or paint in this mode, artwork is visible above the other objects in the illustration (**Figure 31b**). However, as soon as you're done drawing, the new artwork is automatically moved back behind all other artwork (**Figure 31c**).

Figure 31b While drawing in Draw Behind mode, artwork initially appears above other art.

Figure 31c Finished brush strokes automatically moved behind existing artwork.

Draw Inside mode is available only when a single drawn shape is selected. When Draw Inside is activated, the selected artwork is surrounded by a dashed corner selection border (**Figure 31d**). As long as that border is visible, all new artwork will be created *inside* the shape, even when you deselect the shape to start drawing other objects. Draw Inside creates clipping masks as you're working, saving you the trouble of doing so after the artwork is completed.

Figure 31d Draw Inside mode activated for the body of the car.

An additional benefit of the Draw Inside mode is that allows you to paste artwork inside of other artwork. There is no Paste Inside command in Illustrator, but when you're in Draw Inside mode, all pasting is done inside the selected object.

Figure 31e A copied path with a variable-width pattern brush applied pasted into the Draw Inside object. Only the parts of the path within the shape are visible.

To exit Draw Inside mode, double-click anywhere else on the artboard to return to Draw Normal mode.

#32 Creating Bristle Brushes

Illustrator CS5 introduces a new kind of brush that's designed to mimic the appearance and behavior of natural media brushes. To do this required the addition of a background physics engine that understands a brush's size, shape, length, the number of bristles it contains, and each bristle's thickness and stiffness.

This feature greatly benefits artists using a pressure-sensitive tablet and stylus, because the physics engine and brush attributes respond to the orientation and tilt of the stylus, and to the pressure applied to it. This creates a beautiful "painterly" appearance with what is, in fact, 100 percent vector-based artwork.

You select a Bristle brush by choosing New Brush, then Bristle Brush to open the Brushes panel menu. The Bristle Brush Options dialog box available in that panel has a Shape pull-down menu for the different categories of brushes. There are five brush types—point, blunt, curve, angle, and fan—and each has both a flat and round version. Including brush size, each of these ten brush types has six customizable attributes (**Figure 32a**).

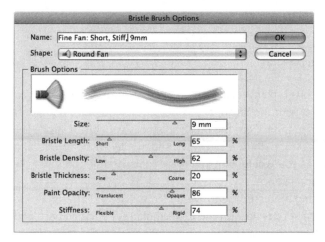

Figure 32a A custom bristle brush established in the Bristle Brush Options dialog box. Note that brush names will appear only when the Brushes panel is in List View.

There's a range of settings within each of these attributes, so by mixing and matching brush types and attributes, you have a nearly infinite number of brushes at your disposal, faster—and much cheaper!—than you could ever have with real paint brushes.

How Does It Do That?

The Bristle brush mimics the effect of actual bristles on a surface by creating individual overlapping filled objects for each stroke. If you were to expand the appearance of a Bristle brush stroke (Object > Expand Appearance), you'd see each individual bristle mark as a filled object.

Bristle Brush Attributes Explained

Bristle Length (Short to Long). Longer bristles have more flexibility as you paint; short bristles barely bend.

Bristle Density (Low to High). This sets the number of bristles in the brush tip and how close they are to one another. Low density means a lot of space between bristles.

Bristle Thickness (Fine to Coarse). This refers to the thickness of individual bristles. In natural media brushes, fine would be something like a sable hair brush and coarse would be like a hog's hair brush.

Paint Opacity (Translucent to Opaque). In digital painting—unlike real painting—you use the brush to control paint transparency. The less opaque the paint, the more shows through it as you paint. Semi-transparent strokes are akin to the look of watercolors or transparent acrylics.

Stiffness (Flexible to Rigid). This refers to how much the bristles bend. Flexible bristles bend more and are softer. Rigid bristles produce hard, discernible bristle patterns.

Change Your Brush on the Fly

Don't worry too much about defining the size of your brush when creating a new Bristle Brush. Instead, set the size based on either (a) how well the preview in the Bristle Brush Options dialog shows you the brush appearance, or (b) the size you expect to use most often in your artwork. The brush size can be increased on the fly by hitting the right square bracket key, or decreased with the left square bracket key.

(continued on next page)

Just as Adobe has always respected typographic conventions designers are used to, it now shows that same reverence for traditional brushes artists are accustomed to. Illustrator CS5 ships with a Bristle brush library (choose Open Brush Library > Bristle Brush > Bristle Brush Library from the Brushes panel menu) containing 14 preset brushes based on real-world painters' brushes (**Figure 32b**).

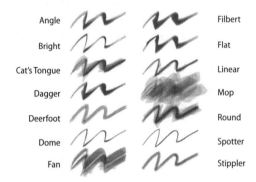

Figure 32b Samples of each brush in Illustrator's Bristle Brush Library. All strokes are the same weight. Their appearance is affected by brush thickness and other brush-specific attributes.

The Bristle brush paints using the path's stroke color, not its fill. You can either paint with the Brush tool, or select existing paths and apply a Bristle brush to them from the Brushes panel. Every brush stroke is a fully editable vector path. You can move and modify anchor points and Bezier curves as you would with any drawn path and still preserve the brush stroke appearance.

If you're using a pressure-sensitive tablet and stylus with the Bristle brush tool, a cursor preview on the tool simulates the appearance and angle of the brush tip, matching the orientation and tilt of the stylus as you move and tilt it (**Figure 32c**).

Figure 32c A Brush tool cursor preview—specific to the current position and angle of a drawing stylus—is displayed when working with a pressure-sensitive tablet and stylus.

Performance and Printing

The Bristle brush's creative potential is limited only by your imagination. But what about more practical considerations like system performance and printing? The more bristles you have in a brush, the more complex it is, and all that beautiful overlapping transparency comes at a price.

Complex brushwork can potentially cause rendering speed and printing issues. If you plan to use the Bristle brush, Adobe recommends 4GB of RAM (well above the 1GB minimum requirement), and the fastest available processor for optimum Illustrator performance.

Even with gigabytes of RAM and a killer processor, you'll see a warning dialog about the amount of transparency in your file when you try to save it to EPS, PDF, or any other format that requires flattening.

When your artwork's final, make a copy of the file and rasterize complex Bristle brush artwork in that copy in Illustrator (Object > Rasterize) before placing it in InDesign or into a Postscript process that requires flattening for output. This will avoid PDF or RIP rasterization, which is much slower.

A related keyboard shortcut increases or decreases the paint opacity. Hit the 1 key for 10% opacity, 2 for 20% and so on up to 90%. Hit 0 for 100% opaque paint coverage.

Previewing a Bristle Brush in Color

The Bristle brush and the Brush panel are limited to grayscale displays of a brush's appearance. To preview what a Bristle brush effect will look like in color, select a path and apply a stroke color and weight. Then, either apply an existing brush to that stroke, or define a new brush with the Preview check box selected in the Bristle Brush Options dialog.

#33 Using Multiple Artboards

The multiple artboard feature introduced in Illustrator CS4 enabled designers to collect many Illustrator assets and layouts into a single file, stored on independent artboards (**Figure 33a**). The presentation and organizational benefits of multiple artboards were a big hit, and Illustrator CS5 builds upon the feature to make it more versatile and powerful.

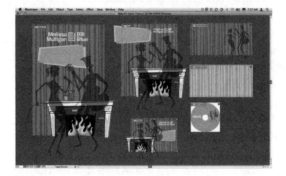

Figure 33a A multi-artboard Illustrator CS5 document containing various components of a design project: poster, flyer, postcard, CD booklet, and disc label.

Artboards now have their own dedicated panel (Window > Artboards) from which you can select, rename, and reorder your artboards (**Figure 33b**). Clicking any artboard name in the Artboard panel makes it the active artboard, and double-clicking fills your document window with that artboard.

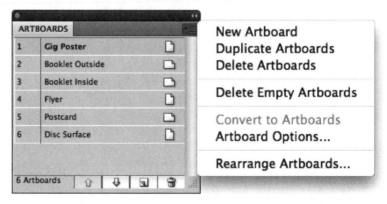

Figure 33b Illustrator CS5's new Artboards panel displaying six artboards and the panel's menu options.

When you create a new document, you can add multiple artboards of identical size in the New Document dialog box. In an existing document, you can use the Artboard tool ▣ to add artboards of varying sizes at any time. A single Illustrator document can contain up to 100 artboards.

With the Artboard tool, you can select entire artboards, resize them by pulling on any of the corner/edge handles, or reposition them on the Illustrator canvas by clicking and dragging (**Figure 33c**). For precise control over artboard size, use the width and height fields in the Control panel to specify the artboard's size, and the x and y coordinates to control its position on the Illustrator canvas.

Figure 33c Resizing (left) and repositioning (right) artboards with the Artboard tool.

By default, everything on the artboard moves with it, except locked objects and objects on locked layers. However, artwork doesn't scale when the artboard is resized. To move the artboard *without* moving the art on it, deselect the Move/Copy Artwork with Artboard button ⊕ in the Control panel.

Same Button, Different Behavior

The Artboard panel and the Control panel each have a New Artboard button, but they behave a bit differently. Both will create a new artboard at the size of the currently active artboard, but that's where they part company. When you use the Artboard panel to create a new artboard, it's added at the far right of the canvas, aligned with the top of the topmost artboard in your document. The Control panel, however, leaves artboard placement up to you. When you click the New Artboard button from the Control panel, your cursor gets "loaded" with an artboard and wherever you click is where that artboard gets dropped on the canvas.

116

Lose the Board, Keep the Art

When you delete a page in InDesign, everything on it is also deleted. But that's not the case with artboards in Illustrator. Deleting an artboard—by clicking the trash can icon in the Control or Artboard panels—deletes the artboard, but the art itself is preserved in place.

Controlling Artboard Sizes

You can quickly draw out new artboards with the Artboard tool by clicking and dragging out an area. When you have Smart Guides turned on (the default), a measurement cursor displays the current size of the drawn artboard. To get more precise control over the artboard size and its position on the page, either enter the size and position values directly in the Control panel, or click the Artboard Options button to define your artboard's parameters in the Artboard Options dialog.

In CS4, artboards were identified only by a number, making it hard to keep track of what each artboard contained when selecting, printing, or exporting individual artboards. In CS5, artboards can be given names that are displayed in the Control panel (when the Artboard tool is in use), the Artboard Navigation pop-up menu (**Figure 33d**), or in the Artboard panel.

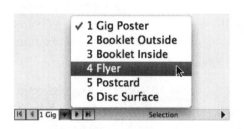

Figure 33d Artboards listed in the Artboard Navigation menu.

The fastest way to name artboards is *not* from the Artboards panel, however. That process requires selecting the artboard name, choosing Artboard Options from the panel menu, renaming the artboard in a dialog box, then clicking OK. It's much more efficient to switch to the Artboard tool (Shift-O), select the artboard to be renamed, and enter a name in the Name field of the Control panel. While that tool's still active, you can select other artboards and quickly rename them as well.

Rearranging artboards in the Artboard panel does not rearrange them visually, just hierarchically. The Artboard panel sequence and appearance of artboards on the Illustrator canvas are not dynamically related. To arrange your artboards on the canvas so they reflect the order in the Artboard panel, choose Rearrange Artboards from the Artboard panel menu, and specify your desired arrangement options (normal order or reverse order, horizontal or vertical distribution, number of columns, and spacing between artboards) in the dialog box (**Figure 33e**).

CHAPTER FOUR   Working with Illustrator

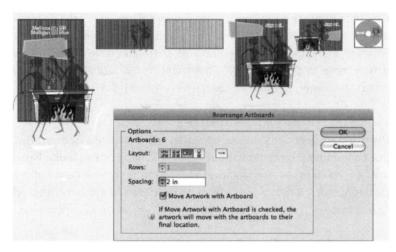

Figure 33e Artboards rearranged in a single row by using the Rearrange Artboards dialog box.

Whether or not you rearrange your artboards visually, their sequence in the Artboards panel plays a key role when the document is printed or exported. The numeric order of artboards in the panel acts as the document's page order when printing and saving as a PDF.

Other print- and export-related artboard improvements include:

- A new Auto-Rotate default in the Print dialog box sets all artboards to the proper orientation for the destination page size, allowing you to print portrait- and landscape-oriented artboards simultaneously.

- You can now save native Illustrator (.ai) files from individual artboards using Save As. This allows you to save a multi-artboard file as separate files in Illustrator CS3 (or earlier) format for backward compatibility.

- When exporting to non-native formats (EPS, JPEG, and so on), select the Use Artboards check box in the export dialog to create separate files from each artboard. A "root" name is required for the exported files (i.e., campaign.jpg), but the files are named with their artboard name or number appended after that shared root name (i.e., campaign_postcard.jpg).

Cut, Don't Copy, When Using Paste on All Artboards

Two new artboard-centric options—Paste in Place and Paste on All Artboards— have been added to Illustrator CS5's Edit menu. Paste in Place pastes anything copied to the clipboard at the exact same x, y coordinates from which it was copied. Paste on All Artboards does the same thing on every artboard in the document at once.

When using Paste on All Artboards to copy artwork from one artboard onto all others, remember to use the Cut command, not Copy. Paste on All Artboards includes the *current* artboard, so it will make a duplicate of the copied artwork on the same artboard while adding art to the others. Using Cut avoids this problem.

#34 The Power of Appearances

One of Illustrator's most powerful and underutilized features isn't really a feature, it's a panel: the Appearance panel (Window > Appearance or Shift-F6). Many designers may know it's there and have perhaps used it from time to time, but few understand its full scope or exploit its potential…largely because Adobe has never given it the hype it deserves.

Understanding Appearances

Paths and anchor points have no appearance. They define shapes, or lines, but contain no information about how that shape or line looks. Paths are like skeletons, and appearances are the attributes that flesh out the skeleton, giving it recognizable form (**Figure 34a**). All attributes applied to an object—fill, stroke, effects, opacity, etc.—make up its appearance.

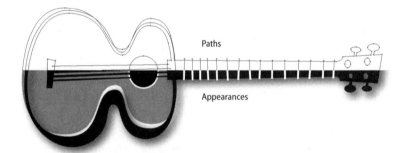

Figure 34a A series of paths (top) as seen on the Illustrator artboard vs. those same paths with appearances applied to them (bottom).

The Appearance panel is a direct conduit to all appearance settings for an object. It also shows you all the appearance attributes of a document, and reveals the stacking order of all appearances applied to a selected path or object at a glance. This one panel gives you one-click access to the panels and dialog boxes for any fill, stroke, opacity settings, and live effects that are part of an object's appearance (**Figure 34b**).

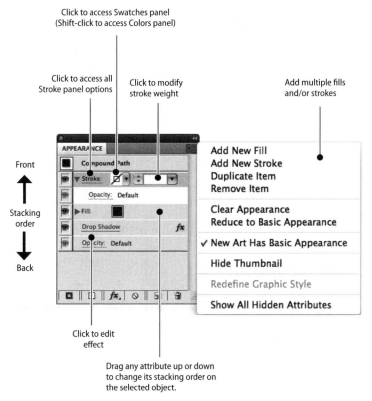

Click to access Swatches panel
(Shift-click to access Colors panel)

Click to access all
Stroke panel options

Click to modify
stroke weight

Add multiple fills
and/or strokes

Front

Stacking
order

Back

Click to edit
effect

Drag any attribute up or down
to change its stacking order on
the selected object.

Figure 34b The Appearance panel and its options at a glance.

Selecting vs. Targeting

Paths get selected, but appearances are targeted. When you select a path, you're selecting the entire object. Illustrator does basic appearance targeting for you at this level (fill and stroke only), so you can change basic appearance attributes.

If an object has more than one stroke, simply *selecting* the object targets its topmost stroke only. Targeting any stroke below that requires clicking the specific attribute name in the Appearance panel.

Targeting an appearance attribute allows you to work exclusively on that attribute, not the entire selected object. A targeted attribute can also be moved up and down in the Appearance panel to change its position in the stacking order for selected object, just as you drag items up or down in the Layers panel to change the stacking order for a document.

Adding Multiple Fills or Strokes

Illustrator creates all artwork with what's called a "basic" appearance, meaning one stroke, one fill, and no effects. But you can achieve a "complex" appearance for any object, ranging from one or more effects to multiple fills and strokes (**Figure 34c**).

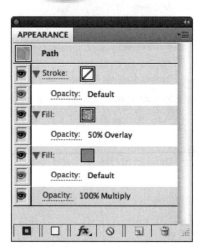

Figure 34c The guitar illustration has complex appearances applied but uses no more paths than the simple version in Figure 34a. The body of the guitar (left Appearance panel) has two fills—a solid color and a pattern fill (with a 50% overlay blend mode) above it in the stacking order. Both the body and the neck (right Appearance panel) have two strokes—a thin white stroke stacked above a wider black one—and a drop shadow. The frets along the neck are individual paths, each with two strokes applied via the Appearance panel.

Saving Appearances as Graphic Styles

Once established, any appearance can be saved as a Graphic Style (Window > Graphic Styles or Shift-F5) that applies all appearance attributes saved within it in a single click. A change to the style changes every object in the illustration to which that style has been applied.

To create a Graphic Style from an appearance, select an object with the desired appearance, then drag the small thumbnail of the appearance next to the object name (Path, Compound Path, etc.) into the Graphic Styles panel (**Figure 34d**). You can double-click its thumbnail in the Graphic Styles panel to give it a useful name. Once defined, that style can be applied to any other object with a single click on the style thumbnail.

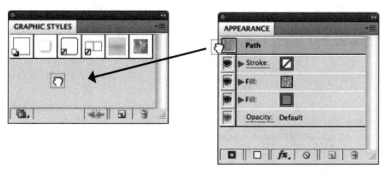

Figure 34d Creating a Graphic Style from a specific appearance is as easy as clicking the Appearance thumbnail (right) and dragging it into the Graphic Styles panel (left).

Assigning Appearances to Layers

Appearances can be applied to an entire layer, so that all art drawn on or moved to that layer automatically has that appearance. This can be an enormous time-saver in complex, layered illustrations like maps, where common appearances (i.e., road lines) are applied to many objects.

To assign an appearance to a layer, select any object that uses the desired appearance and locate it in the Layers panel by expanding the disclosure triangle for the layer it's on. The selected object will have a solid colored square next to its name, and you'll see a small gradient circle indicating that a complex appearance is applied (**Figure 34e**). Option-click (Alt-click) the gradient circle, drag it up to another layer in the panel, then release the mouse. You'll see a gradient circle applied at the layer level in the panel for that layer (**Figure 34f**).

Redefining Graphic Styles

Unlike InDesign's Object Styles, you don't make changes to Illustrator's Graphic Styles from the Graphic Styles panel. Instead, you make your changes to a selected object via the Appearance panel, then choose Redefine Style from the panel menu. This updates the Graphic Style to match the appearance of the current selection, and every other object to which that style is applied will reflect those changes.

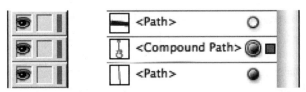

Figure 34e A selected object (with square at far right) in the Layers panel. The gradient circle indicates that a complex appearance is applied, and the circle around that indicates that the appearance is targeted. The path above it has a hollow circle, indicating only basic appearance in use. The path below it also has a complex appearance, but it is not targeted.

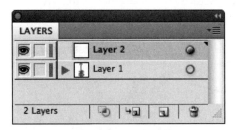

Figure 34f A layer with a complex appearance assigned to it, indicated by the gradient circle at the layer level in the panel.

Note that once the appearance applies to the layer, the objects on that layer do not need to have any appearance applied to them. The layer handles all of that (**Figure 34g**). Any appearance attributes applied directly to an object on that layer will be added to the layer-level appearance. Also, as soon as you move an object off of that layer, the object loses all layer-based appearance attributes.

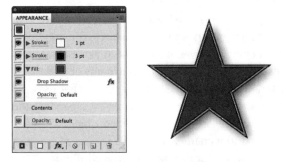

Figure 34g An object with 100 percent layer-based appearance applied. Note that all appearance attributes in the panel are attached to the layer. The only attribute under "Contents" is a default opacity setting.

#35 Creating Crisp Artwork for the Web

With its strong typographic capabilities, fast and flexible drawing capabilities, and tight integration with Flash CS5 Professional, Illustrator is a great tool for Web graphics creation. Since it started as a resolution-independent application for print, however, there are some things you need to know to properly work with Illustrator to create artwork for the Web.

Even though all artwork appears razor-sharp at any magnification in Illustrator, the same is not true when that art is rasterized (converted from vectors to pixels) for the Web. Artwork gets fuzzy when exported for the Web due to anti-aliasing, which blurs edges to smooth the appearance to the naked eye (**Figure 35a**). Illustrator CS5 includes a new Pixel Preview (View > Pixel Preview) mode that allows you to see just what your artwork will look like when rasterized.

Figure 35a Artwork as it normally appears in Illustrator (top) and the same artwork after it's been rasterized (bottom).

But *seeing* a problem with rasterization isn't much help if you can't *fix* it. Fortunately, there are new Illustrator features for that, too. The first is the Align to Pixel Grid option, which is available either for individual objects (**Figure 35b**), or on a document-wide basis. To align one or more objects to the pixel grid, select the objects, open the Transform panel (Window > Transform), and select the Align to Pixel Grid check box. To make this behavior persistent throughout your document, choose Align New Objects to Pixel Grid from the Transform panel menu.

Figure 35b The same rasterized buttons from Figure 35a aligned to the pixel grid. Notice the improvements around the edges of each button.

The Pixel Grid

When you zoom above 500 percent in Photoshop, the pixel grid becomes visible. In Illustrator, however, the pixel grid doesn't appear until you zoom to 600 percent. If you prefer to disable the pixel grid, deselect the Show Pixel Grid check box in the Grids & Guides area of Illustrator's Preferences dialog.

Automate Your Alignment

When you save artwork as a symbol, you'll see an "Align to Pixel Grid" option in the Symbol Options dialog box. Every time a symbol with Align to Pixel Grid enabled is placed, it will automatically snap to the pixel grid. If you know before you create a document that your destination is the Web, and you'll want all art aligned to the pixel grid, select the Align New Objects to Pixel Grid option in the New Document dialog box.

Aligning artwork to the pixel grid solves your rasterization problems for drawn shapes, but typography requires extra attention. The Character panel (Window > Type > Character) in Illustrator CS5 now includes the same type anti-aliasing options that Photoshop has had for many versions (**Figure 35c**). Choosing the correct option will depend entirely on the typeface in use and its size, color, and interaction with the colors around it.

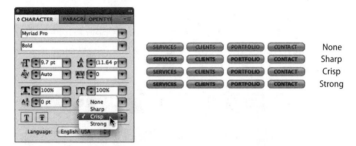

Figure 35c Anti-aliasing options in the fully expanded Character panel (left) and the results of each setting (right).

Getting Pixel Dimensions You Can Trust

When you select an object with a stroke applied to it in Illustrator, the Control panel displays the height and width for the path used to draw that object, not for the full extent of the stroke applied to that path (meaning the thickness beyond the path edge). Illustrator strokes, by default, are distributed along both sides of the path. This means you won't get accurate pixel dimensions for stroked artwork, since strokes add pixels to an object's overall size.

When you're working in a document that's intended for the Web, you can compensate for this discrepancy by changing a preference. In the General options of Illustrator's Preferences dialog, select the Use Preview Bounds check box to force all dimensions displayed for an object to include its outermost boundaries, not just the extent of its path.

#36 Preparing Scalable Web and Print Graphics

A long-standing frustration about creating Illustrator graphics was how objects distorted when scaled. Everything looked fine when an object was scaled in the same proportion, but if it was scaled more in one direction than another, rounded corners became stretched and horizontal and vertical stroke weights became inconsistent (**Figure 36a**).

Figure 36a When Illustrator artwork (left) is scaled in one direction only (right) the corner shapes are distorted, and the horizontal and vertical stroke weights become inconsistent.

For several versions, Illustrator has supported 9-Slice Scaling—an intelligent object scaling method used by Flash. Symbols created in Illustrator and destined for Flash could have 9-Slice Scaling guides established in Illustrator before they were exported (**Figure 36b**). Until Illustrator CS5, however, this kind of scaling worked only after the art was exported to Flash. Illustrator itself could not take advantage of the feature. Now you have the benefit of the same kind of intelligent scaling Flash has supported for all Illustrator artwork, whether destined for print or the Web.

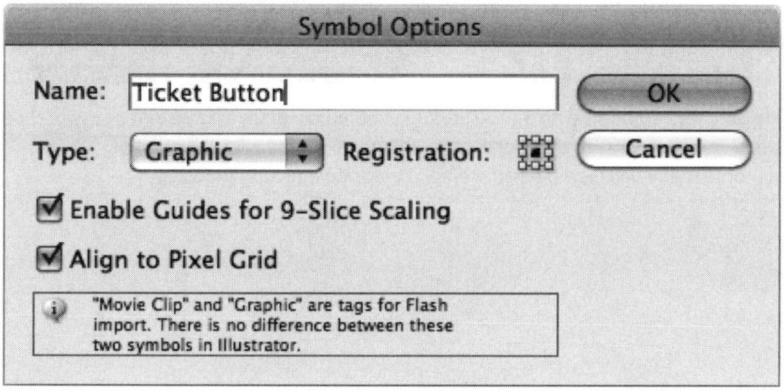

Figure 36b Enabling 9-Slice Scaling when creating a symbol allows for intelligent object scaling in both Illustrator CS5 and Flash CS5 Professional.

Any Way You Slice It

Illustrator CS5 has improved another kind of slice behavior to make your Web workflow more effi-cient. Artwork created in Illustrator that has been sliced for eventual use in a Web layout (Object > Slice), is much easier to selectively export with the addition of the Slice Selection tool , which shares a spot in the Tools panel with the Slice tool. Defined slices can be selected and more eas-ily exported with the new Save Selected Slices com-mand (File > Save Selected Slices…) without having to export the entire layout. You can even have Illustrator generate the HTML neces-sary for the selected slices.

What 9-Slice Scaling does is establish four guides (two horizontal and two vertical) on the symbol, dividing it into nine regions (**Figure 36c**). You can position the guides so that rounded or other stylized corners are "locked off" from scaling. The top and bottom center regions scale horizontally, and the left and right center regions scale vertically. Only the center region scales in both directions. When the object is scaled dis-proportionally, stroke weights remain consistent and custom corners are unchanged (**Figure 35c**).

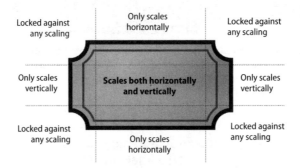

Figure 36c The four scaling guides divide an object into nine regions, each with its own scaling behavior.

Figure 36d Symbols with 9-Slice Scaling enabled maintain a consistent stroke weight and keep the four corner regions consistent with the original symbol's shape (left), even when scaled in only one direction (right).

CHAPTER FIVE

Working with InDesign

InDesign has matured rapidly since its debut ten years ago. Now in its seventh version, it's as robust and powerful as applications like Photoshop and Illustrator that have been around twice as long. As publishing grows beyond the printed page, InDesign has grown in the same direction. Now, in addition to gorgeous printed pieces, you can generate interactive PDFs, Flash animations, and rich media documents that include video, interactivity, and navigation.

InDesign CS5 hasn't forgotten its roots, however. It's still a page-layout powerhouse, and many of its new features are geared toward simplifying how designers work on the printed page, boosting productivity, improving automation, reducing repetitive tasks, and working collaboratively. Let's start with the print-centric techniques you'll want to master in this version.

#37 Creating Multiple Page Sizes

InDesign CS5's support for multiple page sizes in a single document offers many benefits to designers. When working on a stationery project, for example, it's helpful to have the letterhead, business card, and envelope layouts in a single file where styles and swatches can be centralized. Projects like three-panel brochures and gatefolds typically require one "short" flap for proper folding, and creating pages at the proper size in a single document simplifies the production process.

You still create new documents at one fixed size in the New Document dialog—but within a document, you can modify the size of any page using the Page tool 🔲 (Shift-P) in the Tools panel. When this tool is active, you can select pages either by clicking the page itself, or by clicking its thumbnail in the Pages panel.

Tip
Shift-clicking pages or thumbnails with the Page tool selects a range of pages, and Command-clicking (Ctrl-clicking) selects multiple noncontiguous pages.

Once one or more pages are selected, the Control panel offers up options related to the size of the selected page(s) (**Figure 37a**). All resizing options and behaviors work the same for both document pages and master pages.

Figure 37a The Control panel in Page mode.

Resizing occurs from any of the nine points on the proxy image in the Control panel, and the point chosen there determines how the resized page is positioned relative to other pages on the spread (**Figure 37b**). The y coordinate value determines the vertical position of a resized page relative to other pages on the spread. The x coordinate cannot be changed.

Figure 37b From left to right, the results when pages are resized from the top, center, and bottom.

To change the position of pages relative to one another, select a page with the Page tool and drag it to the desired vertical position. To move both the page and the objects on it, click the Objects Move with Page check box (if you do not, the page items will remain where they are and only the page will move).

The new Multiple Page Size feature works in combination with InDesign's existing Layout Adjustment feature. If that feature is off (which it is by default), select the Enable Layout Adjustment check box in the Control panel to activate it prior to resizing the page. With Layout Adjustment active, objects and guides (except those on master pages) will be repositioned, redistributed, and/or resized according to the new page dimensions.

Using the Master Page Overlay

When pages of different sizes share a master page, you can reposition the master page items on the document pages without overriding or detaching them from the master. Click the Show Master Page Overlay check box in the Control panel, and a blue overlay of the master page and everything on it appears on the document page.

Click, hold, and drag any edge of that overlay to reposition the master over the document page. The entire master (and all objects on it) moves to the new position on the selected document page, but the master page itself remains unaffected. The resized document page remains dynamically linked to that master page, and will reflect any subsequent changes made to it.

Document pages of varying sizes can share a master page, regardless of its size. Master page margins are maintained on the resized document page, so a letter-sized master page with half-inch margins maintains a half-inch margin around any page using that master, regardless of the page size. Master page items and guides, however, *do not* adapt to resized document pages. Their position on the resized page is determined by the point selected on the Proxy icon when the page size was modified (**Figure 37c**).

Figure 37c A letter-sized master page (left); a tabloid-sized page based on that master page (middle), resized from the top left corner; and a half-letter-sized page based on the same master page (right), resized from the center.

With the flexibility afforded by master pages that can be shared by many different page sizes, there's no need to create a new master for every page size in every document. However, it may be easier to do so for some projects. For example, when creating a stationery package—typically consisting of letterhead, business card, and envelope—consider creating an InDesign template (.indt file) that includes master pages for an 8.5-by-11–inch letterhead, 3.5-by-2-inch business cards (in both horizontal and vertical orientations), a 4.125-by-9 inch #10 envelope, and a 9-by-12-inch envelope (**Figure 37d**). The next time you land a stationery project, you'll be ready to dive right into it.

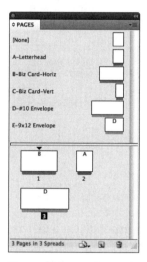

Figure 37d Master pages for varying sizes of standard stationery components in one InDesign document.

#38 Using the Revamped Layers Panel

Using the Layers Panel to Work with Groups

You can use the Layers panel to target and select any object in a group by Option-clicking (Alt-clicking) its name in the panel. This puts you in Group Object Selection mode, and you can then click other objects in the group directly in the layout to select and modify them. This behavior persists until you exit the group by either hitting Esc or clicking off the group.

The Layers panel also simplifies adding objects to or removing them from a group. Ungrouping is no longer a required first step. Simply Option-click (Alt-click) the desired object name, drag it outside the <group> hierarchy, and release the mouse. You can release a grouped object to its current layer only, but once it's released, you can drag it to any layer in the panel.

Adding an object to a group is even easier. Select any object in the layout, or Option-click (Alt-click) its name in the Layers panel, then drag the object's name into the desired group in the panel.

With each new version of InDesign, it seems that one feature gets the "extreme makeover" treatment by Adobe engineers. In CS5, it's the Layers panel: In this latest version, it's been torn down and rebuilt to look and work like Illustrator's Layers panel. Each layer now sports a clickable disclosure triangle next to its name that reveals a complete, object-by-object hierarchy of everything in that layer (**Figure 38a**).

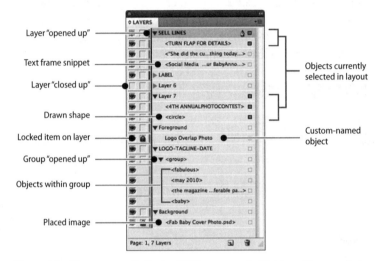

Figure 38a The revamped InDesign CS5 Layers panel with hierarchies revealed.

The new Layers panel automatically assigns every object a generic name, such as "line," "rectangle," and "group." Each set of grouped objects has its own nested hierarchy within the layer, which is revealed by clicking the disclosure triangle next to the group name. Placed images bear the original filename, and text frames are named with their first 32 characters. Default names are enclosed in angle brackets, and you can rename any object by triple-clicking its name in the panel.

The Layers panel can be a handy alternative to the Selection tool, especially in complex layouts where directly clicking a desired object might be difficult. You can use the Layers panel to select objects on the page by clicking the small, hollow square at the right of an object name, or Option-clicking (Alt-clicking) an object or layer name. Alternatively, you can select multiple object names in the Layers panel, then right-click and choose Select Item(s) from the context menu. Another option, available only for single-object selections, is Select Item and Fit, which selects the targeted object on the page and positions it in the center of the document window.

Tip

You can select a continuous range of object names by Shift-clicking; Command-click (Ctrl-click) each object name for noncontiguous selection.

Advantages to the New Layers Panel

- An at-a-glance under-standing of the structure and stacking order of your entire layout, and the ability to re-arrange that order without selecting items on the page.

- Individual Hide/Show and Lock buttons for each object allow a granular level of control over visibility and edit-ability. In previous ver-sions, you could only hide, show, or lock an entire layer.

- A means of naming every object on the page that's recognized by other fea-tures like the new Ani-mation panel. This also makes objects easy to target and refer to with scripts.

#39 Setting Up Span/ Split Columns

Building Span/ Split Options Into Paragraph Styles

The best way to use Span Columns is to build its options into your paragraph styles for one-click application to headlines, decks, and more. Since spanning is a paragraph-level attribute, the option has been added to the Paragraph Styles dialog.

For maximum flexibility, take advantage of the Based On feature. Create a "parent" style (let's call it "Headline") with spanning set to None. Then create a few "child" styles, each with spanning set to the desired number of columns. The first child style would span two columns and be named "Headline (Span 2)," the next would span three columns and be named "Headline (Span 3)," and so on. Any changes made to the original Headline style will be inherited by those child styles, but each of them will maintain its unique spanning attribute.

You can use the same strategy with your bulleted or numbered list styles, using the Split Column Paragraph Layout option instead.

In previous versions of InDesign, creating a layout in which text spans multiple columns required an excessive number of threaded text frames, delicate balancing, numerous adjustments, and a lot of patience. **Figure 39a** illustrates just how complex even a relatively simple text flow can be. Achieving the desired look—a headline and deck that span three columns, an intro paragraph that spans two, a bulleted list split into two columns, and a footer that spans three columns—requires eight threaded text frames, three of which include text wrap settings.

Figure 39a Multi-column paragraphs set up in InDesign CS4 or earlier.

Not only is this cumbersome to set up, but it also offers no flexibility whatsoever when text is changed. Any significant copy changes require repositioning, resizing, and rebalancing every frame, often multiple times.

InDesign CS5 eliminates all of this toil with the new Span Columns dialog, which allows you to extend a paragraph across the columns in a multi-column frame. Span Columns also includes options that would have allowed the bulleted list in Figure 39a to stack in two columns within a single column. With Span Columns, the layout in Figure 39a could be achieved within a single frame. More than that, its text would re-flow perfectly if edited, with no frame adjustments required.

Access to Span Columns is available several ways. The Control panel (in Paragraph mode 🔳) offers easy access to the basic settings. More settings are available in the Span Columns and Split Column Paragraph Layout options (**Figure 39b**), which are available from either the Paragraph panel menu or the Control panel menu when text is selected.

Figure 39b The Span Columns dialog's span (left) and split (right) Paragraph Layout options.

When you compare the "old-fashioned" method in Figure 39a to the single-frame way it can now be done in InDesign CS5 (**Figure 39c**), there's no denying this feature will simplify your work significantly.

Figure 39c The same look as Figure 39a, using one text frame with Span Columns and Split Column settings.

Adding Space Before/ Space After

For both Span Columns and Split Column, you can build in a space before or after the span/split. This setting will include any existing space before/after settings in the paragraph's Indents and Spacing options, rather than add to it. In other words, a paragraph with a 1-pica space after defined in Indents and Spacing that also has a 2-pica space after in its Span Columns settings will *not* have a 3-pica space after. It would simply be the greater of the two values— in this case, 2 picas.

Split Column Options

The Split Column settings include additional options for the gutter between the split and the gutter outside the split. The outside gutter helps establish an indented appearance where the split is applied, and the gutter controls the space between the columns.

There are a few limitations to be aware of. Span Columns does not work with footnotes, nor can you use span or split options within a table cell. Also, you can't totally control the columns that text will span. For example, a two-column span applied to text in the third column of a four-column frame will span the second and third columns (**Figure 39d**), not the third and fourth, which might be more desirable. Spanning is initiated from the column in which the paragraph resides, and moves toward the columns to its left, when applied anywhere other than the first column. This can make the spanned text appear to be in the wrong reading order, since text from the column to its left is flowed around the spanned column.

Figure 39d Spanning pushes to the left when applied anywhere except in the first column.

#40 Working Efficiently with Objects

Page layout applications have always followed certain conventions: Different tools are used for frames and content; guides and rulers are the go-to methods for aligning objects; and transformations are made via dialog boxes. InDesign CS5 shatters those conventions with a collection of new features that will transform and simplify how you work with objects on the page.

Let's talk about switching tools. How often do you alternate between the Selection and Direct Selection tools to work with frames and their content, respectively? Too often, right? You may wonder what the Direct Selection tool was for once you start using the new Content Grabber—that ghosted "doughnut" at the center of all graphic frames in InDesign CS5.

Whenever you hover over an image, the Content Grabber appears. Because it's semi-transparent, it's visible over any image. Simply click and hold the Content Grabber, then start moving your image around in the frame. Once it's where you want it, release the mouse button and you're right back to the Selection tool, ready to keep working (**Figure 40a**).

Figure 40a To use the Content Grabber, hover your pointer over the image (top left), click and hold (top right), drag the image to the desired position in the frame (bottom left), and release (bottom right). You're done!

Impatience Gets Rewarded

As you move objects within frames, you may notice that you no longer need to enter "patient user mode" to see a live draw of the image and any bleed that extends beyond the frame edge. In InDesign CS5, this is now instantaneous. If this slows down your document's performance, you can opt to switch the Live Screen Drawing setting—in the Application preferences Interface options—from the new default of Immediate to either Delayed or Never.

Tip
You can disable the Content Grabber by choosing View > Extras > Hide Content Grabber, if you just can't get used to it. But it's a useful new layout tool you should give a fair chance.

A useful new InDesign feature that borrows from Illustrator is a rotation cursor ⤵ that automatically appears when you hover the cursor just beyond a corner point on any selected frame or object. This avoids a switch from the Selection tool to the Rotate tool. Once the object is rotated and you move your mouse from the corner, you're back to the Selection tool again.

Speaking of rotating…you can also rotate multiple selected objects whether or not they're grouped. When several objects are selected, there's an overall selection border in addition to all of the selected frame edges (again, very much like Illustrator). The rotation cursor, under those conditions, rotates *everything* that's selected (**Figure 40b**).

Figure 40b Using the rotation cursor on a selection (left) to easily rotate one or more objects simultaneously (right) without grouping.

One of our favorite object transformation enhancements in InDesign CS5 is Live Distribute, which dynamically redistributes the space between multiple selected objects as you move them around. When more than one object is selected, you can activate Live Distribute by clicking any handle on the selection boundary, then holding down the spacebar before dragging. Moving the cursor toward the center of the selection reduces the spacing between all objects, and moving it away increases that spacing (**Figure 40c**). Holding down the Shift key as you drag proportionally distributes the space (along the x and y axes), and holding down Option (Alt) performs the redistribution from the center of the selection outward.

Figure 40c Live Distribute moves multiple objects (left) closer to or farther away from (right) one another.

Resizing and Scaling Multiple Objects

Clicking and dragging any corner or edge point on a selection resizes all of the objects. Holding the Shift key constrains the proportions of the resized frames. The Command (Ctrl) modifier resizes the content within frames as they're resized, and Shift-Command (Shift-Ctrl) does so proportionally. So in addition to avoiding switches between the Selection and Rotate tools, you won't need to temporarily group, then ungroup, objects. You won't need to do much with the Scale tool anymore, either.

#41 Using the Gap Tool

Anyone with formal art or design training has had it drilled into them that the negative space (commonly called *white space*) on a page is just as important as the positive space (the text, images, shapes, and so on). Historically, however, the only way to work with the negative space in InDesign has been to select and move the objects that make up the positive space. InDesign CS5's new Gap tool |↔| gives white space its due.

The Gap tool modifies the negative space (the gaps) between two or more items, or between any one or more items and a page edge (**Figure 41a**). The tool detects these gaps, highlighting them in gray as you move over them. Moving a gap modifies every page item that shares that gap. Drag to move a gap and resize all items aligned to the gap's edges.

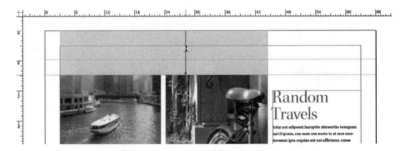

Figure 41a The Gap tool's gap detection and highlighting in action.

Enhancing the Gap Tool with Auto-Fit

As you transform objects by modifying the gaps they share, your placed images will get cropped by smaller frames or float within larger ones.

To dynamically resize those images, enable the new Auto-Fit feature for your frames *before* making your Gap tool adjustments. On wide monitors, the Control panel displays an Auto-Fit check box when one or more frames is selected. The option is also available in InDesign's frame fitting options (Object > Fitting > Frame Fitting Options).

Auto-Fit is semi-intelligent image scaling that honors the cropped state of your image as its frame is resized. This lets you scale the frame vertically, for example, but maintain the image's left and right horizontal cropping.

(continued on next page)

The Gap tool is a fantastic way to rapidly transform layouts and experiment without needing to select each object, draw guides, use the align panel, and painstakingly measure distances between page items. What once involved multiple tools and steps can now be accomplished entirely with the Gap tool in a fraction of the time (**Figure 41b**).

Figure 41b With only the Gap tool, and in only seven clicks, the static, boxy layout on the left was modified to the more pleasing arrangement of frames on the right.

Table 41a Gap Tool Keyboard Modifiers

Keyboard Modifier	Gap Tool Behavior
Shift	Changes the gap between the two objects closest to the cursor.
Command (Ctrl)	Increases the size of the gap as you drag outward, and decreases it as you drag inward.
Option (Alt)	Moves, as one unit, all of the objects sharing that gap. Does not reposition or resize the gap.
Shift-Command (Shift-Ctrl)	Increases or decreases the gap between the two objects closest to the cursor
Shift-Option (Shift-Alt)	Moves the two objects closest to the cursor
Command-Option (Ctrl-Alt)	Increases or decreases the gap by moving the objects, without resizing them.
Shift-Command-Option (Shift-Ctrl-Alt)	Increases or decreases the gap between the two objects closest to the cursor by moving the objects, not resizing them.

When combined with the other frame fitting options, the scaling gets even smarter. You can choose from which point an image scales when Auto-Fit resizes it. For example, choosing the lower-right corner on the alignment proxy ⊞ sets Auto-Fit to scale from that point.

When used in combination with keyboard modifiers, the Gap tool's power and flexibility increases dramatically (**Table 41a**), allowing for fast, consistent adjustment of the white space on a page.

#42 Using the Gridified Tools and Super Step-and-Repeat

Many traditional designers adhere to a grid structure upon which they "hang" all of their page elements. InDesign has always provided tools to continue this tradition, including Document Grid, Margins and Columns, Baseline Grid, and Frame-based Grid. In InDesign CS5, frames, shapes, and lines have been "gridified" too.

When you draw any rectangle, ellipse, polygon, line, or text frame on a page, you can press an arrow key to create multiple instances of that object. The right arrow key adds objects in a horizontal row, and the up arrow key adds objects vertically. Conversely, the left arrow key reduces the number of horizontal objects, and the down arrow key removes vertical duplicates.

For some time, InDesign has allowed multiple file placing via the "place gun"; the new gridified behavior extends to the placing of multiple images on the page as well. With two or more images loaded in the place gun, you can create all of the frames for those incoming images—horizontally, vertically, or in a grid—as you place them (**Figure 42a**). You can put all objects on the page at the same time, in equally sized frames and at the same distance from one another (**Figure 42b**). You can even do this with a mix of file types including graphics, PDFs, text files, spreadsheets, and other InDesign documents.

Figure 42a With three images loaded in the place gun (left), tapping the right arrow twice while dragging out a frame on the page creates two additional frames to receive all three incoming files.

Figure 42b The three images placed in separate frames.

Gridification by the Numbers

If you prefer your Step and Repeat the old-fashioned way—by dialog box—you'll find that's been gridified, too. A new "Create as a grid" option allows you to specify the number of rows and columns of duplicates you want to create.

If you've already got objects on your page and you want to take advantage of this gridified behavior to make duplicates of those objects (picture a high school yearbook page of standard-sized photos and captions), you don't need to visit the Step and Repeat dialog to create those duplicate objects. Simply Option-drag (Alt-drag) the object you want to copy to its farthest position, then press either the right arrow key for horizontal duplicates or the up arrow key for vertical duplicates. Each press of an arrow key fills the space between the original and the copy with an additional duplicate (**Figure 42c**).

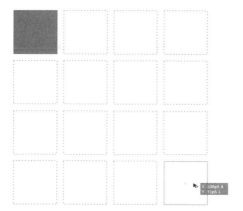

Figure 42c Super Step and Repeat creates on-the-fly duplicates (left) as you hit the arrow key.

#43 Using Live Corner Effects

Rounded corners have always been a part of InDesign, but the feature never offered much in the way of choice. You could apply five different corner types, and only to every corner on the object at once. Anything more ambitious required using a script—Corner Effects—which helped, but it generated "drawn" corners, not "live" corners, so changing the size of the frame once you ran the script distorted the effect.

InDesign CS5 offers per-corner settings in the Corner Options dialog, so you can apply an effect to just one corner, use alternate corner effects (top left/bottom right, for example), or mix and match different corners on a single object (**Figure 43a**).

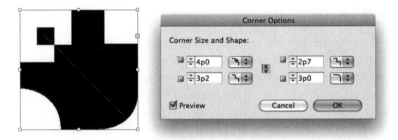

Figure 43a   Four different corner effects applied to a single frame.

This would be a positive improvement all by itself, but the engineers took it one step further. Now, the dialog box isn't even necessary for rectangular frames. You can apply corner effects directly to any rectangular text or graphic frame right on the page. Every selected rectangular frame now sports a small yellow square on its top-right side. Click that, and the object's corners display small yellow diamonds. Click, hold, and drag the diamonds? inward—rounded corners that span the distance you drag appear (**Figure 43b**).

Figure 43b Applying live rounded corners (left, top-to-bottom): click the yellow square on the frame, click the yellow diamond that appears and drag to desired corner size.

It's not all about rounded corners, though. There are five other corner types available: None, Inset, Bevel, Inverse Rounded, and Fancy. Rounded is by far the most common choice, so it's the default, but you can toggle through all of the other options by Option-clicking (Alt-clicking) the yellow diamond (**Figure 43c**). Once you get to the corner you want, click off the object, and you're done.

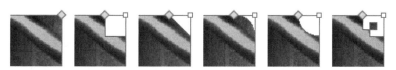

Figure 43c Option-click (Alt-click) the live corner diamond to cycle through different choices.

Corner Customization

Shift-Option-clicking (Shift-Alt-clicking) a yellow diamond on any corner of a frame will cycle through the different corner effect options for that corner only, regardless of the effects applied to any of the other corners.

Apply Your Corner Effects with Speed… and Style

To truly turbo-charge your corner effects, make Object Styles (Window > Styles > Object Styles) for those you use most often. For example, if your project's visual style calls for a rounded top-left and rounded lower-right corner, but no effects on the bottom-left and top-right corners, build those attributes into the style's Stroke and Corner Options for one-click application to any rectangular frame. You'll avoid both the Corner Options dialog and the multiple clicks and drags required to add the effects object-by-object throughout your document.

#44 Creating an Interactive Slide Show

InDesign CS4 included some bare bones export-to-Flash/SWF capability, but a slew of new features and tools in expand InDesign CS5's ability to produce interactive content. One such feature is the multi-state object, with which we'll set up a basic image-based slide show with button navigation that can be previewed directly in InDesign without having to first export to SWF.

The document in **Figure 44a** includes four graphic frames containing the images for the slide show, and two grouped objects that will ultimately become buttons that will control the user's navigation through the photos in the slide show.

Figure 44a The building blocks of an interactive image slide show (the graphic frames are staggered to show their layering in the document).

The first thing we need to do is convert the four separate image frames into one multi-state object. We'll select all of the graphic frames and use the Align panel (Window > Object & Layout > Align) to align the frames along the left and top edges, so they all sit directly atop one another. While they're still selected, we'll go to the Object States panel (Window > Interactive > Object States), and click the Convert Selection to Multi-state Object button 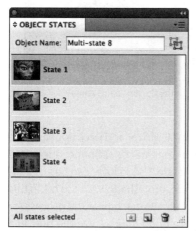 at the bottom of the panel. This combines the four separate graphic frames into a single frame with four distinct "states" (**Figure 44b**). It's a good idea to name both the object and its respective states right away so that each can be easily referred to later when setting up button actions.

Figure 44b A new multi-state object created from four graphic frames with default names (left), and after customizing with appropriate names (right).

Mix Up Your Multi-states

Although this example uses four images and equally sized graphic frames, multi-state objects do not have any limitations regarding the size or proportions of the objects in each state, or even what kind of objects they are. Your multi-state object can have an image in one state, a text frame in another, a drawn InDesign shape in another, and so on, in any combination. That makes the potential uses for multi-state objects limited only to how clever you choose to get with this amount of flexibility.

Make Button Appearances a Push-Button Process

A button's various appearances—Normal, Rollover, and Click—are usually just a variation in color, stroke, transparency effects, or other basic attributes. When you're setting up a number of buttons in an interactive document, the fastest method is to create Object Styles for each of the button's appearances. Assigning a Rollover appearance then becomes as easy as clicking the Object Style name when that appearance is selected in the Buttons panel.

Not only is this the fastest way to *apply* your button appearances, it's also the most flexible. When you (or your client) have a change of heart about a particular appearance, changing attributes in one Object Style will update that appearance in every button in your document. This saves you the tedious chore of selecting every button and modifying one (or more) of its appearances one button at a time.

Now we need to turn the left and right arrow graphics in the layout into buttons that control the multi-state object. This is as simple as selecting one of the two graphics, opening the Buttons panel (Window > Interactive > Buttons), and clicking the Normal appearance in the panel (**Figure 44c**).

Figure 44c Clicking the Normal appearance in the Buttons panel converts a selected object to a button.

To provide user feedback, we can add Rollover and Click appearances to the button. Clicking [Rollover] in the Appearance subpanel duplicates the appearance of the button's Normal state. The rollover can be any variation of that appearance—a color change, drop shadow, and so on. In this example, a simple color change is enough. We can repeat the process for the Click state as well (**Figure 44d**). It's a good idea to give the button a logical name like "Previous," too.

Figure 44d The button named "Previous" with Normal, Rollover, and Click appearances.

Now we've got to tell this button what to do. In the Button panel's Event and Actions options, the default event is On Release, meaning the button carries out its action when the user has clicked, then released, the mouse. That's exactly what we want. For the button named "Previous," click the Add Action icon 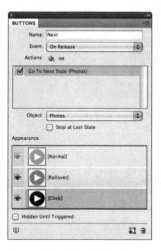 and choose Go to Previous State.

Since there's only one multi-state object in this layout, it's chosen by default from the Object pull-down menu that's revealed in the Buttons panel. If there were more than one multi-state object in the document, they would all be listed as available targets for the button.

Follow the same steps to set up the right arrow button—select the graphic, convert it to a button, establish its appearances, and add the necessary action to control the same multi-state object. This button, however, should be named "Next," and its Action should be set to Go To Next State (**Figure 44e**).

Figure 44e The finished Next button options in the Buttons panel.

How Much Can a Button Do?

Whether you're creating an Interactive PDF or exporting a SWF file, buttons perform a number of actions. A button can go to a destination (a specific page, external file or bookmark), or to the first, last, next or previous page in the current document. Buttons can also go to a URL, control placed audio and video files, and even be used to show or hide *other* buttons.

Button actions available only for SWF export can also play, stop, pause, reverse, or resume an animation, or go to any document page or object state.

PDF-specific button actions can zoom the view of a PDF page, go to the previous view (not the previous page in document order, but rather *the page you just looked at previously*) or next view, or open an external file.

Button events—the user activities that trigger the button's action—include On Release, On Click, On Roll Over, and On Roll Off (for both SWF and PDF), and On Focus and On Blur for PDFs only.

A Power User's Guide to the Preview Panel

By default, the Preview panel opens no wider than most other InDesign panels. However, you can resize the panel to get as large a preview as you need.

The three buttons in the Preview panel's lower right corner let you choose how much or how little of the document's interactivity and animation you want to preview: The first limits the preview to the current selection; the second previews only the current spread; and the third previews the entire document. Since InDesign is actually rendering out a temporary SWF file to play in the preview panel, limiting the preview to only what you need to see speeds up that process.

Another preview performance tip: Each time you click the Play button in the preview panel, a new temporary SWF is rendered and displayed in the preview panel. If you just want to replay the preview (not create a new preview), Option-click (Alt-click) the Play button.

Want to see how this all looks? In CS4, looking at your Flash output from InDesign meant exporting the final SWF file, then viewing it in a browser. But CS5 adds in-document viewing of all interactive content from the new Preview panel (Window > Interactive > Preview), where you can view and interact with your slide show, including all rollover behavior and button functionality (**Figure 44f**).

Figure 44f Viewing and testing interactive content in the new Preview panel. Note the rollover state of the Next button when the mouse is positioned over it.

If you're happy with your slide show, all that remains is to export it to SWF. We'll look at those options in tip 46, "Exporting to SWF and Flash Professional."

#45 Creating an Animation for the Web

As we distribute content across print pages, computer screens, smart phones, and tablets, the definition of what a document is continues to change, and InDesign continues to keep up with that changing definition.

InDesign CS5 includes features that let you create animations quickly and easily right in your favorite page layout application. As an example, we'll animate a simple ad (**Figure 45a**) that contains an image and a few text frames using built-in animation presets and absolutely no code.

Figure 45a A simple, one-page layout ready to be animated.

Know Where Your Document's Headed

InDesign CS5's New Document dialog includes an option to create documents with either a Print or a Web intent. When you choose Web (a good choice when starting a project you know will be animated), the measurement system changes to pixels, and the document's orientation changes to landscape. All documents created using the Web intent have a Transparency Blend Space setting of Document RGB, and all default color swatches are RGB.

InDesign's animation interface is not timeline based, like Flash and Photoshop; the settings are instead distributed across several panels (**Figure 45b**). You use the Animations panel to create an animation in InDesign, and you give the animation a specific sequence in the Timing panel. You can see how your animation is coming along at any time using the Preview panel.

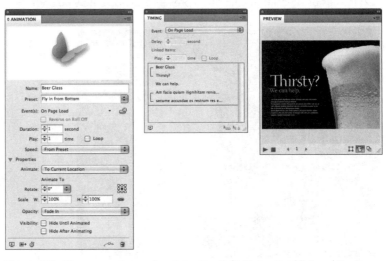

Figure 45b Three separate panels—Animation (left), Timing (middle), and Preview (right)—share the animation tasks in InDesign CS5.

We'll add a basic animation to the layout in Figure 45a: The beer glass will move from the bottom of the page to its final position in the layout. After that, the text frames ("Thirsty?" "We can help"), will fade in one after another.

When the beer glass frame is selected, the Animation panel (Window > Interactive > Animation) displays its object name in the Name field, but no animation is assigned. We'll open the Preset menu and choose Fly in From Bottom; a butterfly proxy shows us what that animation will look like (**Figure 45c**).

Figure 45c An animation preset applied to the beer glass in the layout.

If we want to make that animation play a little longer, we can change the Duration, and if we don't want it to fade in as it starts (which is the default for this preset), we can set the Opacity to None in the Properties area of the panel. This makes our preset now "Custom" since it no longer matches the original preset settings.

Where'd My Butterfly Go?

The sample butterfly animation at the top of the Animation panel is a helpful visual guide to what that preset does. Unfortunately, as soon as you make a change to the default preset, the butterfly animation is disabled and you're on your own.

154

Editing Motion Paths

Motion paths can be modified like any other path in InDesign. Select any point on the motion path with the Direct Selection tool to move it, or use the Pen tool to add points and convert corner points to Bezier curves, or vice versa. Any path you draw in InDesign can be converted to a motion path. Simply select the path and the object you want to apply it to, then click the Convert to Motion Path icon at the bottom of the Animation panel.

Add Your Own Presets

Once you've customized an animation preset to your needs, you may want to use that preset again in the same project—or later in another project. To save yourself time later on, save your customized preset by choosing Save from the Animation panel menu. Saved presets are available application-wide, so they're available in your current document and all other documents. Any preset you save in InDesign can also be loaded into Flash Professional.

Motion presets include a motion path along which the animated object travels, which appears as a green line attached to the object (**Figure 45d**). To extend this motion path so that the beer glass begins its journey from the bottom of the page, just drag the bottom of the path down to a position well below the bottom edge of the page.

Figure 45d An extended motion path on an animated frame. Note the small icon on the bottom right of the graphic frame, indicating that animation is applied to it.

Note:
Animations are automatically given the same name they have in the Layers panel. Before starting any animation work in InDesign, it pays to name your objects in the Layers panel. This makes objects and animations easy to identify in the Animation and Timing panels.

Next, we'll animate the text frame for the headline, using the same steps, but with a simpler preset. With the "Thirsty?" headline frame selected, we'll choose Fade In from the Preset menu in the Animation panel to have that frame fade in. To start the animation with the text frame already "invisible," we'll also select Hide Until Animated in the Visibility options. The "We can help" frame and the body copy text frame can be animated the same way, using the same preset and options.

Next, it's time to set the order in which the animations occur. By default, animations play in the order in which they were created, which is listed from top to bottom in the Timing panel (**Figure 45e**). But you can change that order by dragging any animation's name above or below another. You can also set two animations to play simultaneously by selecting both in the Timing panel and clicking the Play Together icon 🐾 at the bottom of the panel.

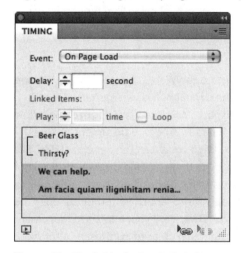

Figure 45e The finished animation's timing sequence, with the first two animations set to play simultaneously, followed by the last two.

As a final adjustment, the "Thirsty?" animation can be set to a delay of 2 seconds in the Timing panel so that it doesn't begin until the beer glass animation is two thirds of the way through its 3-second-long animation time. **Figure 45f** shows various stages of the completed animation.

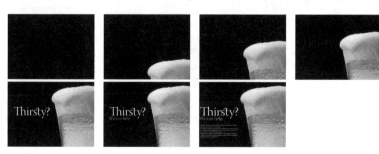

Figure 45f In the final animation, the beer glass animates up into the empty page, the "Thirsty?" headline fades in, followed by "We can help," then the body copy.

The Animation Encyclopedia

The Adobe engineers have hidden a little animation-related gem in the Scripts panel (Window > Utilities > Scripts) called Animation-Encyclopedia. You run that script by double-clicking its name in the Scripts panel. The script creates a new document with six pages of examples of InDesign animations and animation events (those user actions that trigger an animation). Other examples demonstrate the effect of settings like Ease In and Ease Out, the animation origin point, From/To Current Appearance, and more. You can save the document for future reference, or you can always just run the script again.

#46 Exporting to SWF and Flash Professional

Once you've tested your interactive document or animation in the Preview panel and you're satisfied with your work, it's time to take it to the Web by exporting to either Flash Player (SWF) or Flash Professional (FLA). But which one? The answer is simple. If your interactive document or animation is 100 percent ready to debut on the Web, with no additional work required, export to SWF. If there's more to be done—like linking the document up to dynamic online content, or adding functionality like ActionScript—then export to FLA.

Exporting to SWF

Assuming you're ready to publish to the Web, choose File > Export, and select Flash Player (SWF) from the Format pull-down menu.

The General options in the Export SWF dialog box (**Figure 46a**) allow you to export a page, a range of pages, an entire document, or just the current selection on the page to SWF. If you select the Generate HTML File check box, InDesign will also produce the HTML file that will display your SWF file. Selecting the View SWF after Exporting check box (available only if Generate HTML File is checked) will also launch your browser once the export is complete and display the HTML file. If your interactive document includes video or sound files, or other SWFs placed in InDesign, all of those external assets will be gathered into a single folder named "yourexportedfilename_Resources" in the same directory as your exported SWF file.

Figure 46a The options in the Export SWF dialog box.

You can export at the same size as the InDesign document, set the exported SWF to fit to a standard resolution like 640 by 480, or customize the width and height to a specific size.

The Background option sets the color that appears behind nonrectangular objects on the page. It's built into the SWF file, and does not affect the background color of the HTML file that InDesign generates (if you selected that option). When Paper Color is chosen, you can take advantage of any InDesign page transitions you may have set in the document, or activate the Interactive Page Curl feature, which creates an animated page-turning effect. If Transparent is chosen, your SWF will have a transparent background, allowing you to place it on an HTML page with a background color, but the options for page transitions and Interactive Page Curl are disabled.

The options in the Advanced panel (**Figure 46b**) offer more specific control over whether the layout's text is converted to Flash Classic Text (meaning scalable, crisp, and with almost no impact on file size), converted to outlines (also scalable and crisp, but with more file overhead), or converted to pixels (neither scalable nor crisp, and with more image-based information adding to the size of the final SWF). You can also set the exported file's frame rate, image compression format, quality, and resolution.

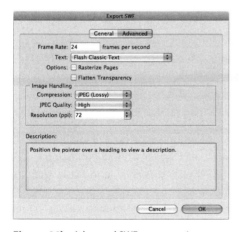

Figure 46b Advanced SWF export options.

Changing the HTML Background Color

All HTML files exported from InDesign have a gray background written into their HTML as <body bgcolor="#999999">. To change this to white or any other color, edit the HTML file in Dreamweaver or any text editor and change the bgcolor hexadecimal value.

Understanding Image Compression Formats

JPEG compression is "lossy," which means it will compress with some degree of quality loss depending on your choice from the JPEG Quality menu. PNG compression makes files smaller with no quality loss, making it an ideal choice for SWFs containing many images where quality is a primary concern. If you're not sure which of these options to choose in the Advanced panel, select Automatic to leave the decision up to InDesign. The application evaluates all images in the file and assigns a compression scheme based on what it finds.

158

Interactive Features in Flash Professional (FLA) Files

- Animation, motion paths, and motion presets
- Multi-state objects
- Buttons (but button names are not preserved)
- FLV video and MP3 audio
- Flash Professional's new TLF text engine

ActionScript in SWF vs. FLA

ActionScript is the code that plays and times your animation and interactivity. InDesign CS5 allows you to create animations and interactivity without code by writing it in the background for you when you export to SWF. However, that Action-Script is not preserved when you export to FLA. All of your InDesign images and text are brought into Flash, converted to movie clips, and placed on the Flash stage, but you have to re-establish all animation and timing settings (like easing, fades, duration, and looping), and all button functionality in Flash Professional CS5 using ActionScript and code snippets.

Exporting to FLA

If your file is going to be handed off to a developer—or if you want to work with it in Flash Professional—choose Flash Professional (FLA) from the Format menu when exporting your document.

Many of the options in the Export Flash CS5 Professional (FLA) dialog box (**Figure 46c**) echo those in the Export SWF dialog, with a few notable exceptions. You can opt to rasterize your pages, converting all text and images to pixels, but this will limit editability in Flash Professional. Similarly, you might choose to flatten transparency to reduce file size or improve compatibility with Flash, but this could limit your ability to manipulate those flattened objects when you open the file in Flash Professional.

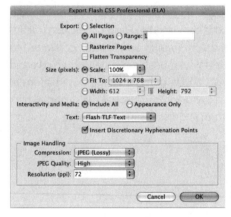

Figure 46c InDesign's Flash CS5 Professional (FLA) export options.

There's an additional text export option set by default for FLA export: Flash TLF Text, the new text engine built into Flash CS5 Professional. TLF supports typographic features previously unavailable in Flash, such as ligatures and threaded text frames.

The Interactivity and Media choices determine whether the actual media—video, audio, SWF—in the InDesign document get built into the exported FLA file, or if only a placeholder image with no media attributes is passed on to Flash.

#**47** Exporting an Interactive PDF with Video

For some time now InDesign has made it possible to create interactive documents in the form of interactive PDFs complete with button navigation, audio, and video. InDesign CS5 supports more rich media formats (including SWF and FLV), and additional export options.

The example shown in **Figure 47a** is a layout in which an FLV video file was placed onto the page. Video and audio files are placed just as you would any image file, but legacy formats are initially displayed with no preview and show up in the frame as a pattern of diagonal lines. For newer video formats, like FLV, InDesign automatically generates a "poster frame" using the first frame of the placed video.

Figure 47a A page layout with a placed video.

Note
InDesign CS5 supports the MOV video format, but the options for this format are less robust than for FLV.

InDesign's Interactive PDFs

When you use InDesign to create an Interactive PDF, you can

- Embed and control audio and video, including MP3, MOV, and FLV files

- Create button- and text-based navigation to go from page to page, play a sound, control a video, and show and hide document content

- Embed SWF files that play in and scale with the PDF

- Use InDesign's page transitions (except interactive page curl) to add effects like fade, dissolve, and wipe between pages in the PDF

Play on Page Load— Use With Caution

A video in an interactive PDF will either play when clicked or when its controller is used, or it can be controlled by custom buttons you create directly in your layout. The Play on Page Load setting will start the video playback without any user interaction as soon as the page opens in the exported PDF (or SWF). As a matter of general courtesy, you should consider whether or not this is appropriate, or if it's best left up to the user.

FLV Support Brings New Controller Options

Since InDesign now supports FLV video, the Controller options include many of the controllers available when exporting video from Flash Professional. A Flash-based controller appears as a "skin" over the video that appears and disappears as the mouse moves over or off the video on the page. It can include or exclude options like volume control, full-screen view, and captions.

All rich media placed in a document can be viewed, modified, and controlled via the new Media panel (**Figure 47b**). From here, you can watch the placed media, set its playback options, designate a poster frame, assign a controller, and add Navigation Points.

Figure 47b The Media panel displaying a selected video.

The Poster pull-down menu lets you assign a "poster" for the movie, meaning a static image that appears on the page until the movie is played. This can either be a frame from the movie, or you can select an external image file (**Figure 47c**).

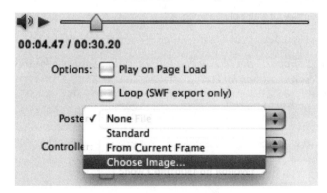

Figure 47c Selecting an image to use as a poster frame for a placed movie.

New to InDesign CS5 is the ability to add navigation points to a placed video (**Figure 47d**). Using a navigation point is like jumping to a particular scene in a DVD. Navigation points set in the Media panel can be called upon by InDesign-created buttons, offering segment-by-segment access to any placed video from within the exported PDF or SWF (**Figure 47e**).

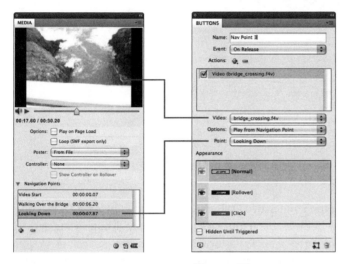

Figure 47d Video navigation points added in the Media panel.

Figure 47e An InDesign button set to jump to a specific navigation point in a movie.

When your layout is done, and your video controls are set up to your liking, it's time to export your file as an interactive PDF. In reality, there's little difference between an interactive PDF and any other PDF: An interactive PDF includes a number of options specific to the handling and display of media files and interactive elements like buttons. In InDesign CS5, Adobe added an Adobe PDF (Interactive) format choice to the Export options, consolidating the interactivity-related options into a single, simplified dialog box (**Figure 47f**) and eliminating the print-related PDF options.

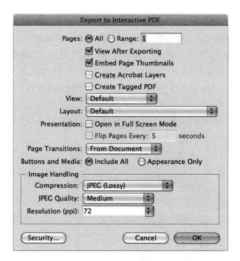

Figure 47f The Export to Interactive PDF dialog box.

The resulting interactive PDF, when displayed in Acrobat Professional or the free Adobe Reader (**Figure 47g**), will display all button interactivity and play any video or audio file included in the InDesign document. Note that all interactive PDFs from InDesign export as spreads, not single pages.

Figure 47g A video playing in Adobe Reader 9, with its controller overlay visible.

#48 Exporting for EPUB

While EPUB export isn't new to InDesign, many of the options in CS5 are new—and very welcome. This tip consists of a handful of must-dos and best practices for successfully exporting EPUB documents (or EPUBs) from InDesign CS5, starting with several features that have been around long before this version.

The Web may have taken the precision out of your design, but you lose even more control with EPUBs. Pagination becomes meaningless when readers can adjust the font size, and simply turning a device like Apple's iPad changes the width and orientation of the "page" through which the text flows. With EPUBs, all you can lock in is the base formatting of the content and the markers for navigating through the document.

Preparing Your Document

If you're exporting to EPUB, you need to perform several tasks to prepare your document.

Use Paragraph, Character, and Object styles. Once your InDesign file is exported as an EPUB, you can modify the CSS that's generated to format the book. An EPUB exports as a collection of XHTML files plus a CSS template. Each of your InDesign styles generates a CSS class that you can easily customize and apply immediately document-wide.

Insert all images as inline graphics. EPUBs don't structure pages to match how we design them for print. They're "read" either in a left-to-right, top-to-bottom order, or according to the document's XML structure. To ensure that images appear near related text content, all photos and graphics should be inserted as inline anchored objects, on their own lines.

Split up long documents and use the Book panel. Multiple documents are easier to manage and build a navigation scheme for than one very long file. The Book panel allows you to designate one file as the "style source" for all styles and other attributes (text variables, numbered lists, and so on) shared by documents in the book. The style source document holds all the metadata necessary for the exported EPUB.

Keep the cover separate. If the book's cover is in its own document, it remains separate and doesn't flow into the beginning text of the EPUB. Also, covers that are made up of images and text frames should be converted to a single image. Otherwise, the cover text will be considered part of the readable flow, not as a part of the cover design.

What's EPUB?

EPUB is an open, industry-standard, device-independent format for delivering books to reading devices like Sony's Reader or Barnes & Noble's Nook, or for viewing on a computer using an EPUB reader like Adobe Digital Editions, Calibre, or Stanza. EPUBs offer a fluid presentation, as opposed to the fixed view of a PDF. An EPUB presents a continuous flow of text that's intended to be scalable depending on both the device and the choices made by the user viewing the content.

Build an automated table of contents. InDesign's Table of Contents feature is 100 percent style-driven. Without paragraph styles, you can't create an automatic TOC, which is the *only* navigation scheme that an exported EPUB will recognize. You must also save your TOC settings as a TOC Style.

Add metadata. EPUB readers and Web search engines rely on metadata for the book's title, author, and description. Choose File > File Info to add the necessary metadata into your InDesign document (**Figure 48a**).

Figure 48a This File Information dialog box contains the minimum metadata necessary for EPUB export.

EPUB Export Options

When you're ready to generate your EPUB, choose File > Export for > EPUB. If you're exporting from the Book panel, choose Export Book to EPUB from the Book panel menu. The export dialog is split into three panes—General, Images, and Contents—each dealing with a specific aspect of the export process.

General options. All CS5-generated assets are given a unique identifier, which is revealed in this dialog (**Figure 48b**). That identifier becomes part of the EPUB's metadata, along with what you entered in the File Information dialog. If you use bullets or numbering in your book, be sure you map them to unordered and ordered lists, respectively. To see the results of your export in Adobe Digital Editions immediately, check View eBook after Exporting.

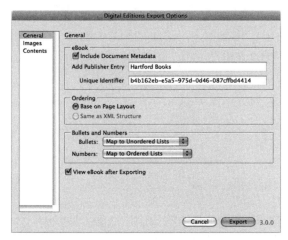

Figure 48b EPUB General export options. The dialog still uses the Digital Editions name from CS4 and earlier versions.

Image options. All images destined for an EPUB are converted to a resolution of 72 pixels per inch, in either JPEG or GIF format. Which of those formats is used can be up to you, or you can leave it up to InDesign by choosing Automatic Image Conversion. When setting your image export options, be sure to select the Formatted check box to preserve all cropping, rotation, borders, effects, and other InDesign-based modifications made in your layout. If Formatted is not selected, the full canvas (for Photoshop files) or Artboard area (for Illustrator files) is exported for use in the EPUB, and all borders, shadows, and other formatting are ignored.

Contents options. The most significant difference between previous EPUB export settings and those in CS5 is evident in the Contents panel (**Figure 48c**). Its expanded options produce an EPUB that's much more "ready for prime time" than earlier versions.

Maximum vs. High Quality

When you set your JPEG image quality options, note that there's no appreciable difference to the naked eye between High and Maximum, but there is a big difference in file size. High is probably more than enough for good-looking images in most cases, and it'll keep your EPUB files nice and lean.

EPUB Formats

There are two formats for EPUBs: XHTML and DTBook (digital talking book). The more common of the two is XHTML, which produces XHTML pages and a CSS style sheet document. It's also the easier of the two to customize and troubleshoot before releasing to the world.

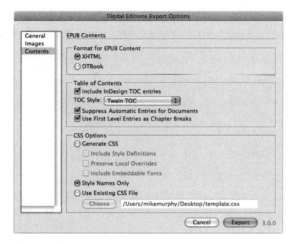

Figure 48c EPUB Contents export options.

Here's where your work setting up both an InDesign TOC and a TOC Style pay off. The InDesign TOC builds the necessary bookmarks into the document, and choosing the appropriate TOC Style here converts your InDesign TOC into the EPUB's TOC. Since page numbers are meaningless in a reflowable eBook, they're dropped in the EPUB.

The Suppress Automatic Entries for Documents option prevents each section from being nested within a hierarchy that includes the document's name. With this check box selected, you'll see "Chapter 1" as a top-level navigation item, rather than "DocumentName" as a top-level item with "Chapter 1" nested within it. The Use First Level Entries as Chapter Breaks option also capitalizes on your InDesign TOC settings by using the level hierarchy established there to force each chapter to start on a new page in the final EPUB.

Finally, InDesign CS5 includes several options for handling the CSS used to format the EPUB, including the least desirable option: generating a CSS based on the styles in the InDesign document. Most of the fonts we use in our layouts aren't supported by browsers, reading devices, or eBook software, so it's best to choose either Style Names Only (which creates empty CSS declarations and relies entirely on the device's defaults for presentation) or Use Existing CSS File. The former includes no formatting information, so you'll need to open up the EPUB's CSS after exporting your InDesign file and add formatting attributes to all CSS classes. The latter requires that you have an established CSS document with class names that match the style names in your document.

Once exported, you should view your eBook with more than one EPUB reading application (**Figure 48d**) and device to see if its appearance and navigation match your expectations.

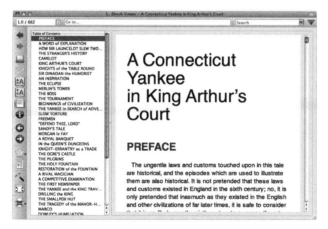

Figure 48d The same EPUB viewed with its TOC in Adobe Digital Editions (top) and Calibre (bottom).

Making Your EPUB Perfect

Some trial and error is inevitable before your EPUB looks as good as it can on as many devices as possible. It's unlikely that your EPUB will be 100 percent perfect without some tweaking of the exported EPUB files, the CSS, or both. EPUBs are essentially zip-compressed files that can be opened and modified (carefully) with tools like Adobe Dreamweaver or other utilities like Springy (on the Mac OS). There are many options on the market—and more to come.

Once you've customized a CSS file and tested it on your target devices, you can re-use it in other EPUBs by replacing the InDesign-generated CSS file with your well-tested version. Note, however, that this technique requires paragraph and character styles in the InDesign document that are named consistently with those in the CSS file.

CHAPTER SIX

Working with Dreamweaver

Dreamweaver has come a long way since its acquisition by Adobe and inclusion in Creative Suite 3. For some designers, though, getting a toe in the water with the application has been a challenging, sometimes intimidating, experience. Although Dreamweaver offers a WYSIWYG working environment and helpful site-management tools, it's inevitable that designers will, at some point, have to work with code and understand more about what's going on "under the hood" than they might care to.

Rather than denying that reality, the Dreamweaver CS5 team instead added many new features specifically designed to lessen the "scary" factor for newcomers to Web design, Dreamweaver, or both. Site setup is simpler, starter layouts are streamlined and copiously documented, design experimentation is easier and more flexible, and testing and troubleshooting tools are, no pun intended, woven into the fabric of Dreamweaver CS5.

For more experienced users, advanced capabilities for speeding up PHP coding, content-management system integration, working with dynamically linked files on a testing server, and support for both HTML5 and CSS3 are welcome additions to an already robust Web-site creation tool.

#**49** Getting Started with Simplified Site Setup

In previous versions of Dreamweaver, setting up a site was a complex process involving an intimidating dialog box with up to 15 screens of options. Getting started in Dreamweaver CS5 is incredibly fast and easy. You can now define a site by choosing New Site from the Site menu, giving the site a name, and pointing Dreamweaver to a local folder where site files are—or will be—stored (**Figure 49a**). After that, you're ready to dive right in and start designing your site.

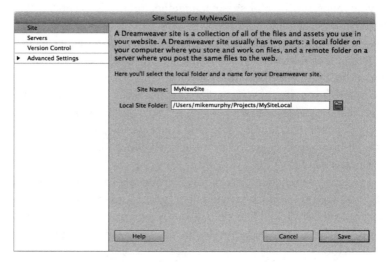

Figure 49a Dreamweaver CS5's simplified Site Setup dialog eliminates some of the site information requirements and many of the confusing options found in earlier versions.

At any point as you design your site, you can add more information in other areas of the Site Setup dialog, allowing Dreamweaver to make more of its advanced features available to help you manage your Web site. When Dreamweaver requires information from you—i.e., when you try to add or test server-based code—it will prompt you.

Two parameters you might want to add early on are a default images folder (defined under Advanced Settings > Local Info in the Site Setup dialog), where Dreamweaver will store any images it creates, and information about the remote Web server to which Dreamweaver will upload your local files.

Speed Up the Setup Dialog Access

When you need to get back to the Site Setup dialog to define more site-related information (testing servers, remote servers, etc.), you can avoid going to the Site menu, choosing Manage Sites, selecting the site you want to further define, and clicking Edit. Instead, you can use the site pull-down menu in the Files panel. If you're working on the site you want to define, just select its name from the menu and release the mouse. The Site Setup dialog for that site will open. To access the Site Setup dialog box for another site, select that site's name from the Files panel to make it the active site, then click the site name in the menu again.

Methods of Relativity

Under the Advanced Settings in the Site Setup dialog, you can establish whether links created by Dreamweaver are relative to the current document (the default) or the Site Root.

(continued on next page)

Working with Dreamweaver

FTP (File Transfer Protocol) is the most common way to connect your local computer to your remote server, and the default option when setting up a remote server. When necessary, Dreamweaver will use FTP to transfer your local site files to the remote server. To add a remote server, go to the Servers section of the Site Setup dialog and click the large plus sign (+) (**Figure 49b**). In the resulting dialog box, put in the appropriate server information (**Figure 49c**).

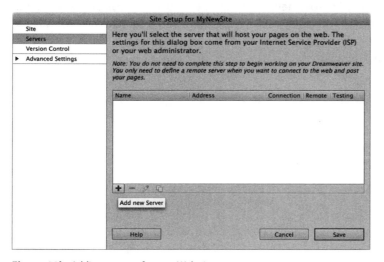

Figure 49b Adding a server for your Web site.

Figure 49c Basic options for setting up a remote server using FTP.

In other words, if a page is located at `rootfolder/content/articles/story01.html` and it links to an image located at `rootfolder/content/images/image01.jpg`, a Site Root scheme would use the path `content/images/image01.jpg` to call on that image starting from the main (root) directory of the site as defined in the Site Setup dialog. A Relative linking scheme would refer to the image with `../../images/image01.jpg`, pointing the browser out two levels in the folder structure (to the articles folder, then to the content folder) starting from the location of the story01.html file.

Remote vs. Testing Servers

By default, a new server added in the Site Setup dialog is set up as a Remote server, meaning it's a destination only—the online repository for storing your finished files.

(continued on next page)

Testing servers are used by Dreamweaver to execute server-based functionality (PHP calls, scripts, includes, etc.) as it would work "live" on the site. If your site doesn't utilize any server-side features, a testing server is not necessary.

Using Dreamweaver's Live View, or choosing Option-F11 (Alt-F11) to preview a page in a browser is considered "testing" a page. The first time you try to test a page that uses server-side code, Dreamweaver prompts you to specify a testing server, if you haven't already done so. When you receive this prompt, click Yes, and the Site Setup dialog opens to the Servers section.

To make a remote server also act as your testing server, just click the Testing Server check box next to the server name in the Site Setup dialog, or add a separate testing server. You may also want to go to the Advanced tab and specify the server model (ASP, ColdFusion, PHP, MySQL, etc.).

As you develop your site, Dreamweaver will prompt you with alerts if you start adding features for which it needs more server-related information. Dreamweaver displays alerts indicating that more site information is required, then brings you to the area(s) of the Site Setup dialog (called out with red Xs to guide you along) where you enter the required information.

This guided and "as needed" approach to site setup and management is a big improvement over the formidable and mysterious site setup approach of earlier versions, enabling you to get started on your site design right away, then add more information at any point in the site's development.

#50 Using Starter Layouts to Kick-Start Site Creation

In the earliest phases of a site's design and development, you may want to take advantage of some of Dreamweaver's basic starter layouts. These are very helpful if you're new to CSS or just looking for a head start for structure and layout. There are more than a dozen standards-compliant layouts to choose from, featuring many common Web-layout schemes. All Dreamweaver starter layouts are compatible with a wide range of modern browsers (IE, Safari, Firefox, Opera) on both Mac OS and Windows.

To create a new page based on one of these layouts, choose File > New or Command-N (Ctrl-N). The Blank Page options for an individual HTML page or an HTML template both take advantage of starter layouts. The default for new pages is <none>, but the list in the Layout column of the New Document dialog includes all starter layout options, and a preview for each is displayed to the right of that list for the currently selected layout to help you decide if it's right for you (**Figure 50a**).

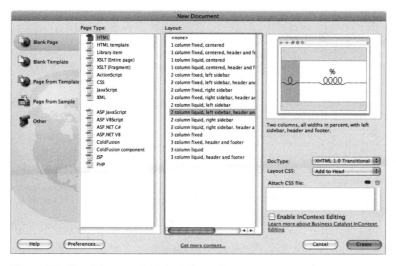

Figure 50a Creating a new HTML page from a Dreamweaver starter layout.

For all starter layouts, Dreamweaver can either add the CSS layout and design to the document head (which is not recommended), create a new external CSS file to be shared among many site pages, or add the CSS required for the layout to an existing CSS file you choose.

CSS in a Nutshell

CSS (Cascading Style Sheets) is the standard upon which all modern Web pages are built. CSS determines not only the formatting of text, but also the positioning of objects on the page, and the margins, padding, and borders on the page itself, and each object on the page. Like Styles in InDesign—but even more powerful—CSS makes consistent site-wide page design (and subsequent changes to that design) manageable, typically from a single file (a style sheet) that is called upon by all pages on the site to instruct the browser how to render the content.

Breaking Down the Starter Layouts

Dreamweaver's starter layouts combine a handful of options to create a number of different page structures. Combining these options puts most Web-site page structures at your fingertips with a few clicks in the New Document dialog.

One option in the mix is the number of columns in the layout.

(continued on next page)

Many sites divide page layouts into two columns, with one (the "sidebar") acting as a navigation area, and the other containing the page content (the "content well"). This two-column layout scheme can use the sidebar on the left or right. A three-column layout would have sidebars on both sides of the content well.

Your design may require a header and/or footer, which is another option you can choose from the starter layouts.

The last option is whether a layout is liquid or fixed. Column widths in a liquid layout expand along with the browser window and are defined in the CSS by what percentage of the layout they occupy. A fixed layout does not adapt to the width of the browser window, and its columns are defined in specific pixel widths.

Download Super-Charged Starter Designs

The Adobe Developer Connection (www.adobe.com/devnet) offers a series of starter designs specifically created to use with Dreamweaver.

(continued on next page)

The CSS generated for the layout is copiously commented with explanations for each CSS rule and warnings about potential problems that could occur when certain rules are edited (**Figure 50b**).

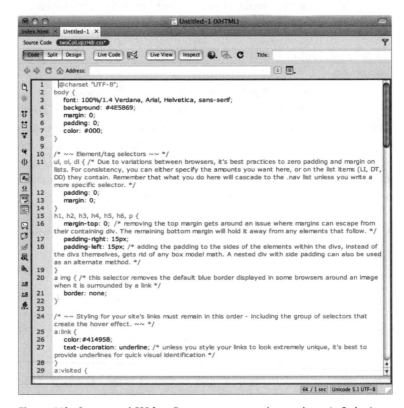

Figure 50b Commented CSS for a Dreamweaver starter layout, shown in Code view.

Each starter layout generated this way includes text that acts as both placeholder and instructional guide (**Figure 50c**). The paragraphs of text in the content well describe how the page's CSS layout is built, and provide explanations and advice for customizing its attributes. The updated starter layouts in Dreamweaver CS5 even use different color palettes for liquid layouts (a blue palette) and fixed layouts (earth tones).

Working with Dreamweaver

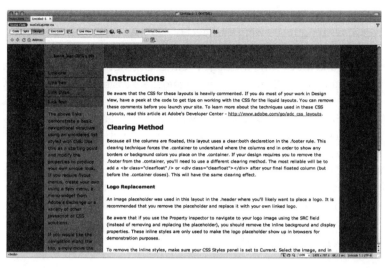

Figure 50c A Dreamweaver starter layout applied to a new document with a liquid layout.

Bear in mind, starter layouts are not meant to be your final site design. They provide a structural framework upon which you apply your beautiful design touches. However, if you've never used CSS layout before and you want to start on a solid foundation of browser-compatible, standards-compliant CSS-based layout, they're a great starting point. The CSS and page structure is entirely customizable, so you can modify the code however you choose to get you closer to your ultimate design goals.

Each template comes with the source Photoshop files containing the exact slices used in the final designs. These templates are a great starting point if you want to leapfrog defining the structural elements and navigational functionality of your site, and concentrate on its content and customizing the look and feel. An instructional video accompanies each set of templates.

The first five templates are both CS4- and CS5-compatible, and can be downloaded at http://www.adobe.com/devnet/dreamweaver/articles/dreamweaver_custom_templates.html and include features like Spry accordions, menus, and tabbed panels.

Four newer templates—compatible with CS5—are available at http://www.adobe.com/devnet/dreamweaver/articles/dreamweaver_custom_templates_pt2.html and include features like custom jQuery functions and a custom-developed WordPress theme.

#51 Experimenting with Design Using CSS Enable/Disable

Fast and flexible design experimentation has never been one of Dreamweaver's strengths. Viewing the effect of CSS changes on your layout has always required modifying or deleting one or more properties, saving the CSS, and previewing the page in either Live View or a browser. With the addition of CSS Enable/Disable, changes are easier to make, faster to see, and simple to either keep or undo.

CSS Enable allows you to temporarily enable and disable specific properties of a CSS rule so you can experiment with design options. To disable a property, click in the space just to the left of the property name in the CSS panel in Current mode. This adds a circle-and-line icon and grays out the property name in the panel (**Figure 51a**). That same icon appears next to disabled property names in Code Navigator.

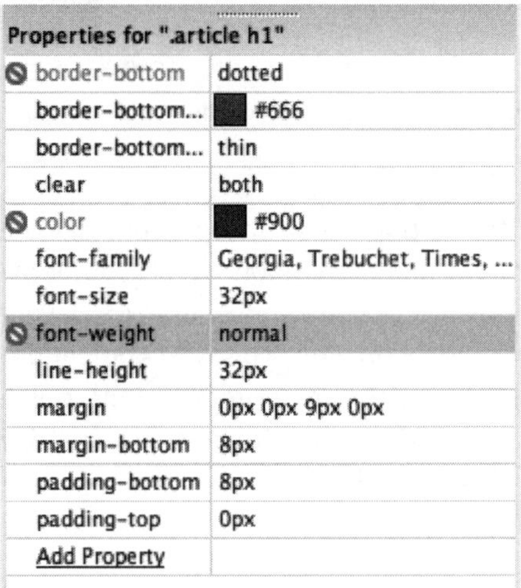

How "Disabling" Works

A disabled property remains in your CSS, but it's "commented out" (surrounded by an opening /* and a closing */ to indicate to the browser that it's a line of code to be ignored) with [disabled] added at the beginning of the comment. This is what Dreamweaver uses to know that something in the CSS is temporarily disabled by the CSS Enable/Disable feature. These disabled property comments should not be modified in code view, or it won't be possible to re-enable the property again from the CSS Styles panel.

Properties for ".article h1"	
⊘ border-bottom	dotted
border-bottom...	■ #666
border-bottom...	thin
clear	both
⊘ color	■ #900
font-family	Georgia, Trebuchet, Times, ...
font-size	32px
⊘ font-weight	normal
line-height	32px
margin	0px 0px 9px 0px
margin-bottom	8px
padding-bottom	8px
padding-top	0px
Add Property	

Figure 51a Disabled properties in the CSS panel.

In Design view, you can immediately see the change that results from the disabled property without going into the code or committing to the decision by actually modifying the property in the CSS panel or Rule Definition dialog (**Figures 51b and 51c**). Until the property is enabled again, it's just ignored. If you don't like what you see, simply click the circle-and-line icon and the property is restored.

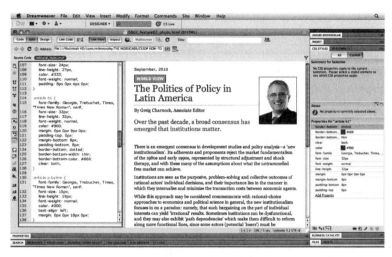

Figure 51b This layout uses an h1 class that customizes the article headline's color, weight, font, border, and other attributes.

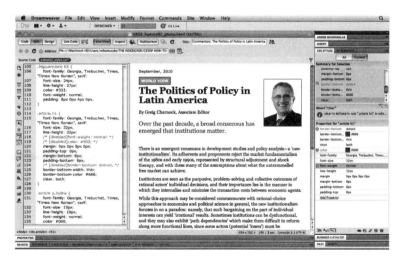

Figure 51c The same layout with the bottom border, font color, and font weight properties of the "article h1" rule disabled using CSS Enable/Disable. The style document on the left of the split view shows the dynamically generated comments that Dreamweaver adds to the disabled attributes in the CSS rule.

Before you go live with your site, you'll want to commit to either enabling (removing Dreamweaver's comments from the code) or permanently disabling (removing both the comments and properties) to keep your CSS file size to a minimum. To do so, select something on the page for which you've disabled one or more properties, right-click a disabled property name in the Properties area of the CSS Styles panel, and choose either Delete All Disabled in Selected Rule or Enable All Disabled in Selected Rule from the context menu (**Figure 51d**).

Go to Code
New...
Edit...
Duplicate...
Rename Class...
Enable
Enable All Disabled in Selected Rule
Delete All Disabled in Selected Rule
Apply
Delete

Use External Editor

Attach Style Sheet...
Design-time...

Figure 51d The CSS panel's context menu with final Enable and Disable options.

#52 Testing Your Design with BrowserLab

As part of its CS Live online services, Adobe has brought designers a tool that enables them to preview and compare their Web pages in multiple browsers on both the Mac OS and Windows platforms. This new tool—called Adobe BrowserLab—takes your local Dreamweaver HTML file (or any URL you point it to), loads it into as many different browser versions and platforms as you specify, and delivers back a JPEG screen shot of how that page renders in each browser. This eliminates the need for designers to have multiple computers running multiple operating systems and browsers.

With an HTML document open from a Site project (Dreamweaver's BrowserLab preview will not work unless the page you want to preview is within a defined site), do any of the following:

- Go to File > Preview in Browser > Adobe BrowserLab, or Shift-Command-F12 (Shift-Ctrl-F12).

- Choose Preview in Adobe BrowserLab from the Preview/Debug in Browser button at the top of the document window.

- Click Preview in Dreamweaver's Adobe BrowserLab panel (**Figure 52a**).

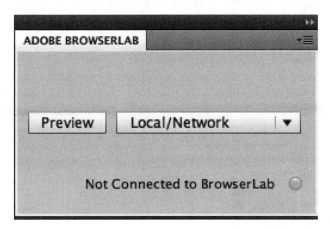

Figure 52a Dreamweaver's Adobe BrowserLab panel (Window > Extensions > Adobe BrowserLab).

If you've never used Adobe BrowserLab before, you'll be required to sign in with your Adobe ID to do so. If you don't have an Adobe ID, you'll be prompted to create one.

180

Make Efficient Browser Sets

The more browsers you include in a single Browser Set, the longer it takes for BrowserLab to generate and return screen shots. Instead, use multiple Browser Sets (BrowserLab allows up to 10) and request a narrower group of browsers within each that suit specific testing needs. If, for example, you only want to see how your page renders in the oldest browser versions, create an "Older Browsers" set. If you're most interested in comparing the oldest version of a particular browser with its most recent version, make an "Oldest/Newest Browsers" set with just those two browsers included.

Once logged in to BrowserLab, you can create one or more testing environments by clicking Browser Sets and choosing from the available browsers (**Figure 52b**). Currently, BrowserLab supports Internet Explorer versions 6 through 8 (Windows), Mozilla Firefox 2.0 through 3.6 (Windows/Mac OS), Safari 3 and 4 (Mac), and Google's Chrome 3.0 (Windows).

Figure 52b Browser Set options in Adobe BrowserLab.

You can view the JPEGs rendered by BrowserLab individually or compare them using BrowserLab's various view modes (**Figure 52c**). The 2-up View compares two of the rendered screen shots side by side (**Figure 52d**) and Onion Skin lays one of the JPEGs over another at 50 percent opacity, allowing a pixel-by-pixel comparison (**Figure 52e**). This is a great way to track down very subtle variations in browser renderings of the same page.

Figure 52c View options for screen shots in BrowserLab.

Figure 52d Firefox 3.0 (Windows) and Internet Explorer 7.0 (Windows) renderings of the same page compared side by side with BrowserLab's 2-up View.

Figure 52e The same two screen shots from Figure 52d viewed in Onion Skin mode. A slider control above the screen shots allows you to shift the opacity more toward one browser or the other to help you better determine which may be rendering the page in an unexpected fashion.

Delaying a Screen Shot

Some pages may contain content—Flash movies, Ajax data, animations, etc.—that requires a bit of time to complete after that page loads. By setting a time (up to 10 seconds) in BrowserLab's Delay box, you can pause the rendering of a screen shot by that amount of time.

Table 52a. BrowserLab Keyboard Shortcuts

Key	Action
Down arrow	Displays screen shot from the next browser in the current set
Up arrow	Displays screen shot from the previous browser in the current set
+	Zooms in (BrowserLab does not zoom below 75%)
-	Zooms out
1	Displays the screen shot in 1-up View
2	Displays screen shots from two browsers in 2-up View (side by side)
3	Displays the screen shots in Onion Skin view
Left arrow	In Onion Skin view, increases the opacity of the rendered page from the browser specified on the left, decreasing the visibility of the screen shot taken in the browser specified on the right
Right arrow	In Onion Skin view, increases the opacity of the rendered page from the browser specified on the right, decreasing visibility of the screen shot taken in the browser specified on the left
R	Shows or hides rulers
Ctrl/Cmd	Switches the cursor to a hand, allowing you to drag the page
Shift	Creates a duplicate cursor on the right or left image (2-up View only)

To save a screen shot, right-click (Ctrl-click) the image in BrowserLab and choose Save Locally from the context menu.

#53 Troubleshooting Your Design with CSS Inspect

Many Web designers and developers rely heavily on plug-ins like Mozilla's Firebug or WebKit's Web Inspector to test page behaviors and trouble-shoot design issues. The downside of these great plug-ins is that they require you to load your page in a browser and activate the plug-in. This is a very inefficient process for basic CSS troubleshooting.

Some of the functionality of these plug-ins has now been folded into Dreamweaver in the form of CSS Inspect, which allows you to visualize the box model of the HTML elements on your page just by hovering over them with the mouse. The feature is limited to the width and height of content (text, images, etc.), and that content's margin and padding.

Clicking the new Inspect button (**Figure 53a**) automatically acti-vates Live View, if it's not active already, because the two features work together. When you switch to Inspect mode, Dreamweaver nicely sug-gests that you avail yourself of a workspace that maximizes the feature's usefulness (**Figure 53b**). This workspace activates Live Code mode and Split view, and opens the CSS Styles panel in Current mode. All of these features are "plugged in" to Inspect.

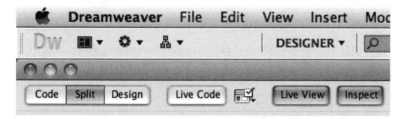

Figure 53a The Inspect feature is designed to work in Live View. Both must be turned on to dynamically highlight content, padding, and margins.

ⓘ Inspect mode is most useful with certain workspace settings. Switch now | More Info...

Figure 53b Dreamweaver prompts you to modify your workspace when you turn on Inspect.

184

Can't Hover Over What You Want?

If there's some complexity in your page structure, and hovering with the mouse isn't revealing the content, margin, and padding you seek, press the left arrow to go up the CSS hierarchy in the Tag Selector and dynamically highlight and inspect parent elements, or press the right arrow to drill farther down.

Reverse-Engineering Site Layouts You Admire Using Dreamweaver

Keep in mind that Dreamweaver's Live View is, in fact, a WebKit-based browser. When you're in Live View you can use Dreamweaver to browse to any Web site, then use tools like Inspect to visually peek under the hood at any site page's elements. Here's how:

1. Open any local HTML page (a page must be open to access the Browser Navigation toolbar).

(continued on next page)

With these workspace settings, Live Code will dynamically highlight the HTML for any element you hover over, and the CSS Styles panel will dynamically display the summary, rules, and properties of that element (**Figure 53c**). In addition, the Tag selector reflects what element is currently in focus (**Figure 53d**).

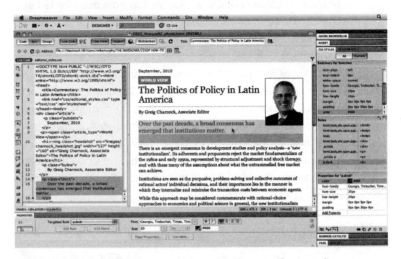

Figure 53c Dreamweaver's Inspect-optimized workspace reflecting information about the page element currently under the mouse. The paragraph being inspected is also dynamically highlighted by Live Code on the left.

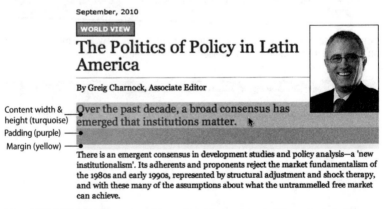

Figure 53d With the mouse over the paragraph, the extent of its content, padding, and margin boxes are highlighted in Live View. In this example, Inspect reveals both padding and a margin on this <p> element.

If you're curious about why certain spacing is occurring in your layout, or can't figure out which rule is causing a puzzling layout problem, hovering over adjacent elements in Inspect mode helps you understand how elements interact and align.

Once you've found the source of any unwanted layout property, click on the highlighted element to "freeze" the highlighting in place, then go to the CSS Styles panel to make changes to that element's margin or padding. As soon as you click, you're automatically kicked out of Inspect mode. Once you've modified the problem property, turn on Inspect again to verify that all is as you expected (**Figure 53e**).

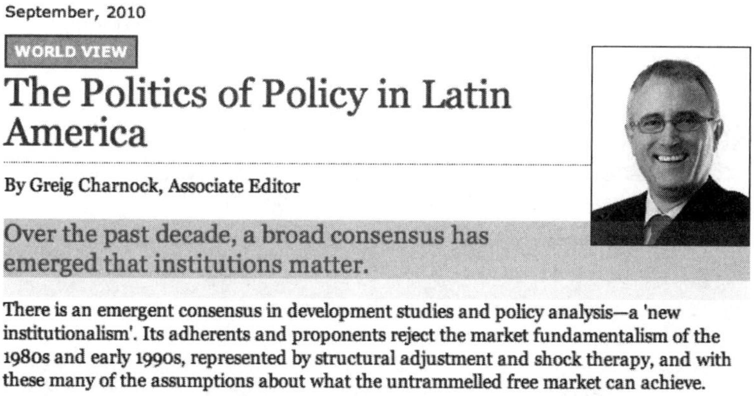

September, 2010

WORLD VIEW

The Politics of Policy in Latin America

By Greig Charnock, Associate Editor

Over the past decade, a broad consensus has emerged that institutions matter.

There is an emergent consensus in development studies and policy analysis—a 'new institutionalism'. Its adherents and proponents reject the market fundamentalism of the 1980s and early 1990s, represented by structural adjustment and shock therapy, and with these many of the assumptions about what the untrammelled free market can achieve.

Figure 53e The <p> element viewed using Inspect after all padding was removed. Bottom spacing is controlled solely by the `margin` property, as highlighted here.

Inspect doesn't fully replace a plug-in like Firebug, which can also analyze a site's network activity and measure JavaScript performance, and which offers debugging of XML and JavaScript. For resolving layout and CSS problems, however, working with CSS Inspect in Dreamweaver—with your layout visible and your code editable—is a great workflow improvement and time-saver.

2. Click Inspect to activate both Inspect and Live View.

3. Enter a URL in the Address field of the Browser Navigation bar (View > Toolbars > Browser Navigation).

4. Roll over elements to see how they're constructed. If you're using Dreamweaver's Inspect-optimized workspace, you'll also see where the elements are in the source HTML via Live Code.

#54 Using Live Code and Live View

(continued on next page)

Under the hood of Dreamweaver's Live View is the same WebKit-based rendering engine behind Apple's Safari and Google's Chrome Web browsers. When viewing a page in Live View, the layout should be reasonably close to what you'll see when it's viewed in most modern, standards-compliant browsers.

Live View is a noneditable mode, meaning you won't be able to make changes directly in the layout as you can in Design view, but you will be able to edit the code and refresh the page to see those changes.

In Live View, "reactive" page elements like rollovers, Ajax widgets, and Spry accordions all work as they would on the page in a modern browser. Activating Live Code view (**Figure 54a**) in addition to Live View allows you to see what happens in the background—in other words, how your code dynamically changes according to the state of the page (**Figures 54b and 54c**).

Figure 54a Live Code mode activated in Dreamweaver CS5.

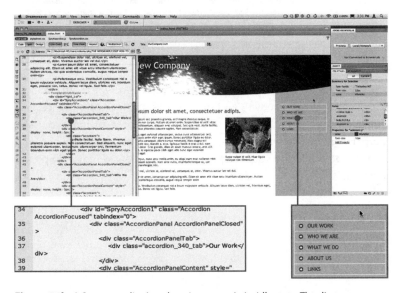

Figure 54b A Spry accordion's code as it appears in its idle state. The div tag uses a class of `AccordionPanelTab`.

Working with Dreamweaver

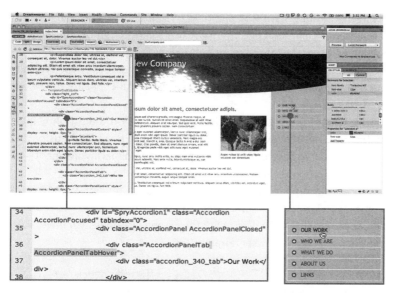

Figure 54c When you roll over the Our Work link in the accordion (bottom right), the `AccordionPanelTabHover` class is added to the `div` tag dynamically and highlighted by Live Code (bottom left).

Live Code is a new CS5 feature that dynamically highlights and reveals parts of the code when you interact with page elements in Live View. When you turn Live Code on, that also puts the code into a noneditable mode, preventing you from making any changes until you turn off either Live Code or Live View.

Live Code is especially useful when you're working with pages connected to content-management systems (a.k.a. CMS frameworks), and dynamic sites like WordPress blogs, which rely heavily on PHP includes and server-side page generation. Live View reveals stage changes on the page; Live Code reveals all of the content code that gets delivered to the browser, even if the blog template page is little more than a handful of PHP calls and includes.

While Live View is a good sample of what a WebKit-based browser will display, it does double duty as a debugging and learning tool when used together with Live Code. The two viewing modes provide something a browser doesn't—the ability to see in real time what's happening as code is generated by the server and returned to the user's browser.

Beyond just viewing single pages for which you type in a URL, you can also follow links on any Web page (or on any of your local site pages) by Command-clicking (Ctrl-clicking) the link. If the link is within the current site, the view refreshes with the page you requested. You can navigate through the site to any number of pages, and get back to the page you started from at any time by clicking the home button in the toolbar.

If the link is to another site, a new document window opens (in Live View) in another tab and the page is displayed there.

Don't Stop at Live View

Remember that WebKit is but one of several rendering engines. Live View is not meant to eliminate previewing your page in the browsers your site needs to comply with, either locally or using Adobe BrowserLab. However, as you're starting the development process, Live View is a fast and easy way to view your design in a true standards-compliant browser environment without ever leaving Dreamweaver.

#55 Using the Widget Browser

For many designers without a coding or scripting background, getting the kind of rich, interactive site most users expect can be challenging. Advanced user-interface components like sliding panels, accordion widgets, slideshows, and lightboxes are not something novices can typically build from scratch, but often exactly the sort of functionality they want for their Web sites.

The Widget Browser is an Adobe AIR application that's tightly integrated into Dreamweaver, allowing you to browse, download, customize, and insert publicly available Ajax widgets with minimal involvement—or in some cases none—with the widget's code.

Since it's a separate application that works in tandem with Dreamweaver, you'll need to first download and install the Widget Browser before you can use it. To do so, click the Extend Dreamweaver menu icon and choose Widget Browser (**Figure 55a**).

Figure 55a Accessing the Widget Browser from within Dreamweaver.

Once the Widget Browser is installed and launched, you'll need to sign in using your Adobe ID. After logging in, you'll see the available widgets on the Adobe Exchange (**Figure 55b**).

Figure 55b Available widgets on the Adobe Exchange displayed in the Widget Browser application.

The number of widgets on the Adobe Exchange continues to grow as developers share new widgets. Currently, the types of widgets available include functionality like slideshows and lightboxes, a Google Maps widget, dynamic rollover image zooming, jQuery-based tabbed interfaces, calendar-style date pickers, and more.

Where Do Widgets Come From?

Some widgets on the Adobe Exchange come from Adobe, but many are uploaded and shared by outside developers who share their efforts freely with other members of the Dreamweaver community. Although most of us will use the Widget Browser to avail ourselves of existing components and UI elements, the Widget Browser is, in fact, a two-way street. Developers can also use the Widget Browser to package and upload their widgets, making them available on the Adobe Exchange.

Click on any widget in the Widget Browser window to see details about the widget's functionality, its developer, and browser compatibility. Clicking the Preview button loads a working version of the widget in the Widget Browser, where you can view and interact with all of its functionality (**Figure 55c**).

Figure 55c The "jqzoom" widget in Widget Browser's preview mode displays a fully functioning example of the widget and alternate preset behaviors you can test out before downloading.

When you've found a widget that suits your needs, click the Add to My Widgets button in the bottom-right corner of the Widget Browser window. You'll be required to accept the licensing terms of the widget, after which you can start customizing the widget immediately by clicking Go to My Widgets in the resulting dialog box.

From the My Widgets view in the Widget Browser, click Configure in the lower-left corner of the application window. How customizable a widget is depends on both the widget and the developer, and how many settings they've "exposed" for the widget browser. Some widgets offer very few options, and further customization requires getting into the code yourself. Others, however, make many options available, and the

Widget Browser application facilitates the process by providing a simple user interface through which various parameters of the widget can be quickly modified and immediately previewed (**Figure 55d**).

Figure 55d The LightBox Gallery Widget is highly customizable, and different aspects of the widget are organized into accordion-style collapsible panels, including General, Gallery, Thumbnails, Icons, and other settings.

To save your settings as a preset, name your settings in the Name field under the live preview and click the Save Preset button. Any presets you save with the widget will be selectable options when you later insert the widget in your Web page from Dreamweaver (**Figure 55e**). Adding a widget to a Web page in Dreamweaver is as simple as clicking Widget in the Inspect panel or choosing Insert > Widget… from the Dreamweaver application menu. In the Widget dialog, select both the desired widget and the appropriate preset, then click OK.

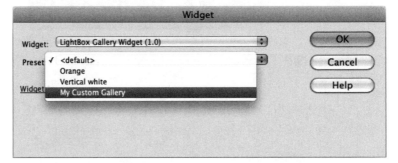

Figure 55e Widget selection and preset options when inserting widgets.

The inserted widget—and all of its related functionality—is added to your page, and can be fully interacted with in Dreamweaver's Live View (**Figure 55f**).

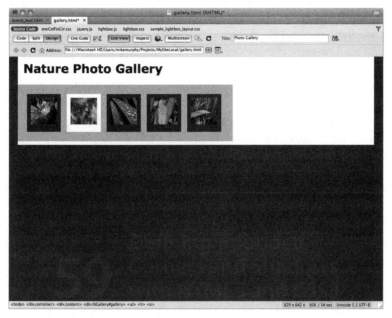

Figure 55f The LightBox Gallery Widget inserted in an HTML page in Dreamweaver and shown in Live View. Customizing the images requires going into the code and replacing the demo image references with references to your own images, and creating corresponding thumbnails to replace those used in the demo.

Using the Widget Browser, tweaking a few settings, and with little or no delving into code, you can add advanced user-interface controls and components to your Web pages without needing to become an expert in JavaScript or any other coding language.

#56 Reveal Dynamic Files on a Web Server

Setting Up a Test Server and Installing WordPress

Accessing dynamic server files requires first setting up a testing server either on the Web or locally on your computer (using software like MAMP for the Mac OS or XXAMP for Windows) that's running the blog software you're working with. For detailed information about installing this server software, read the online tutorial at http://imageready.info/ devnet/dreamweaver/ articles/setting_up_php.html.

For step-by-step instructions on installing WordPress on a local testing server, read the online tutorial at http:// imageready.info/devnet/ dreamweaver/articles/dw_ wordpress_pt2.html.

When working on a site project that has a test Server set up (see "Setting Up a Test Server" and "Installing WordPress"), Dreamweaver can track activity on that server and report back all of the related files that make up a dynamically generated Web site. By "discovering" related files on the server, Dreamweaver can both render the site's pages and display the code that's dynamically delivered to the browser.

This new capability can help take the mystery out of a robust and complex content-management system (CMS) like WordPress, Droopl, or Joomla. If you're interested in customizing an existing WordPress theme, for example, doing so from the WordPress admin's site appearance settings using only the blog's CSS files can be intimidating and slow. Working exclusively in the WordPress admin makes it difficult to grasp the context and scope of the CSS rules and cumbersome to preview or undo your changes. With Dreamweaver's support for these dynamic CMS frameworks, understanding and modifying a blog's page structure and appearance can be accomplished more quickly and intuitively than ever before.

When you first open a page from a WordPress site (index.php, for example), Code view shows you very little, and Design view shows you nothing at all (**Figure 56a**). That's because pages in a WordPress site are dynamically generated, requiring page elements and content to be delivered up according to the PHP calls made to the server.

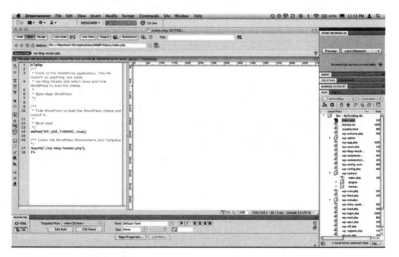

Figure 56a A WordPress index.php file opened with Live View turned off displays only PHP calls in Code view, and no content at all in Design view.

Working with Dreamweaver

If your testing server has been set up properly, Dreamweaver CS5 can "discover" the related files necessary to both display the page in Live View and reveal dynamic code changes in Live Code. The application prompts you to allow it to discover those files when it loads a PHP page such as a WordPress index.php file (**Figure 56b**).

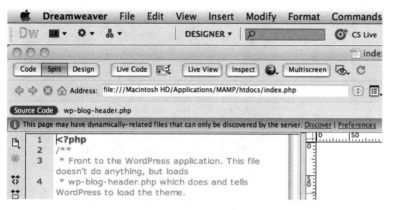

Figure 56b Dreamweaver prompts you to discover the related files necessary to properly display a PHP-based site such as a WordPress blog.

Once discovered, the related files are listed in a row across the related files panel above the Code and Split views (**Figure 56c**). Files for the blog's header, configuration files, CSS style sheets, and XML data files are all listed and editable by Dreamweaver just by clicking their names in the panel.

Figure 56c The related files panel reveals the PHP, CSS, XML, and other files required to properly render the site's pages and deliver its content.

When Live View is activated, the PHP page fully renders in the Design view pane, but Code view still shows only the minimal PHP calls used to

Automate File Discovery

Rather than go through the process of permitting Dreamweaver to discover related files each time you open one of your PHP pages, you can change Dreamweaver's preferences to do so automatically. From the General options of the Dreamweaver preferences dialog, change the setting for Discover Dynamically-Related Files from Manually to Automatic.

Filter Dynamically Related Files

CMS frameworks like Word-Press are complex. To be as dynamic as they are, they use many related files. This can make the row of related files listed in the Related Files toolbar tough to navigate through. To make it easier for you to find the file types you want to work with, you can filter the list of files. Click the Filter icon 🜚 at the right end of the Related Files toolbar and deselect the file types you're not interested in seeing in the toolbar, keeping only what you want checked.

build the page from other related files (**Figure 56d**). When Live Code is turned on, however, everything that the index.php file requests from the server is brought in and displayed in the Code view pane (**Figure 56e**).

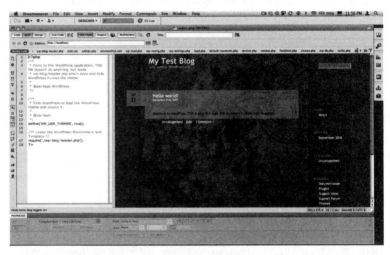

Figure 56d With Live View turned on, the blog page fully renders in the Design view pane, but Code view (on the left) does not change.

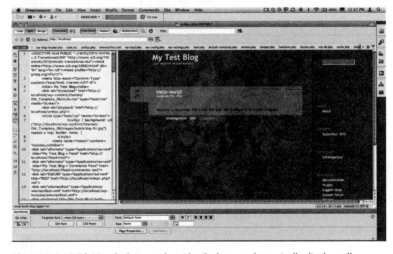

Figure 56e With Live Code turned on, the Code pane dynamically displays all server-based content delivered to the browser as if the site were live.

#57 Taking Advantage of PHP Code Hinting

PHP code hinting debuted in Dreamweaver CS4, but was lacking some key functionality, such as support for custom variables and functions defined in related files (external files required by a page to render it as intended in a browser). Custom variables and functions were only hinted when they were defined *in the same document* (**Figure 57a**).

More often than not, however, functions and variables should be defined in separate files and called upon in the Web page at runtime (when the file is delivered to the user's browser). This allows many pages to share those functions and variables, just as many pages share the same CSS.

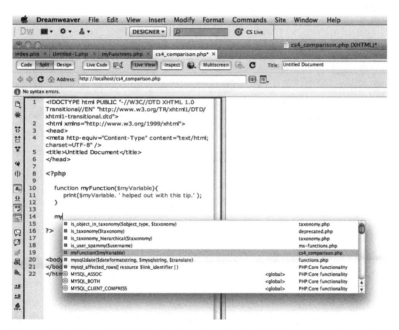

Figure 57a PHP code-hinting behavior as it worked in CS4. The custom `myFunction` hint appears because the function itself is defined within the same document.

Dreamweaver CS5 now provides code hints regardless of where those functions are defined on the site. To take advantage of this feature, the following must be true:

- The page from which you're calling the functions or variables, and the file(s) being called upon, are part of a defined Dreamweaver site (See Tip #49, "Getting Started with Simplified Site Setup").

- You must have allowed Dreamweaver to discover related files for the site (See Tip #56, "Reveal Dynamic Files on a Web Server").

When the above conditions are in place, you can write functions and variables in a separate file (**Figure 57b**) for maximum efficiency, and still rely on the ease of code hinting. If you want to see the result of the PHP calls in Live View, the site you're working on must also have a testing server defined and running.

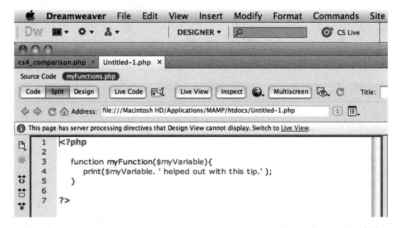

Figure 57b A separate file named myFunctions.php is set up to store one or more functions or variables for a site.

To use the functions contained in that related file, you must first use a PHP include to point your Web page to it with a basic statement such as: `<?php include('myFunctions.php'); ?>`.

Once Dreamweaver knows that the custom variables and functions in that file are to be included, it will include all of them in pop-up PHP code-hinting mode as you start typing them in the source code of individual site files (**Figure 57c**). To invoke code hinting, press Control-Spacebar (Mac and Windows) after you start typing the desired code. The more you type, the closer code hinting gets you to the appropriate matching code.

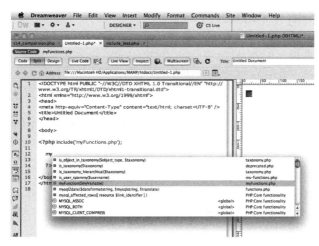

Figure 57c With the association made between the current document and the myFunctions.php file by the include statement, Dreamweaver can offer up all of the custom functions and variables contained in that file as code hints. In this instance, it identifies not only the myFunction function, but also displays the syntax that indicates what variable—in this case, myVariable—is part of that function, and shows the PHP filename from which the function originates.

As with all other code hinting in Dreamweaver, the hints get narrowed down the more you type, and scrolling to the appropriate match and hitting Return (Enter) completes the code for you. PHP code hinting goes one step beyond this, keeping a persistent tooltip visible if there are variables built into that function. This is both a helpful reminder of what variables the function requires and a way to spare you more typing (**Figure 57d**).

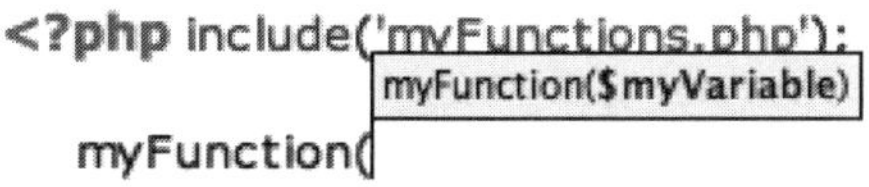

```
<?php include('myFunctions.php');
                 myFunction($myVariable)
    myFunction(
```

Figure 57d A tooltip specific to the syntax of myFunction provides additional context for PHP code hinting.

200

Context Is Everything

In addition to hints about your custom code, Dreamweaver's code hinting provides additional context about standard PHP functions at the bottom of the code-hints pop-up. Each of these structural tips is actually a clickable link to the page on www.php.net that provides comprehensive information about that function.

Code Hinting in Related Files

For sites based on CMS frameworks like WordPress, Droopl, and Joomla, the CMS will already have existing PHP functions and variables in place after you install the CMS on your server. Dreamweaver can now scan through such a site's related files and add site-specific code hinting to make working with that CMS's PHP code more efficient.

This feature is not on by default, so before you start modifying, for example, a WordPress blog, go to the Dreamweaver Site menu and choose Site > Site-Specific Code Hints. In the resulting dialog, Dreamweaver defaults to WordPress as the site's structure and displays a directory and file tree for the site (**Figure 57e**), and every file and folder necessary to build that site's pages dynamically is set to be scanned for custom functions and variables.

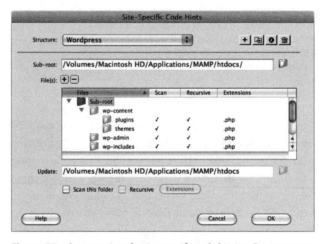

Figure 57e Setup options for site-specific code hinting. Dreamweaver allows folders to be scanned for custom PHP functions and variables to add to its code-hinting feature. The Recursive option means that all files and subfolders within a given folder will also be scanned.

If you opt to customize any of the settings for site-specific code hinting—to exclude unwanted themes or to add custom files not included in the default WordPress structure defined by Dreamweaver—you'll be prompted to create a custom site-structure setting (**Figure 57f**). Once saved, the file appears in the files list of the Site panel as "yourstructurename_codehinting.config."

Working with Dreamweaver

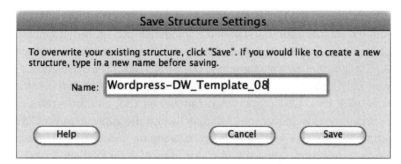

Figure 57f Saving a custom site-specific code-hinting structure.

Once site-specific code hinting has been established for your site, typing in the start of any site-specific functions or variables in code-hinting mode will make your site's specific code available (**Figure 57g**).

Figure 57g Site-specific WordPress "get" functions listed as code hints.

#58 Working with HTML5 and CSS3 in Dreamweaver

What Is HTML5?

The HTML5 specification is the World Wide Web Consortium's (W3C) fifth major revision to the Hypertext Markup Language that is the core of the World Wide Web. It adds new features to help Web-application authors, and new markup elements that reflect authoring practices that have become de facto standards since the last HTML specification. HTML5 also aims to define clear standards for maximum cross-browser (or cross-device) compatibility and consistency. The standard also incorporates features like video playback, which has historically relied on browser plug-ins like Adobe Flash Player or Microsoft's Silverlight. HTML5 will also drop a number of outdated elements like <font>, <center>, and <frameset>.

(continued on next page)

Dreamweaver CS5 debuted with no support for HTML5—the emerging (but still not fully adopted) standard for modern browsers. Within a month of its release, however, a downloadable extension was made available on Adobe Labs that natively supported the HTML5 DOCTYPE declaration, as well as HTML5 structural elements and CSS3 properties. A few months later, with the 11.0.3 update to Dreamweaver CS5, all the features of that extension were incorporated directly into the application via CS5's automatic updates feature (see Tip #6 "Keeping CS5 Design Premium Up-to-Date"), eliminating the need for users to download and install a separate extension.

After updating Dreamweaver to add this expansive new functionality, you might not even notice what's changed. On closer inspection, however, you'll see a new Multiscreen button in the Document toolbar (see Tip #60 "Testing Alternate Designs with Multiscreen Preview") and, when you create a new document, there are two HTML5-based starter layouts in the New Document dialog (**Figure 58a**).

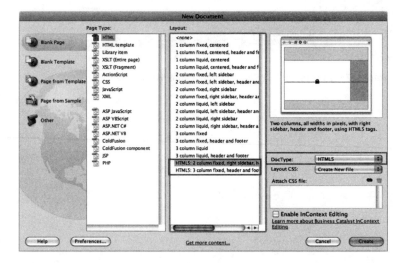

Figure 58a HTML5 starter layouts available in the New Document dialog.

When you open Code view in one of these HTML5 starter layouts, you'll see familiar tags, such as <div> , <h1>, <ul>, and <p>, along with new HTML5 tags such as <header>, <footer> , <nav> , <article>, and <section> (**Figure 58b**).

```
1    <!DOCTYPE HTML>
2    <html>
3    <head>
4    <meta http-equiv="Content-Type" content="text/html; charset=UTF-8">
5    <title>Untitled Document</title>
6    <link href="file:///Macintosh HD/Users/mikemurphy/Projects/MySiteLocal/
     HTML5_twoColFixRtHdr.css" rel="stylesheet" type="text/css"><!--[if lt IE 9]>
7    <script src="http://html5shiv.googlecode.com/svn/trunk/html5.js"></script>
8    <![endif]-->
9    </head>
10
11   <body>
12
13   <div class="container">
14     <header>
15       <a href="#"><img src="" alt="Insert Logo Here" name="Insert_logo" width=
         "180" height="90" id="Insert_logo" style="background: #C6D580; display:block;
         " /></a>
16     </header>
17     <div class="sidebar1">
18       <nav>
19         <ul>
20           <li><a href="#">Link one</a></li>
21           <li><a href="#">Link two</a></li>
22           <li><a href="#">Link three</a></li>
23           <li><a href="#">Link four</a></li>
24         </ul>
25       </nav>
26       <aside>
```

Figure 58b The HTML5 DOCTYPE declaration and new tags (including header, nav, and aside) in a Dreamweaver starter layout.

Unfortunately, Dreamweaver's implementation of HTML5 is not 100 percent integrated into the application, so new elements like <section> and <nav> aren't available from the Insert panel or accessible from the Property inspector. Until HTML5 is woven in throughout the application, you'll be able to work more efficiently with HTML5 elements in Code view—taking advantage of code hinting, which fully supports HTML5 tags (**Figure 58c**)—than you will in Dreamweaver's panels and other interface elements.

Figure 58c Code hinting in action for the new HTML5 <canvas> tag.

Keep in mind that the HTML5 specification is still new and continues to evolve. Even when it's adopted, it will not entirely eliminate cross-browser issues. To learn more about the HTML5 Specification, go to http://www.w3.org/TR/html5 or http://www.w3schools.com/html5/html5_reference.asp.

HTML5 Browser Support

The HTML5 DOCTYPE is designed to be backward compatible. Even Internet Explorer 6 recognizes the HTML5 DOCTYPE declaration (just not any of the HTML5 tags), so it's safe to use with current pages. The new standard is designed so that older browsers can ignore the new HTML5 syntax, and render pages according to an older standard.

Speed Up Your HTML5 Coding

Dreamweaver continually looks at your code as you work to determine when a closing tag is needed. By default, as soon as you type an open angle bracket and backslash, Dreamweaver looks for the nearest unclosed tag and autocompletes the closing tag for you. Since HTML5 and CSS3 coding requires that you work more in Code view than Design view, this can be a helpful time-saving feature. To speed things up a bit more, you can change the default so that Dreamweaver adds the closing tag immediately after you type the opening tag's final angle bracket (>) rather than waiting for you to start closing it. You set this autoclosing behavior by going to Preferences > Code Hints, and selecting "After the opening tag's >". As you code with this setting turned on, your cursor will automatically be placed between the opening tag you type and the closing tag Dreamweaver autoinserts, so you can keep working without worrying about closing tags manually.

Despite the incomplete integration of HTML5 and CSS3 into its panels, features like code hinting that do support these emerging standards will take some of the tedious tasks out of working directly with code. Also, the CSS Styles panel does recognize and list CSS3 properties that you've defined in Code view when you select elements to which that code is applied. Because of this, you can still take advantage of features like CSS Enable/Disable (see Tip #51, "Experimenting with Design Using CSS Enable/Disable").

#59 Defining Rounded Corners and Shadows with HTML5 and CSS3

At the dawn of digital design, drop shadows were all the rage, but the Web 2.0 aesthetic is all about rounded corners. Rounding helps disguise the underlying box model of CSS and soften Web-page designs in general. Historically, this look had to be achieved with image-based workarounds. CSS3, however, includes a new border-radius property that displays page elements with rounded corners without the need for any images. The same is true for drop shadows, which can now be rendered with a properly structured shadow property (**Figure 59a**).

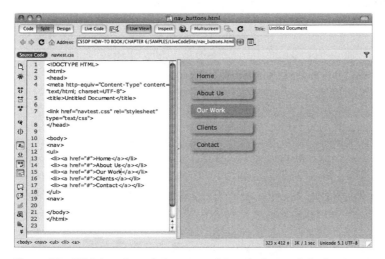

Figure 59a HTML-based rounded corners and drop shadows coded using standard ul and li tags within the new HTML5 nav tag.

Both of these CSS3 properties are among several that are not yet fully supported by all browsers. Even in browsers where they are understood, they need to be referred to in a browser-specific way until HTML5 and CSS3 are fully adopted.

For rounded corners, the standard CSS3 property syntax is border-radius, followed by a colon and the value of the radius (i.e., 6px) and a semicolon. However, the rendering engines that support the property don't yet support it in this standard format. Opera supports the property, but WebKit (Safari, Chrome, etc.) and Mozilla (Firefox) do not. Those rendering engines require a specific prefix on the border-radius property. For WebKit, that prefix is -webkit- and for Mozilla, it's -moz-. For the few

Use Code Hinting to Determine Browser Support

When you start typing in one of the browser-specific variations for a CSS3 property, turn on code hinting by hitting Control-Spacebar (Mac and Windows). When you type the leading dash, the following code hints pop up: moz-, o-, and web-kit-. Once you complete that browser-defining part of the property, code hinting displays the CSS3 properties that must be defined specifically for those browsers. If a hint doesn't appear in the list, you don't need to include a browser-specific version of that property. Opera, which has the most CSS3 support, has the fewest code hints.

properties that Opera doesn't natively support, the prefix would be -o-. These browser-specific properties must go first in your CSS rules, followed by the standard form of the tag as shown below.

```
-moz-border-radius: 6px;
-webkit-border-radius: 6px;
border-radius: 6px;
```

The new shadow property defines drop shadows in terms of color, opacity, offset, and blur. The first two are defined with the rgba attribute. The RGB values (from 0 to 255) define the amounts of red, green, and blue in the color. The "a" in that attribute stands for the color's alpha channel, with values from 0 (fully transparent) to 1 (fully opaque). For the navigation buttons in **Figure 59b**, the shadow is offset by 4 pixels both horizontally and vertically, with a 6-pixel blur. The full property is defined as:

```
box-shadow: rgba(0,0,0,0.4) 4px 4px 6px;
```

In Figure 59b, the alpha value of 0.4 equates to 40 percent. The color is 60 percent transparent. The alpha setting is different from the opacity declaration in CSS3, which sets how opaque an element *and all of its children* are. The alpha value in an rgba color sets the opacity only for that color declaration, not any other elements.

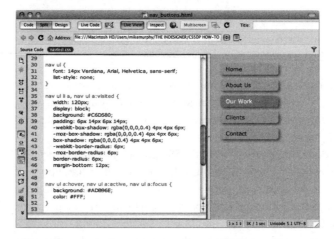

Figure 59b The CSS style sheet—with browser-specific code for both the border-radius and box-shadow properties—that defines rounded corners and drop shadows in the navigation buttons, shown side by side in Dreamweaver's Split view.

Since Dreamweaver is WebKit-based, you'll only see these properties in Live View if you've included the -webkit- iteration of the property in your CSS. Live View will not render the standard version of the property, nor will it render the Opera- or Firefox-specific iterations (**Figure 59c**).

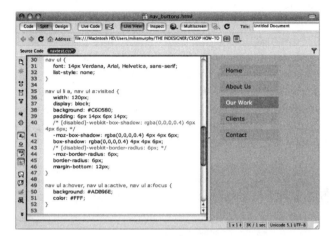

Figure 59c Using CSS Enable/Disable, the WebKit-specific properties have been commented out, and Dreamweaver's Live View does not render the rounded corners or shadows, even with the standard border-radius and shadow properties present in the CSS.

#60 Testing Alternate Designs with Multiscreen Preview

CSS3 media queries give designers the ability to change a page's layout and style properties depending on what kind of device that page is delivered to. It's not the specific device or browser that's detected, however; it's the size of the viewing area available for the page that determines what CSS rules are used to display the pages.

A desktop browser offers the most screen real estate, and most Web-page layouts are optimized for that. A tablet device like the iPad offers somewhat less screen space, and a smartphone provides the smallest viewing area. Rather than implementing complex browser detection with JavaScript and creating multiple pages for the same content, CSS3 and media queries can reconfigure the page according to alternate CSS rules you define for each screen resolution, allowing you to use one HTML page to deliver three different layouts (**Figures 60a, 60b, and 60c**).

Figure 60a A Web page designed for desktop-browser viewing. Note the large page heading and the positioning of secondary information in a column on the far right. This layout works fine when viewed on a screen large enough to fit it all.

Figure 60b The same Web page using CSS3 rules and media queries that optimize the layout for tablet viewing. Note the slightly smaller page headline and the positioning of the secondary information below the main content, rather than to the right of the image.

What Is a Media Query?

A media query is a logical expression that is either true or false. An example of a media-query syntax is:

`media="screen and (min-width: 321px)"`

or

`media="screen and (min-width: 321px) and (max-width: 768)"`

In this context, the media query determines whether that minimum-width screen parameter exists or doesn't exist. If the condition is true, the CSS associated with the media query is applied. If not, it's ignored.

Figure 60c The same page again, displayed on an iPhone, its layout optimized for a mobile device's small screen. The page heading is significantly reduced, and the navigation buttons are smaller and arranged more tightly, and the CSS prevents the photo from displaying at all.

In the HTML source code for the example in Figures 60a through 60c, two media queries are included in the document head (**Figure 60d**). One declares a minimum width of 0 pixels and a maximum of 320 pixels, and points to an external style sheet to be used by mobile devices like smartphones. The other establishes a minimum width of 321 pixels and a maximum of 768 pixels, and points to a different external style sheet to be used by tablet devices or browsers on smaller-screen devices like net-books. A third style-sheet link uses no media queries so that it will be recognized and used by older browsers that do not support media queries.

Figure 60d The style-sheet links for the page in Figures 60a, 60b, and 60c, shown in Dreamweaver's Code view.

Dreamweaver's support for media queries includes a feature called Multiscreen Preview. Clicking the Multiscreen button in the document window opens the Multiscreen Preview panel (**Figure 60e**), where you can see what your page will look like within the confines of three different screen resolutions that correspond to those of a standard desktop browser, tablet, and mobile phone.

Figure 60e A Web page with no media queries or screen-size-based CSS rules as viewed in Dreamweaver CS5's Multiscreen Preview panel. The CSS and layout are designed for a desktop-browser's wider viewport (bottom). In the Tablet viewport (top right), the content to the right of the photo is cut off, and nearly the entire page is cut off in the Phone viewport (top left).

Most tablet or phone browsers would be more likely to shrink the entire page to fit its limited screen width rather than display them as shown in the phone and tablet viewports in Figure 60e, but that would make the text and images too small, and would require the user to zoom in on the parts of the page they want to read, which is also less than desirable.

To optimize the page for multiple devices, the phone.css and tablet.css files called upon by the media queries each contain CSS rules that override specific properties in the main CSS. Only properties that differ need to be defined in these CSS files. For example, the background color does not change for any of the alternate layouts, so it's defined only in the main CSS file, not the phone or tablet CSS files.

Certain elements, however, do need to be changed. The tablet.css file redefines the `div` structure to move the text that appears at the far right to below the content area, among other subtle changes. The phone.css file has far more differences, including redefining the padding around the navigation buttons and their overall size, reducing the size of the headline, and setting the display value for the photo to none so it doesn't

See Alternate Screen Layouts in Live View

Dreamweaver CS5's Design view and Live View fully support CSS3 media queries, and will display pages with the appropriate CSS according to the width of the Dreamweaver document window. As you work in Live View and resize the document window, the layout adjusts to adapt just as it would in a browser that supports media queries.

Follow Links in Multiscreen Preview

The Multiscreen Preview panel is fully interactive—just like Dreamweaver's Live View—so you can mouse over navigation elements or other "live" content in any of the panel's viewports and see how they function. You can also click links to other pages and they'll load in that device's viewport as well.

Making it Work on Apple Devices

The iPhone and iPad scale the viewport to accommodate most standard Web pages on their smaller screens. Each device states its width as the width of the page, not the true width of the screen. As a result, the desktop-sized version of the layout is used, scaled down to fit the screen.

To turn off that scaling and force those devices to honor the CSS3 media queries, add the following line to your html file within the document head:

```
meta name="viewport"
content="width=
device-width;
initial-scale=1.0;
maximum-scale=1.0;
user-scalable=0;" />
```

With that setting in place, both the iPhone and iPad will present the layout according to your media query settings.

appear on mobile devices. All of these differences can be previewed directly within Dreamweaver CS5 from the Multiscreen Preview panel (**Figure 60f**).

Figure 60f The same HTML page from Figure 60e displayed in the Multiscreen Preview panel with all of its media queries honored, and all of the screen-size-based CSS3 rules reconfiguring the tablet and phone layouts accordingly.

Media queries are one of the most promising and powerful new features in the developing CSS3 specification, especially considering the explosion of devices currently—or soon arriving—on the market, from smartphones like the iPhone and Droid, to tablets like the iPad and GALAXY Tab. With media queries, a page can be delivered in three completely different configurations from a single HTML file.

CHAPTER SEVEN

Flash Catalyst

If you purchased Adobe Creative Suite 5 Design Premium you probably noticed a new program among the old stalwarts like Photoshop, Illustrator, and InDesign. That new kid on the block is Adobe Flash Catalyst. Flash Catalyst is positioned as the interactive application for those who don't want to write code. It was created for designers who are tired of handing off static artwork to developers to breathe life into their design before placing it onto the Web or into an interactive desktop environment. Although in its infancy, Flash Catalyst delivers on its promise. Want to make a box into a button? Select it and it's a button. Need a scroll bar? Drag an object onto the project that looks like a scroll bar and, *shazam!* it's a scroll bar.

#61 Flash Catalyst Basics

Flash Catalyst provides the tools to build interactive content without writing a line of code. Typical Flash Catalyst projects include interactive Web banners or ads, online portfolios, product guides or manuals, and sophisticated application interfaces (**Figure 61a**).

Figure 61a Here's an example of an interactive banner that began life in Adobe Illustrator before its finishing touches were applied in Flash Catalyst.

Among its many key features, Flash Catalyst allows you to design with familiar products like Photoshop, Illustrator, and Fireworks. Taking advantage of what you already know in these programs, Catalyst is designed with a fast learning curve that gets you up and running quickly. Content like images, video, audio, and SWF files can be imported into your project's library and placed with pixel-point accuracy when viewed across varying operating systems and devices.

Drag-and-Drop Components

To quickly comp an idea, you can use the handy Wireframe Components panel seen in Figure 61b. This panel lets you drag and drop common page items like scroll bars or radio buttons into your layout.

Artwork is easily transformed into interactive components, like buttons, check boxes, lists, and scroll bars. Interactive forms can be quickly created using built-in components like text entry and check boxes. Interactions defining component behavior can be added to buttons, for example, to produce smooth transitions between pages or states. Prototyping is also easy using Flash Catalyst's collection of wireframe components (**Figure 61b**).

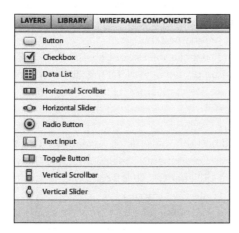

Figure 61b The Wireframe Components panel provides ten useful objects with which to build a quick wireframe of your project.

Built on Adobe's open source Flex framework, Flash Catalyst projects contain three major ingredients: components (buttons, sliders, scroll bars), pages and states (logins, forms, info pages), and transitions. Once a project is laid out, artwork can be imported from Adobe Photoshop, Illustrator, or Fireworks with all original layers intact. Interactions are added like playing a movie, opening a URL, or playing a transition to another state. Once the designer decides the project is complete, Flash Catalyst projects are exported as SWF files that run in Adobe Flash Player for the Web or Adobe AIR on the desktop. Flash Catalyst projects (.fxp) can also be opened in Adobe Flash Builder for further development.

#62 Getting to Know the Flash Catalyst Interface

Unlike most CS5 apps, Flash Catalyst has only two workspaces, Design and Code. Pop-up menus in each workspace let you toggle between them.

The Design Workspace

The Design workspace (**Figure 62a**) is comprised of several key areas. The artboard is the main area, or stage, where the design is built. Above the artboard is the Breadcrumbs bar, which tracks where you are in any point within your project. Above that is the Pages/States panel, which displays a thumbnail of each page or state of a component. Pages and states can be duplicated, removed, added, or renamed this panel.

To the right of the Pages/States panel is the Heads Up Display, or HUD panel. A floating panel that can be placed anywhere, the HUD appears when objects on the artboard are selected. From its drop-down menu, selected objects are easily transformed into working components like buttons, boxes, scrolling panels, or sliders.

In the far-right column you'll find the Tools panel, beneath which sit the Layers, Library, and Wireframe Components panels. Wireframe Components are fully functioning, pre-built generic-styled components, available to be dragged and dropped onto the artboard.

Below this group of panels are the Interactions and Properties panels. Interactions define what happens as users interact with the application. A typical interaction would be a page turn that occurs when the user clicks a defined button. Interactions can also be set up to play animations or videos, or open a Web page.

Directly below the artboard are the Timeline and Design-Time Data panels. The Timeline panel tracks the progression of an animation over time and provides controls to add transitions and effects like fades or dissolves. The Design-Time Data panel provides control over which data (images or text) appear in a prescribed data list.

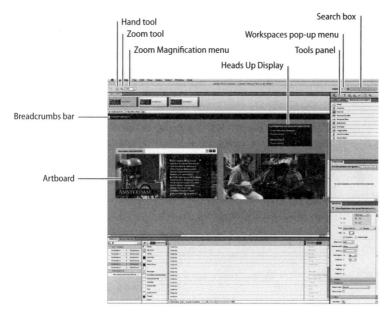

Figure 62a Compared to other CS5 applications, Flash Catalyst has a relatively sparse interface, as seen here.

Under the Hood

All applications built in Flash Catalyst are created on the Flex framework. Flex, an open-source framework for building and deploying applications that run in all major browsers and operating systems, employs the MXML language for developers to define layout, appearance and all Flex behaviors. On the client side, ActionScript 3.0 is the language of choice. When a Flash Catalyst project is published, MXML and ActionScript are combined as a SWF file.

The Code Workspace

To view the underlying application code in Flash Catalyst, use the Code workspace. Like in Dreamweaver, code is generated automatically as you work in Flash Catalyst (**Figure 62b**). But unlike Dreamweaver, the Catalyst Code workspace is read only. All editing must be performed in Adobe Flash Builder.

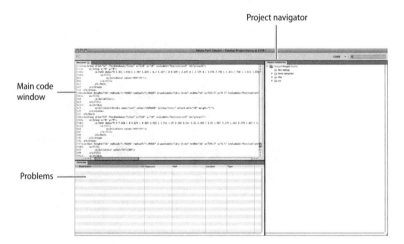

Figure 62b The Code workspace is misnamed, because you can't actually work in it. The workspace is read only, and all editing must be done in Adobe Flash Builder.

#63 Planning a Catalyst Project

Although Flash Catalyst projects can be built from scratch by choosing File > New Project, most projects will originate as static pages in Illustrator, Fireworks, or Photoshop. Working this way is important for two reasons. First, you'll be using tools with which you're most comfortable. Second, with Flash Catalyst a mere 1.0 release, many of its tools are far less robust compared to those found in more mature programs like Photoshop or Illustrator. Most typesetting, for example, is better handled outside Flash Catalyst and then pasted in. The same holds true for objects that need to be aligned or distributed.

This is not to suggest that *all* work need be done outside of Flash Catalyst. For example, a simple effect like creating a drop shadow is better handled in Flash Catalyst than in Illustrator (**Figure 63a**). Adding simple text like button labels is also fine to do in Flash Catalyst.

Figure 63a Drop Shadow is one of six basic filters that can be easily added to objects in Flash Catalyst via the Filters panel.

Whereas originating artwork inside of Flash Catalyst may sometimes seem attractive, remember that once art is created in Flash Catalyst it's there forever. In other words, there's no way to begin a project in Catalyst and then further edit it back in Illustrator, Photoshop, or Fireworks.

What's most important when starting any project, regardless of where you begin, is layer organization and labeling. Without descriptive names for layers and objects, the job of assigning actions and behaviors in Flash Catalyst becomes a confusing mess.

Small Is Beautiful

When you're planning your first Flash Catalyst project, think small and think simple. Don't try to attempt something too complex for your first go-round. If you focus on creating a clean, well-executed project, you'll quickly learn the basics of Flash Catalyst—and you can develop this first foray into bigger and more complex projects going forward.

#**64** Starting in Illustrator

When designing projects in Illustrator, you must give careful consideration to the document structure. The two most common ways to create this structure in Illustrator are to import all your artwork from one artboard into a single page state, or to use multiple artboards to define separate pages and states inside of Flash Catalyst. Either way, giving your artboards and layers descriptive and unique names will simplify their use once they're in Flash Catalyst.

Figure 64a shows an interactive city guide that was built from one artboard employing multiple layers in Illustrator. When viewers click the numbered buttons that are centered on top, images and text panels slide gracefully in and out.

Figure 64a From left to right we see five image panels grouped end to end. The viewer can click a button at the top of the interface to switch between the various screens and text. Although it's hard to see, there is a small text panel in the lower-right corner of the leftmost panel.

If we further examine the Layers panel of our city guide, we see how major components like buttons, panels, or images are all placed on layers (**Figure 64b**).

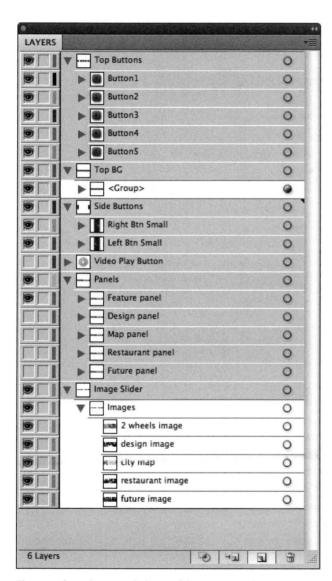

Figure 64b In this expanded view of the Layers panel we get a good look at the way buttons, panels, and images are placed on layers.

Keep It Sharp

Flash Catalyst always wants to make things sharp. To this end, artwork that originates in Illustrator may shift position when imported into Flash Catalyst as it tries to align to a hidden pixel grid. If this shifting has you concerned, always enable Align to Pixel Grid when beginning or choosing New Document profile > Flash Catalyst. This will ensure that vector objects will not be subject to anti-aliasing and instead render with clean, straight lines. To check if lines are aligning to your grid, go to View > Pixel Preview.

The Transform panel is also helpful for this purpose. At the bottom center of the panel is an Align to Pixel Grid option. In addition, the panel's fly-out menu lets you enable the Align New Objects to Pixel Grid feature.

Think Before You Click

Carefully choosing your Fidelity options in Flash Catalyst's Illustrator Import Options dialog box can save you a lot of grief down the road. Let's have a look at what these various choices mean.

Filters

Keep Editable maintains Illustrator filters that are supported in Flash Catalyst, including Blur (Gaussian Blur), Drop Shadow, Inner Shadow, Bevel, Glow, Inner Glow. Following import, filters remain editable in the Flash Catalyst Properties panel.

Expand converts objects with filters into vectors or bitmaps to mimic their original appearance in Illustrator. For example, expanding an object's drop shadow creates a separate drop shadow behind the original object.

Flatten converts objects with filters to a composite, non-editable, raster image

Text

Automatic Conversion: based on the complexity of an item, Flash Catalyst chooses when to keep text editable, rasterize it, or convert it to outlines.

(continued on next page)

When brought into Flash Catalyst, those Illustrator layers are translated into the Flash Catalyst layers seen here in **Figure 64c**.

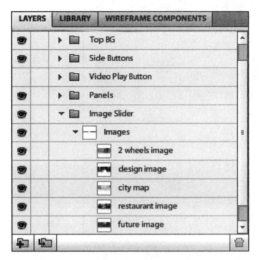

Figure 64c If you strategically organize similar components into Illustrator layers, adding animation and interaction inside of Flash Catalyst is more efficient and less confusing.

Working with Symbols

One of Illustrator's more powerful characteristics is its ability to leverage symbols to reduce file size and lessen complexity. That's because a symbol need only be created once, as each additional copy is considered an *instance* of the original. These instances, or *children*, can be quickly updated therefore by simply updating the originals, or *parents*.

What also makes symbols appealing is how, after import into Flash Catalyst, they are automatically mapped to optimized graphics. It's like importing an already compiled SWF rather than hundreds of independent vector paths.

So does this mean all Illustrator art should be converted to symbols? No, not really. Most simple vector artwork will gain little once converted to symbols. Conversely, complex, multi-path Illustrator objects, objects with embedded images, or objects that repeat many times are strong candidates for conversion to symbols (**Figure 64d**).

Figure 64d In this 365 KB illustration, a stand of trees was created using one tree symbol and multiple instances. When those instances are expanded into individual vector objects, the file size balloons to over 1.7 MB.

As an alternative to using symbols, rasterizing complex Illustrator artwork is another good strategy to reduce file size and to simplify import into Flash Catalyst. (To do this, select Object > Rasterize.) Rasterizing artwork that links to outside image files is also a good idea, particularly when you need to hand off files to other designers. When rasterizing an object, select 72 dpi for your screen resolution and set backgrounds to transparent.

Illustrator Import Options

Once you've completed your project in Illustrator, it's time to import it into Flash Catalyst. To do so locate the Create New Project From Design File section of the Welcome screen and choose From Adobe Illustrator AI File.

Keep Editable imports Illustrator text as editable text objects. Although editable text can lose some fidelity when imported into Flash Catalyst, standard text formatting attributes can be edited from the Properties panel.

Vector Outlines converts live text into static outlines.

Flatten converts text into a raster image.

Gradients
Automatic Conversion: Flash Catalyst decides when to keep gradients live or to rasterize.

Keep Editable keeps objects with Illustrator linear gradients editable. Linear gradients are editable in the Properties panel. Objects with radial or elliptical gradients remain editable (not rasterized), but their gradients cannot be edited in Flash Catalyst. You can change the fill to Solid, Gradient (linear), or None in the Properties panel.

Blend
Automatic Conversion: based on complexity and supported blends, Flash Catalyst chooses when to keep objects with blends live or to rasterize.

Flatten converts objects with blend s into a rasterized image.

Alternatively, choose File > New Project from Design File, which will close any open project and allow you to navigate to another (only one project can run at a time). When the Illustrator Import Options dialog box appears, you'll have several choices (**Figure 64e**).

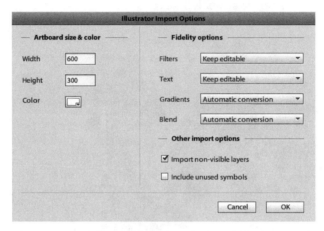

Figure 64e Aside from artboard size and color, Fidelity options and Other import options warrant close attention.

The Illustrator file converts to the FXG format automatically, and then imports into a new Flash Catalyst project. If the Illustrator file uses only one artboard, all artwork is placed in one Flash Catalyst page state. If the Illustrator file includes multiple artboards, each artboard is placed in a separate Flash Catalyst page state. Note that you can also copy and paste artwork from Illustrator into Flash Catalyst. Doing so will trigger this same Illustrator Import Options when copying and pasting. Objects that are outside the Illustrator artboard are not included when you copy and paste artwork to Flash Catalyst.

#65 Starting in Photoshop

Flash Catalyst can also work with projects that originate in Photoshop. Prior to importing your Photoshop file, give some thought to how you'll be working inside of Flash Catalyst. Since each Photoshop pixel layer, adjustment layer, mask, shape, filter, Smart Object, and text layer is converted into separate Catalyst layers, take time to merge and minimize your project's layers to as few as necessary. Reducing a file's complexity before import will make a big difference once it's imported into Flash Catalyst.

Just like when working in Illustrator, take care to descriptively name all layers to avoid confusion after import. Use layer groups to help organize your document into logical sections wherever possible. Finally, be aware that file size affects performance; optimize your graphics and make sure that image resolution is no greater than 72 pixels per inch and that all graphics are saved in the RGB color mode.

Photoshop Import Options

Other than the addition of the Advanced button, importing Photoshop files into Flash Catalyst is almost identical to importing files from Illustrator. **Figure 65a** shows us Flash Catalyst's Photoshop Import Options dialog box, which is invoked from within Flash Catalyst by choosing File > New Project From Design File, or from the Create New Project From Design File > From Adobe Photoshop PSD File section of the Welcome screen.

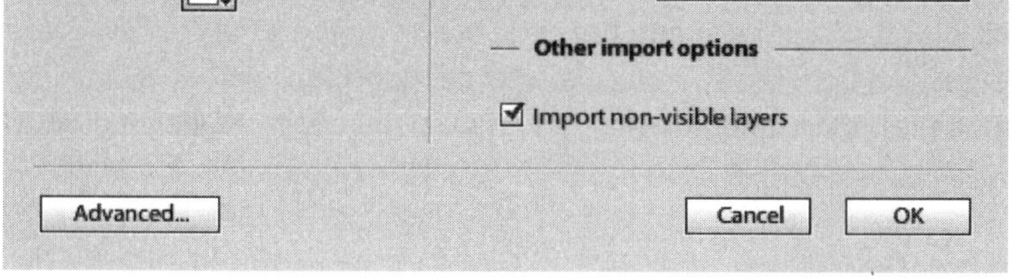

Figure 65a If you're familiar with the Illustrator Import Options dialog box in Flash Catalyst, you'll have no trouble with the Photoshop version. The only difference is the addition of the Advanced button.

Photoshop Import Options Revealed

Overlooking the artboard size & color choices to the left, the Photoshop import fidelity options control how Flash Catalyst imports image, shape, and text layers. Less complicated than Illustrator's Import Options dialog, here's a rundown of the various choices.

Image layers
Keep Editable keeps image layers with effects editable. Layer effects import as separate objects in the Flash Catalyst Layers panel.

Flatten converts image layers with effects into a single raster image.

Shape layers
Crop imports the vector mask that defines a shape, but crops the resulting bitmap to the bounds of the mask.

Flatten converts shape layers with effects into a single raster image.

(continued on next page)

Text layers

Keep Editable imports text layers as editable text objects. Once you import editable text, you can change it, size the text bounding box, and apply text formatting properties in the Properties panel. Editable text can lose some fidelity on import.

Vector Outlines converts text into outlines that approximate the appearance of the text.

Flatten converts text layers with effects into a single bitmap (raster) image.

Way back in the days of Photoshop CS2, a handy feature named Layer Comps was introduced. Simply put, Layer Comps acts as a kind of snapshot of a file at various states of layer visibility. You can click the visibility icon (the eye) in the far left column of the Layer Comps panel to quickly preview different versions of the same document.

Although Flash Catalyst can't natively import Photoshop PSDs containing Layer Comps, clicking the Advanced button shown in Figure 65a provides access to these comps, as seen in **Figure 65b**.

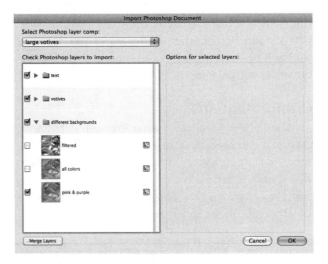

Figure 65b Clicking the Advanced button in the Photoshop Import Options dialog box opens Import Photoshop Document. Here you can see how layer comps can be chosen and how they can be modified upon import.

Clicking the Advanced button in the Import Photoshop Document dialog box drills down into the components of the comp, allowing you to pick and choose what to import from its various pieces. By making multiple imports, multiple page states are created for the Catalyst project.

#66 Round-Trip Editing

With round-trip editing in Flash Catalyst, artwork can be updated in its native application such as Illustrator CS5, Photoshop CS5, or Fireworks CS5. Using the Launch and Edit features in Flash Catalyst, you can open the artwork in its parent application, make your edits, and then return to Flash Catalyst.

Launch and Edit in Illustrator CS5

Illustrator CS5 can be launched from Flash Catalyst to edit vector images. Be aware that only vector objects that have *not* been optimized in Flash Catalyst (Modify > Optimize Vector Graphics) are eligible for round-trip editing. To do so, click and select the object and then choose Modify > Edit in Adobe Illustrator CS5. To help guide you with your task, Flash Catalyst displays a handy dialog box (**Figure 66a**).

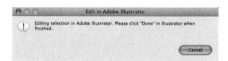

Figure 66a Flash Catalyst tells you to click Done when you've finished editing in Illustrator.

When the object opens in Illustrator you'll see that it appears in Isolation Mode. Only the object itself will be editable. All surrounding artboard objects will be dimmed back to 80 percent opacity and locked (**Figure 66b**). When you finish editing, click Done or click the check icon in the upper bar to commit the changes. This invokes the FXG Options dialog box, seen in **Figure 66c**.

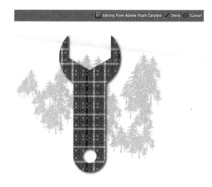

Figure 66b The dimmed background is Illustrator's way of reminding us we're in Isolation Mode and that only items fully visible can be edited.

Best Practices for Preserving Fidelity When Round-Trip Editing

Round-trip editing from Flash Catalyst to Illustrator or Photoshop means you are using the FXG file format to move between applications. These tips from the Flash Catalyst Help pages should be noted to preserve the fidelity of your Flash Catalyst artwork and the edits you make during this process.

- Filters added in Flash Catalyst are editable in Illustrator.

- If you rotate, or apply a filter to a bitmap in Flash Catalyst, you cannot edit it in Photoshop until you rasterize the image. Choose Modify > Rasterize.

  Filters and effects you add in Illustrator convert vectors or bitmaps returning to Flash

(continued on next page)

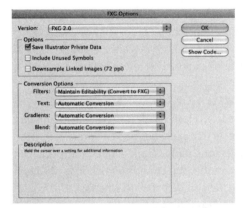

Figure 66c Normally you can expect to accept the default FXG Options and click OK. Adobe has included a description of those options in the bottom portion of the dialog box, which is convenient if you want to change them. Clicking the Show Code button in the upper right opens the file's code in either TextEdit (Mac OS) or NotePad (Windows).

Launch and Edit in Photoshop CS5

Like Illustrator, Photoshop CS5 can be invoked from inside Flash Catalyst when the time comes to edit bitmap images. To do so, select the object on the Flash Catalyst artboard and choose Modify > Edit in Adobe Photoshop CS5. The first time you do this you'll be greeted by the dialog box seen in **Figure 66d.**

Figure 66d Rather than let you suffer needlessly over something that doesn't work, Flash Catalyst kindly explains that to edit your image in Photoshop CS5 you must first download and install a copy of the Photoshop CS5 FXG Extension.

Dismiss the warning if you've installed the extension and prepare to head to Photoshop. Inside Photoshop you'll be greeted not only by your image, but with a warning instructing you run the Simplify Layers for FXG script before leaving Photoshop (**Figure 66e**).

Figure 66e Here we can see Adobe's instruction to run the Simplify Layers for FXG script from the File > Scripts menu. Doing so will remove the yellow band of instructions above the image and send the updated changes back to Flash Catalyst.

Be sure to save a layered PSD copy of your edited FXG file. This way you'll have complete control over all layers, adjustments, masks, and effects if ever you need to further tweak your image.

- Adding layer effects, masks, shape layers, and adjustment layers in Photoshop requires that you run the Simplify Layers for FXG script before returning to Flash Catalyst. There is no harm in running the script. A good practice is to always run the script before returning to Flash Catalyst.

- Always set Proof Colors to Monitor RGB in Illustrator to lessen the difference when comparing colors between Flash Catalyst and Illustrator. To change the setting for Proof Colors in Illustrator, choose View > Proof Colors (to select it), and choose View > Proof Setup > Monitor RGB.

#67 Adding Video and Sound

Codecs for Dummies

If you're scratching your head, wondering what the heck a codec is, read on.

A codec is an encoding/decoding algorithm that controls how video files are compressed during encoding, and decompressed during playback.

- **H.264** is an MPEG-4–based standard for Web delivery. H.264 is recommended for a variety of devices, including high-definition (HD) video, 3GPP cell phones, video iPods, and PlayStation Portable (PSP) devices.

- **On2 VP6** is the standard codec for encoding Flash video (FLV) files for Flash Player 8 and higher.

- **Sorenson Spark** is the required video compression format for Flash Player 6 and 7.

(continued on next page)

Not too many years ago, having a good-looking Web site with a few nice buttons and some sliding panels was considered the height of hip. In those days video looked clunky and chugged away painfully, lurching forward and back, stopping and starting like an old movie in a dirty projector.

Today, with the ubiquity of broadband connections, Adobe Flash Player, and faster computers, high-quality audio and video are often the cornerstones of many professional sites.

Before importing video into Flash Catalyst it's essential to know that Flash Catalyst supports only *encoded* FLV and F4V files. QuickTime, AVI, or other popular video formats that are not encoded won't work.

What's Encoding?

Encoding for Flash Catalyst is the process that converts all video footage to a format compatible with Flash Player. Those formats, or *containers*, are FLV and the newer F4V. In general, FLV files contain video data that's encoded using the On2 VP6 or Sorenson Spark codec. Audio data is typically encoded using an MP3 audio codec. F4V files generally contain video data that's encoded using the H.264 video codec and the AAC audio codec.

For a complete, and completely exhausting, discussion of this subject we suggest you check out Adobe's Video Learning Guide for Flash, which can be found at http://www.adobe.com/devnet/flash/learning_guide/video/.

One final word on encoding: You can use Adobe Media Encoder to convert files to the FLV or F4V file formats (**Figure 67a**). Fortunately, Adobe Media Encoder is installed automatically when you install Flash Catalyst; it's also bundled with After Effects, Flash Pro, and Premiere Pro.

Figures 67a Adobe Media Encoder packs a dizzying array of settings and choices, as these screen captures suggest. On the left is the main window. To get to the window on the right, click the Settings button. From here things quickly become more complicated.

Importing Audio and Video

Once you've properly encoded your video, you're ready to begin import-ing files into Flash Catalyst. To begin, choose File > Import > Video Files/Sound File. Navigate to your file or Shift-click to import multiple files. Once again, only FLV, F4V, and MP3 files are compatible with Flash Catalyst.

Go to the Library panel and expand the Media panel. There you'll see your imported audio and video files (see **Figure 67b**). When you're importing only one file at a time, the file will appear both on the artboard and in the Media section of the Library. When multiple files are imported at once, the files will appear in the Media panel only. You can audition a file in the Library panel. Select the file you want to see or hear and click the Play button in the lower-right corner of the Library panel to test your media.

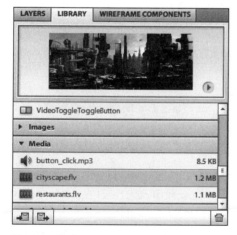

Figure 67b Here we see two video files and one audio file that have been imported into a Flash Catalyst project. To preview file contents, just select the file name and click the Play button in the lower-right corner of the Library panel.

- **MP3** is a standard file format on the Internet and on many portable digital audio players.

- **Advanced Audio Coding (AAC)** is a standardized encoding scheme for digital audio. Designed to be the suc-cessor to the MP3 format, AAC generally achieves better sound quality than MP3 at similar bit rates.

Learn More About Adobe Media Encoder

For more information on using Adobe Media Encoder, stop by http://help.adobe.com/en_US/mediaencoder/cs/using/index.html. Also, have a look at John Dickin-son's excellent free video tutorial, which can be found at http://tv.adobe.com/watch/learn-after-effects-cs5/exporting-with-adobe-media-encoder/.

Importing Audio

Importing audio files such as sound effects is a four-step process. Unlike video, audio files needn't be encoded first, but they must be saved in the MP3 format.

1. Choose File > Import > Video/Sound File. Locate an MP3 file and select Open.

2. Preview the sound file in the Library panel and click Play to preview.

3. Select a transition or action sequence in the Timelines panel. Or, select an interactive object in the artboard.

4. In the Timelines panel, select Add Action > Sound Effect. Choose a sound file and click OK.

Flash Catalyst comes with a small collection of sound effects. These sounds can be found in the C\Program Files\Adobe\Adobe Flash Catalyst CS5\sound effects folder (Windows) or Applications/Adobe Flash Catalyst CS5/sound effects folder (Mac OS).

Setting Video Properties

Once you've imported video into your Flash Catalyst project, you'll want to set its properties. Video properties are found in the Properties panel. Like other objects in Flash Catalyst, video can exist in various states with different attributes.

As you can see in **Figure 67c**, video properties include size, position, opacity, rotation, video controller style, scale mode; check boxes for Auto-Play, Loop, and Muted; and a field to insert accessible text.

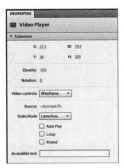

Figure 67c The Video Player section inside the Properties panel. Expanding the Common subpanel exposes controls for attributes such as size, position, opacity, rotation, and scale mode of the player.

#68 Creating and Defining Components

Every button, scroll bar, slider, check box, panel, and scrolling list you see in Flash Catalyst is a component. Once components are built, further life is added by way of interactions and action sequences. Components are created one of two ways:

1. Convert static artwork into a component by using options in the Heads Up Display (HUD) or by choosing Modify > Convert Artwork To Component. You can choose from a list of built-in component types or design a custom/generic component.

2. Add a wireframe component with a generic appearance from the Wireframe Components panel.

Converting Illustrator Artwork to a Component
To convert static artwork from Illustrator into a component, you must first import your artwork using File > Import Adobe Illustrator file. With the imported file selected, select the object. In this example we're using the horizontal scroll bar shown in **Figure 68a**.

Figure 68a This simple scroll bar, drawn in Illustrator using two rounded corner objects, is easy to convert into a live, functioning object inside of Flash Catalyst.

Once the object is imported into Flash Catalyst, select both the long horizontal track and the thumb slider objects. From the HUD, choose Horizontal Scroll Bar from the Choose Component drop-down menu (**Figure 68b**).

Figure 68b Choosing Horizontal Scrollbar from the list of components in the Choose Component drop-down menu.

Available Components

The component types available in the HUD and by choosing Modify > Convert Artwork To Component include:

- Button
- Checkbox
- Radio Button
- Toggle Button
- Text Input
- Horizontal Slider
- Vertical Slider
- Scroll Panel
- Horizontal Scrollbar
- Vertical Scrollbar
- Data List
- Custom/Generic Component

Edit-in-Place

When editing components in Flash Catalyst, all work is done in what's called Edit-in-Place mode. Similar in concept to Isolation Mode in Illustrator, Edit-in-Place is indicated by a dimmed artboard. Only those items currently edited are not dimmed. To Edit-in-Place you can also double-click a component or choose Modify > Edit Component.

The Layers panel behaves differently when performing an Edit-in-Place by splitting in two: the top half shows the components that are being edited, and the bottom half displays all the other layers in your project. Objects in either half of the panel can be dragged and dropped from one half to the other.

After you've told Flash Catalyst that the Illustrator objects are intended to serve as a horizontal scroll bar, the HUD explains what to do next (**Figure 68c**).

Figure 68c Don't you wish all software worked like this? Click on Edit Parts to continue, where you'll be asked to identify the track and the thumb slider.

Select the long thin part and use the Chose Part menu in the HUD to identify it as the track. Do the same for the small rectangle, and identify it as the thumb.

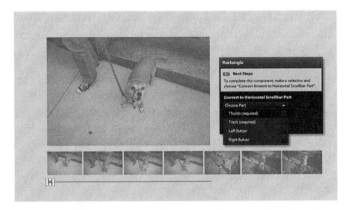

Figure 68d Here we see the small rectangle that's now selected and identified to Flash Catalyst as the thumb.

To test your scroll bar, choose File > Run Project. Flash Catalyst will compile the project, which will open in your browser. Try sliding the thumb left and right on the track to see how it works.

Converting Wireframes to Components

One of the nicer features of Flash Catalyst is its library of wireframe components. Although basic in design and without assigned functionality, these items come in handy during the early planning phases of a Flash Catalyst project and can save you the trouble of designing objects on your own. Once a wireframe object is placed on the artboard, all that's left is to choose its various properties.

Using wireframe components is as easy as dragging and dropping?

1. Select the page or state to which you want to add the wireframe component.

2. Target the layer in the Layers panel where you want to add the component.

3. Drag and drop the Wireframe Component from the panel to the artboard.

4. Position the component with the Select tool (black arrow).

5. Set the properties of the component in the Properties panel.

Customizing a Wire-Frame Component

Wireframe components can be used as-is or customized to your project. Customizing is referred to as *skinning* a component. To customize a wireframe component you must enter Edit-in-Place mode either by double-clicking the component or by choosing Edit Component from the Modify menu. To check whether a wireframe component has been skinned, select the component and then notice its name in the Common section of the Properties panel. Untouched or generic wireframe components retain a skin name of Wireframe. Modified, or custom, components are given a skin name that comes from the name of the component.

#69 Creating Interactions

When you click a button and something happens, you've executed an interaction in Flash Catalyst. The program has many prebuilt interactions you can easily add to components or groups of components. For example, you could create an interaction to transition from page or component states, to play an animation or video, or to go to a Web site (**Figure 69a**).

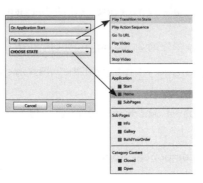

Figure 69a Interactions can be programmed to trigger a change of pages, states, or various actions or action sequences. In this figure we see an interaction that occurs the first time the user encounters the application, known as an On Application Start. From that initial interaction, the user is automatically taken to the application's Home state.

Creating a Simple Button Interaction

Interactions are one of easiest things to create in Flash Catalyst. To create an interaction an object must first be converted into a component (see Tip 68). To add an interaction to a button component to change states, follow these steps:

1. Select the button component and click the Add Interaction button in the Interactions panel (**Figure 69b**).

Figure 69b Click the plus sign (+) to add an Interaction.

2. Select the On Click item.

3. Select Play Transition to State.

4. Select the Tour state from the Choose State pop-up menu (**Figure 69c**).

Figure 69c Select the Tour state from the Choose State pop-up menu.

If the user is in the Tour state you'll want the Tour button to look selected.

Select tour_button in the Tour state. Deselect the Enabled option in the Properties panel (**Figure 69d**).

Figure 69d Deselect the Enabled option in the tour_button Properties panel.

Repeat the above steps for all other button states.

On Application Start Interactions

Some interactions can be triggered without direct user involvement. For example, a movie that starts automatically when the user turns a page is considered an On Application Start interaction. Opening your application to a specific page state is another kind of On Application Start interaction.

To create an On Application Start interaction, go to the Interactions panel. With nothing selected on the artboard, click Add Interaction. Because nothing is selected, On Application Start is your only choice.

#70 The Flash Catalyst Timeline

The Timeline panel works similarly to timelines in other applications like Flash, After Effects, or Premiere Pro. Its job is to graphically allow you to place events over a specified period of time and to apply transition actions such as fades or rotations to those events. The timeline can also be used for controlling playback of sound and video files (**Figure 70a**).

What makes the Flash Catalyst timeline different from timelines in other programs is also what makes it confusing to use: the Flash Catalyst timeline lacks any kind of scrub head or Current Time Indicator (in After Effects or Premiere parlance).

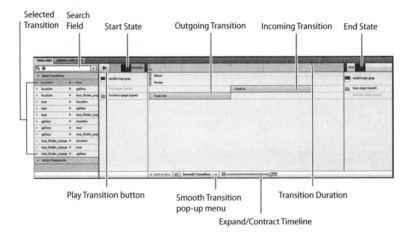

Figure 70a The Timeline panel is used to add transition effects between states or other kinds of interactions. In this figure we see a fade out and fade in effect that's been added when transitioning from the project's Location to Tour states.

#71 Establishing Transitions

Whenever content in one state differs from content in another state, those changes are automatically added in Flash Catalyst as default transitions. Designed as placeholders, default transitions appear on the timeline as very short bars. With a default duration of zero seconds, placeholder bars can then be set to their final duration (**Figure 71a**).

Figure 71a Six default transitions of zero seconds each have been automatically added to the timeline of this Flash Catalyst project.

Smoothing Transitions

If zero second transitions seem a bit fast, don't worry: Flash Catalyst provides an easy way to change their durations via the Smooth Transition Options panel (**Figure 71b**) found at the base of the timeline.

Figure 71b Click the small arrow seen at the bottom of this figure to pop up the Smooth Transitions Options panel. Clicking the words *Smooth Transition* applies your previous settings automatically, bypassing the pop up panel.

Available choices in the Smooth Transition Options panel are:

Duration sets the total transition length from start to finish.

Simultaneous applies smooth transitions to each effect equally, based on the value set in the Duration field.

Smart Smoothing adjusts the duration and delay of each effect by creating a series of staggered effects. Using a logical order of effects, Catalyst begins with objects fading out. After objects fade out, objects resize and move before fading in.

Overwrite Existing Effects applies new settings to any existing transitions.

Smooth Transition can also be applied to page states.

In the State Transitions column of the timeline, select all the displayed states (**Figure 71c**).

Figure 71c The timeline makes quick work out of selecting and applying the same transitions to all page states in your application. Here we've chosen all the transitions in our project. With them all selected, applying the same transition is a snap.

Click on the words *Smooth Transition* at the bottom of the timeline (not the arrow).

Flash Catalyst automatically applies the last settings used to all states.

Tweaking Transitions

Applying Smooth Transitions means all your transitions are the same in every way, including when they start and stop. To give some variety to your transitions you're going to want to stagger not only their durations but also when they start and stop.

Adjusting Duration

To adjust the duration of a transition, click the green bar for the transition in the timeline. Dragging the little handle on the far end will change the bar to blue to indicate it's selected. The effect's new duration will also be visible in the tiny box aside the bar (**Figure 71d**).

Figure 71d Changing the duration of a transition in Flash Catalyst is as easy as dragging the bar handle of the transition to its desired length.

The Properties panel, typically found as part of the column of panels to the right side of your artboard, will also return the effect's duration along with the added benefit of allowing you to set a start delay and an Easing style (**Figure 71e**).

Figure 71e

Easing Styles

Easing styles can be Linear, Sine, Power, Elastic, or Bounce.

Linear starts slowly and eases into the effect. After maintaining a constant rate it begins to slow and ease out toward the end.

Sine eases in, speeds up to the midpoint, and then immediately eases out.

Power eases in to a point and then eases out based on Exponent property. A higher exponent creates greater acceleration and deceleration.

Elastic causes an object to snap back and jiggle upon reaching its destination.

Bounce is similar to Elastic. The object reaches its final destination and then briefly bounces before settling into position.

Adjusting Timing

Timing is an attribute that determines when an object begins and ends its transition. Timing can be easily altered by dragging the Effect bar (not its handle) (**Figure 71f**) in the timeline or by adjusting the Delay value in the Properties panel.

Figure 71f

Repeating Effects

Sometimes you'll find it advantageous to repeat an effect for emphasis. To repeat any effect, select the effect bar in the timeline and choose Repeat in the Properties panel. There you can also set the number of times you'd like the effect to repeat (**Figure 71g**).

Figure 71g If at first you don't succeed... sometimes repeating an effect helps drive it home.

#72 Publishing a Flash Catalyst Project

Just prior to publishing your SWF project it's always a good idea to do a little house cleaning and testing to ensure that everything goes off without a hitch.

1. Delete any unused objects.

2. Optimize vector graphics by using the Optimize Artwork options in the HUD or by choosing Modify > Optimize Vector Graphics.

3. Switch to the Code workspace and review the Problems panel to check that there are no outstanding problems.

4. Choose File > Run Project and test your application before publishing. Check to make sure that all navigation, links, and transitions are working properly.

5. Save your project.

Now that you're ready to publish, your choices are to a deploy-to-Web folder for posting to a Web server, to a run-local folder for local testing of your application, or to an AIR (Adobe Integrated Runtime) folder that creates an application that can run on your desktop (**Figure 72a**).

Regardless of whether your project eventually runs locally on your computer, on the Web, or as an AIR app, if everything works properly as expected, congratulations!

Figure 72a The light at the end of the Flash Catalyst tunnel is this dialog box.

Font Embedding: Yes or No?

If your project uses standard Web-safe fonts (Arial, Courier New, Georgia, Times New Roman, and Verdana) embedding fonts is unnecessary. To embed nonstandard fonts click the Advanced button in the Publish To SWF dialog box. Here you can determine how much of a font is embedded. For example, if you know that your text includes only Basic Latin characters and numerals, then deselect the All option and select Uppercase, Lowercase, Numerals, Punctuation, and Basic Latin. Leave the remaining languages deselected. Remember, the idea here is to embed only what's needed to faithfully render your project. Anything extra only adds unwanted file size.

CHAPTER EIGHT

Working with Flash Professional

Adobe Flash CS5 Professional continues to be the most advanced environment for interactive authoring on the Web. According to Adobe, Flash Player is the most ubiquitous plug-in on Earth, with a penetration rate of nearly 98 percent of all Internet browsers. Despite the ongoing controversy surrounding Flash on the Apple iPhone and iPad, there's currently no better product for creating interactive experiences than Adobe Flash Professional.

More than simply a program for creating vector animation, Flash Professional has evolved into its own platform. Today when we talk about Flash we're really talking about a Rich Internet Application, or RIA, that supports audio, video, and both vector- and pixel-based interactivity.

Although content can be created inside of Flash Professional, most designers take advantage of the application's ability to smoothly import content created in standard design environments like Photoshop or Illustrator. In our first tip, we'll explore that initial process.

#73 Importing Your Illustrator and Photoshop Files

In the past, one of the knocks against Flash Professional was due to its nonstandard (some would say "crude") drawing and image editing tools. Today, that's no longer a problem because the application can now import files originally created in other programs. If you preferred working in Illustrator or Photoshop prior to animating in Flash, you're going to love this improvement.

With Flash Professional CS5, artwork created in Photoshop or Illustrator CS5 can be brought into Flash through the Clipboard, dragged and dropped from the Mac OS Finder or Windows Explorer, or imported via the Import dialog box (File > Import) shown in **Figure 73a**. When you're importing native Photoshop and Illustrator files, Flash Professional converts your artwork and populates the library with elements that match the original file. Other points to keep in mind:

- Text can come in as text or outlines or even bitmaps.

- Vector art is converted to Flash's own vector format.

- Bitmaps are converted to PNG-24, including all transparency.

Figure 73a The Import dialog box contains several options for handling incoming text, layers, and compression from Photoshop—plus the ability to convert layers to movie clips.

If you have applied effects in Photoshop or Illustrator that Flash does not support—such as Photoshop lighting effects or opacity masks in Illustrator—the artwork is converted to a PNG-24 to maintain the appearance and transparency. In **Figure 73b**, we see those incompatible objects flagged by yellow warning triangles.

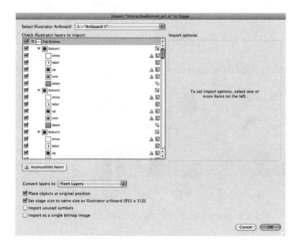

Figure 73b In this figure we're about to import an Illustrator file into Flash Professional. Notice how Flash flags incompatible items with yellow warning triangles.

Imported artwork can also be assigned symbol properties, such as Buttons or Movie Clips. What's more, symbols created in Illustrator are automatically added to the Flash document, including any settings for 9-slice scaling.

Importing Photoshop Layers to Flash Professional

Flash Professional CS5 handles Photoshop layers and layer groups with aplomb. When you're importing a Photoshop PSD with a layer group, avoid the temptation to flatten the group into a single layer. Instead, select the layers and select the "Create movie clip for this layer" check box **(Figure 73d)**.

Once the import is complete, Flash Professional creates layers in the Timeline panel and place elements on the stage to match the layout of the original Photoshop and Illustrator files, as shown in **Figure 73c**.

Figure 73c This is how Flash Professional looks after importing layered Illustrator artwork. Now we're ready to begin!

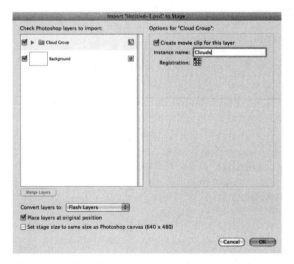

Figure 73d Flash Professional provides an easy path for importing layer groups.

Working with Flash Professional

#74 Round-Trip Image Editing with Flash and Photoshop

New to Flash Professional CS5 is the ability to directly edit imported bitmap images in Photoshop CS5. The process is quite simple, despite an important caveat (see the sidebar). The process is as follows:

1. Control-click (right-click) the object either on the stage or in the Library panel. Choose Edit in Photoshop CS5 (**Figure 74a**).

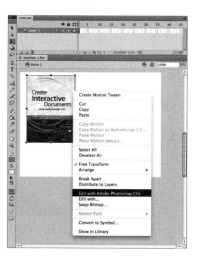

Figure 74a Select the object to edit either on the stage or from the Library panel. Control-click (right–click) and you'll be presented with this context menu, which is your direct connection to Photoshop CS5 or other original parent application.

2. Make your Photoshop edit and save.

3. Return to Flash to see your file modification applied.

The Truth About Round-Trip Photoshop Editing

In the interest of full disclosure, it's worth noting that "round-trip editing" of Photoshop images is in fact a misnomer. This is because when images are imported from Photoshop, Flash Professional converts those files to its own propri-etary format—and images that need to be bitmaps are converted to either PNG-24 or JPEG formats. Because Photoshop bitmap files are converted to PNG-24 or JPEG, you're not technically working with the original Photoshop file—but rather the converted bitmap stored inside of Flash Professional.

In the Flash library, bitmaps can be edited by Control-clicking (right-clicking). Again, these files are converted to either PNG-24 or JPEG formats. When you save from Photoshop, the Flash library is automatically updated.

#75 Importing and Exporting FXG Files

FXG is a cross-platform interchange format that allows files to be moved from Flash Professional to other programs such as Illustrator or Flash Catalyst. Based on a subset of MXML, the XML-based programming language used by the Flex framework, the FXG format helps designers and developers collaborate more efficiently by enabling them to exchange graphic content with high fidelity. When importing FXG files, Flash Professional CS5 needn't do any file conversion to bring in artwork.

The following Adobe applications support FXG:

- Fireworks (export)

- Photoshop (export)

- Illustrator (export)

- Flash Professional (import and export)

- Flash Catalyst (import and export)

- Flash Builder (import and export)

In Flash Professional, you can export content in FXG format in either of two ways:

- To export objects on the Stage as FXG, select the objects and choose Export > Export Selection. Then select FXG format from the File Type menu.

- To save the entire Stage as FXG, choose Export > Export Image and select Adobe FXG from the Format drop-down menu.

When you export a file containing vector and bitmap images using FXG export, a separate folder is created along with the FXG file. This folder has the name <filename.assets> and contains the bitmap images associated with the FXG file (**Figure 75a**).

Figure 75a Expect to see an FXG file and a similarly named folder when exporting files from Flash Professional that contain both vector and bitmap images.

#76 Getting Better-Looking Type in Flash

Achieving better-looking type in Flash is no longer question of TLC, but rather TLF. TLF, which stands for Text Layout Framework, is a rewritten type engine that supports advanced typesetting features like ligatures, baseline shifting, tracking, and more. Multiple columns of text can now be set in one text frame, as in InDesign, and text can flow continuously from container to container (**Figure 76a**).

Figure 76a TLF offers a wide range of typesetting possibilities, as the options found in this collection of panels shows. No longer does type on the Web have to take a back seat to type in print.

Embedding Fonts in Flash

Flash Professional automatically embeds the fonts used in your project when you publish your project. In cases where your SWF file may receive external data, such as a person's name, or stock prices, you will need to embed a full set of characters in order to ensure the SWF file has all the characters it may need.

To embed fonts in Flash Professional CS5, choose Text > Font Embedding. Select the fonts you'd like to embed in the document and click the (+) above the left Font column. Select the sets of characters you'd like to embed from each font family you are embedding. To conserve file size, character sets are broken into commonly used groups, such as numbers only, or Basic Latin (**Figure 76b**).

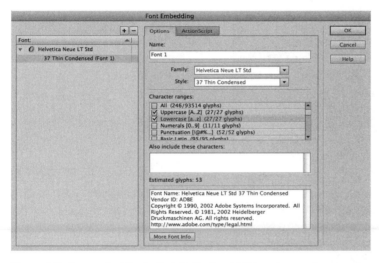

Figure 76b Font embedding in Flash Professional CS5 is no longer a "yes or no" question. Developers now have much greater control over the glyphs they embed. With this degree of control, Flash developers can limit the file size.

Threading Text Through Multiple Text Frames

As in InDesign and Illustrator, TLF text can now link, or thread, through multiple text frames in Flash Professional. This attribute does not apply to Classic text blocks, though. TLF text containers can be threaded from frame to frame, or inside symbols, provided the containers are all part of the same timeline.

#77 Using the Improved Type Composition Options

If you're comfortable formatting type in page layout apps like InDesign, you're in for a pleasant surprise with Flash Professional CS5. Now, for the first time, text frames in Flash can have properties such as insets, borders, background colors, and other professional attributes. A look at the Properties panel reveals a level of control over type previously unattainable in Flash (**Figure 77a**).

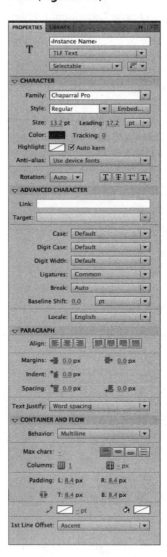

Figure 77a If you didn't know you were in Flash Professional, you might think you're setting type in InDesign. Professional-level typographic attributes such as kerning, tracking, ligatures, frame insets, space before and after paragraphs, and even first baseline offsets are now controllable in Flash Professional.

In addition, text frame linking similar to InDesign improves and simplifies working with type. In **Figure 77b**, we see how text is linked from a two-column frame to other frames in the thread.

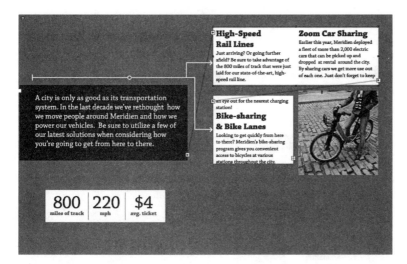

Figure 77b Creating multiple text columns no longer means creating multiple text frames, as shown in this single text frame.

#78 Exploring the Deco Tool

The Decorative, or Deco, drawing tool turns graphic shapes into complex, geometric patterns. In a process known as *procedural drawing,* the Decorative drawing tool uses calculations that are applied to a movie clip or any graphic symbol you create.

After you select a drawing effect, you can customize the way your artwork will be generated. Some options include brushes such as the Flower Brush, Vine Fill, and Lightning Brush. In the case of Vine Fill, Flash Professional generates artwork in an allotted area and fits vector artwork together based on built-in symbols, or custom symbols you create (**Figure 78a**).

Figure 78a Vine Fill is only one of thirteen drawing effects available for the Deco Tool.

Selecting the Tree Brush effect, for example, gives you a choice of 20 different trees and allows you to specify tree scale, branch color, leaf color, and flower or fruit color, as seen in **Figures 78b** and **78c**.

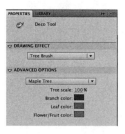

Figure 78b The Deco Tool's Advanced options control overall scaling as well as the color of branches, leaves, and flower or fruit.

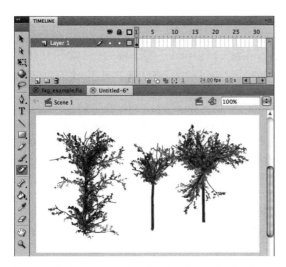

Figure 78c The Deco Tool makes drawing and animating trees almost *too* easy.

#79 Adding Spring to Animations (Inverse Kinematics)

The Bone Tool allows you to add joints to artwork or join together movie clips (referred to as *armatures*) so that movements in one affect the other in a naturalistic way. Using inverse kinematics, Flash Professional will figure out the various angles for all the joints and animate from the first pose to the next (**Figure 79a**).

New Inverse Kinematics settings now allow you to add Spring and Dampening settings to your bones (**Figure 79b**). (Spring is the bounce of objects and Dampening is the force that counters such motion.) Flash Professional applies physics to your motion to create realistic animations with the help of a few simple keyframes.

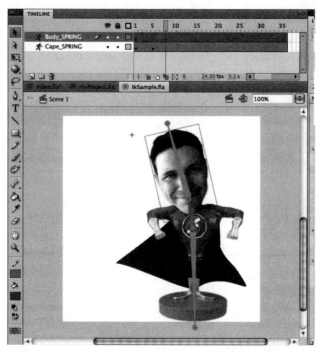

Figure 79a Thanks to Inverse Kinematics, here we see how the cape armature reacts naturally by swaying to the opposite side of the body armature.

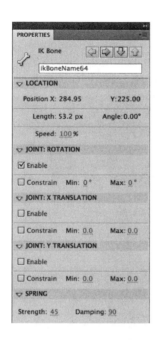

Figure 79b The Properties panel controls settings like Joint Rotation, Spring Strength, and Dampening.

By combining various Inverse Kinematic settings, Flash is able to convincingly animate the toy seen in **Figure 79c**.

Figure 79c Controls over spring and dampening add an extra degree of realism to the body and cape of this toy.

#80 Using Motion Presets

Motion Presets give you a fast way to add animations to your symbols. By applying presets, you can achieve commonly used animation techniques, even with realistic physics properties, such as bouncing (**Figure 80a**). Motion Presets also serve as a solid foundation for learning and studying the principles of Flash for those new to Flash Professional.

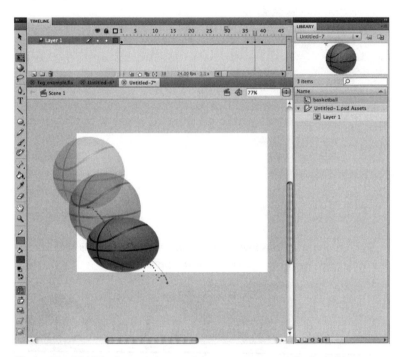

Figure 80a In this basic example, a motion preset turns a static basketball into one that appears to bounce.

Note that motion presets can be applied to motion tweens only. Motion presets can *not* be applied to classic tweens.

To apply a motion preset, select a tweenable object (text or a symbol instance) on the stage and click the Apply button. Only one preset can be applied per object. In the event a second preset is applied to an object, the second preset will overwrite the previous preset (**Figure 80b**).

Figure 80b Motion Presets display a helpful preview in the topmost section of its panel.

Motion presets also contain a specific number of frames. When you apply a preset, the tween span in the timeline contains this number of frames. If the target object already had a tween of a different length applied to it, the tween span adjusts to match the length of the motion preset.

Before clicking Apply to a Motion Preset, right-click the animation option you want and choose from either "start at current location" or "end at current location" as seen in **Figure 80c**.

Figure 80c Motion presets have the added advantage of allowing you to specify whether the effect is applied to the start or end of the animation. You can hold down the Shift key when clicking the Apply motion preset button to end the preset at the current location.

Creating Your Own Motion Presets

Creating your own Motion preset is simple. Follow these steps:

1. Place your object on the stage.

2. Convert the object into a Symbol (Modify > Convert to Symbol).

3. Apply a motion tween (Insert > Motion Tween).

4. Right-click (Windows) or Control-click (Mac OS) on either the object itself on the stage or the frames in the timeline and choose Save as Motion Preset (**Figure 80d**).

5. Give the Motion Preset a unique name and click OK (**Figure 80e**).

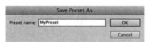

Figure 80d The Save as Motion Preset context menu.

Figure 80e Give your preset a more descriptive name than the one shown here.

#81 Using Code Snippets

The Code Snippets panel (accessed by selecting Window > Code Snippets) provides a fast way to add the necessary ActionScript code to your Flash movie. Simply double-click on a code snippet in the panel and Flash Professional writes and inserts the proper code.

With the Code Snippets panel (**Figure 81a**) you can:

- Affect the behavior of objects on the Stage.
- Control the playhead in the Timeline.
- Add new code snippets that you create to the panel.

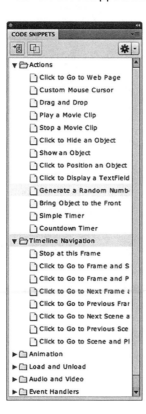

Figure 81a The Code Snippets panel provides a long list of ActionScript 3.0 code that you can easily apply to any object or frame in Flash Professional CS5.

Creating Your Own Code Snippets

You can add new code snippets to the Code Snippets panel by entering a snippet in the Create New Code Snippet dialog box or importing a code snippet XML file.

To use the Create New Code Snippet dialog box:

1. In the Code Snippets panel, choose Create New Code Snippet from the panel menu.

2. In the dialog box, enter the Title, tool tip text, and ActionScript code for your snippet.

You can add any code that is currently selected in the Actions panel by clicking the Auto-Fill button.

3. Select the "Automatically replace instance_name_ here" check box if your code includes the string "instance_name_here" and you want Flash Professional to replace it with the correct instance name when the snippet is applied.

Flash Professional adds the new snippet to the Code Snippets panel in a folder called Custom.

To import a code snippet in XML format:

1. In the Code Snippets panel, choose Import Code Snippets XML from the panel menu.

2. Select the XML file you want to import and click Open.

To see the correct XML format for code snippets, choose Edit Code Snippets XML from the panel menu.

To delete a code snippet, Control-click (right-click) the snippet in the panel and choose Delete Code Snippet from the context menu.

If you have an object selected, such as a button (**Figure 81b**), the code snippet will include the button's name (if it is entered in the Properties panel). If you do not name your object, Flash Professional picks a name, then applies the code.

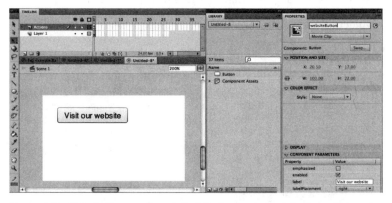

Figure 81b With the button selected, Flash Professional writes the ActionScript using the button name. Notice how the Actions layer is automatically inserted above Layer 1.

Once the code snippet is applied, an Actions layer is created in the Timeline and an ActionScript is applied to the same frame as the button. Opening the Actions panel will reveal the code written by the snippet.

Figure 81c Here we see how the Actions panel displays the applied action, which includes the button named "websiteButton."

#82 Working with Video

One of the most common uses for Flash is for playing video. You can add video to your project by simply importing a video file, or by dragging a video to the stage.

Before you start working with video, it's important to understand the following:

- Flash Professional can support only the FLV, F4V, and MPEG video formats.

- The Adobe Media Encoder (included with Flash Professional) converts other video formats to FLV and F4V (**Figure 82a**).

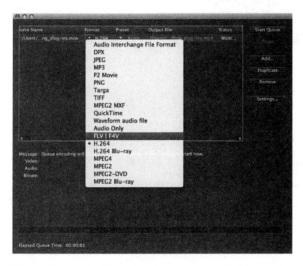

Figure 82a Adobe Media Encoder converts multiple formats to FLV or F4V.

- Flash Professional includes the Video Import Wizard (**Figure 82b**), which opens when you choose File > Import > Import Video. This walks you through the steps for setting up video playback controls.

Figure 82b The Flash Video Import Wizard provides a simple way to select your encoded video. Clicking the Continue button brings up another screen where you can give your video player a custom skin or interface.

- The FLVPlayback component lets you easily add video playback to a Flash file.

  You can use Flash video in different ways:

- As a progressive download from a Web server.

- By streaming video using Adobe Flash Media Server.

- Via embedding video information inside a Flash file.

  In addition, you can use the FLVPlayback component in conjunction with the Component Inspector (**Figure 82c**), and bypass the Video Import Wizard altogether.

Figure 82c Using the Component Inspector together with the Property inspector allows you to make many direct changes to how your video is played and displayed in Flash Professional.

#**83** Publishing Your Flash Projects

The most common format to publish to from Flash Professional is the Shockwave-Flash format, or SWF. This format requires the Flash Player to read and play a SWF file. Typically, Flash Player is found as a Web browser plug-in. **Figure 83a** shows how the Publish Settings dialog box lets you check all possible publish settings prior to proceeding.

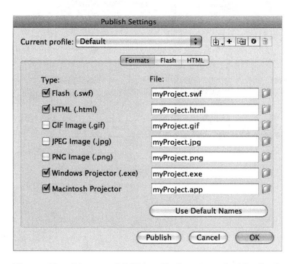

Figure 83a Prior to publishing a Flash project, double-check your settings by choosing File > Publish Settings to ensure everything is ready to go.

In addition to SWF, Flash Professional can also publish to executable projectors (applications) for both Mac OS and Windows (see **Figure 83b**). This format is most commonly used for CD-ROM and kiosk systems. These applications can run on their respective operating systems without the Flash Player being present; its playback capabilities are contained within the projectors themselves.

myProject.exe   myProject.app

Figure 83b These identical icons represent the Windows (left) and Mac OS (right) versions of the self-contained Flash projectors. Only their three-letter file name extensions differentiate the two.

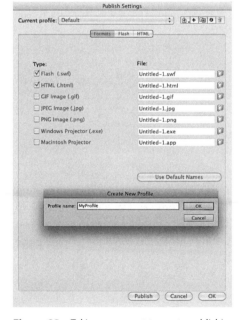

Figure 83c Taking a moment to create publishing profiles can save you lots of valuable production time down the road.

Using Publishing Profiles

In the same way you might create a PDF export preset in InDesign, using Publishing Profiles in Flash Professional can save you a lot of time when faced with repetitive work.

To create a Publishing Profile, choose File > Publish Settings. In the dialog box, take a moment to set everything correctly before clicking the small plus (+) sign in the upper-right area of the dialog box to add your setting. A small dialog will appear (**Figure 83c**) where you can name your new profile. Click the button to the left of the plus (+) sign to import or export existing publishing profiles.

#84 Publishing AIR Applications

In addition to publishing formats targeted at Flash Player, Flash Professional also publishes to Adobe's AIR format (Adobe Integrated Runtime). A cross-platform format that takes advantage of Flash, Flex, HTML, JavaScript, and Ajax technologies, Adobe AIR allows you to build and deploy Rich Internet Applications to the desktop. Users interact with AIR applications in the same way as they would with native apps.

From the Flash Professional publishing options, choose Adobe AIR 2, then Settings and set the properties of your AIR application (**Figure 84a**).

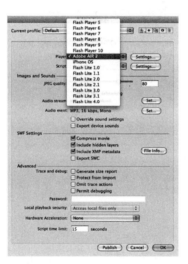

Figure 84a Click the Flash tab in the Publish Settings dialog box to enable this view. Clicking the Player pop-up menu displays the Adobe AIR 2 setting seen here.

Settings for your AIR application include the window style, operating system environment options, custom icons, and finally, the ability to digitally sign your Adobe AIR application before distributing it. After you choose Adobe AIR 2, click the Settings button to the right to invoke the dialog box shown in **Figure 84b**.

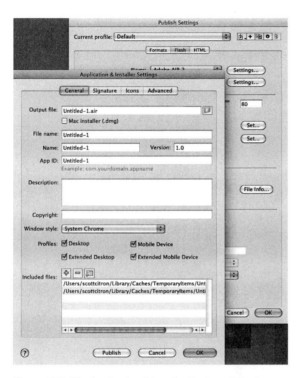

Figure 84b The Application & Installer Settings dialog box offers you a variety of additional settings for your AIR application.

CHAPTER NINE

Using Multiple Applications for Maximum Efficiency

Any one Creative Suite 5 application is good. One or more together is much, much better. Part of the benefit that a suite of compatible applications engineered by one software company offers is that those applications are built to understand one another's file formats. In the CS5 Design Premium edition, Illustrator and Flash Professional understand each other's formats quite well, and Flash Catalyst can use the layer structure of Photoshop and Illustrator files to kick-start a project. However, most of the deep-level integration is between the veteran applications—Photoshop, Illustrator, InDesign, and Acrobat. Because of this, you can play off of the strengths and capabilities of one application to maximize your efficiency in another.

#85 Generating Live Metadata Captions with InDesign and Bridge

What's Metadata?

Metadata is a set of standardized information about a file that's stored as XML data in the file itself, so it "travels" along with the file no matter where it's copied to or sent. Digital cameras, for example, attach at least some basic information—height, width, file format, date and time, etc.—to the images they record. Some record more detailed information like exposure, ISO speed, white balance settings, and even location information if the camera has GPS capabilities.

You can add much more metadata—such as author name, resolution, color space, copyright, and keywords—to any file from Adobe Bridge either in the Metadata panel, or by right-clicking any image thumbnail in the Content panel, choosing File Info, and entering metadata in the resulting dialog box.

Adobe Bridge is an excellent photo-management tool, and part of its strength is support for comprehensive image metadata. The metadata that you store in Bridge can now be leveraged to automate caption creation in InDesign CS5.

To add metadata to images in Bridge, it's helpful to switch to the Metadata workspace to optimize the Bridge environment for metadata entry (**Figure 85a**). The most likely metadata fields for eventual use as captions in InDesign include Description, Title, Copyright, and Credit, but InDesign's Live Captions feature supports more than 60 metadata fields.

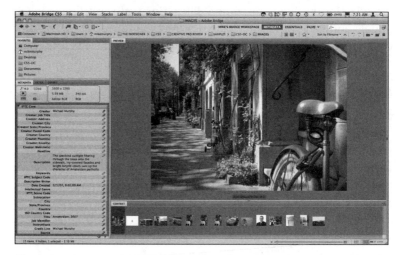

Figure 85a An image viewed in Bridge's preconfigured Metadata workspace showing metadata in the Creator, Description, Date Created, Title, and Credit Line fields.

With the metadata added to your images in Bridge, you can use InDesign CS5's Caption Setup dialog box to specify which pieces of metadata it should use to generate captions. Simply right-click an image, choose Caption Setup, and select the desired metadata field(s) that you want to use (**Figure 85b**).

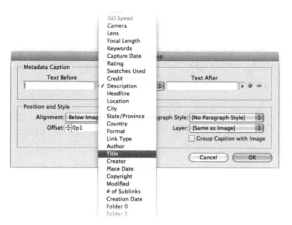

Figure 85b
Metadata selection in InDesign CS5's Caption Setup dialog box.

More Metadata Per Caption

To add more than one piece of metadata to the caption, click the plus sign (+) to the right of the Text After field. Another row is added to the dialog below the first. You can choose other metadata to include and define static text before and after it, if desired. Metadata is included in the caption in the order that it appears, top to bottom, in the Caption Setup dialog. Each metadata entry defined in the dialog is separated by a hard return in the generated caption, so a caption defined with three pieces of metadata will be three lines deep.

You can surround the metadata you select with static text by adding that information to the Text Before and Text After fields. For example, if you're using the Copyright metadata field to dynamically pull in a photographer's name for a placed image, you can put the copyright symbol and a space in the Text Before field, and a comma, space, and the text "Used by Permission" in the Text After field to generate a caption in the format "© Photographer Name, Used By Permission" where "Photographer Name" is whatever name exists in the image's Copyright metadata field.

In the Caption Setup dialog box, you can also specify whether the caption's text frame is created below, above, or to the left or right of the image. Captions aligned to the left or right of the image will be rotated to run "downhill" or "uphill," respectively, making them ideal for photo credits (**Figure 85c**).

Figure 85c The "Left of Image" and "Right of Image" caption alignment options rotate text frames 90 degrees clockwise or counterclockwise, respectively.

Build Better Custom Captions

One disadvantage of the Caption Setup dialog box is that it puts each piece of metadata on a separate line if your caption uses multiple metadata fields. To customize the structure of a multi-metadata caption, bypass the Caption Setup dialog box and build your caption in the Text Variables dialog box: Open the Type menu, then select Text Variables and Define. Click the New button and choose Metadata Caption from the Type menu.

By setting up one variable for Title, and another for Description (each must be saved as a separately named variable), you can create a dynamic-caption text frame by inserting the Title variable, any separator you want (a colon, en space, etc.), then the Description variable. You can also style each variable placeholder to customize its formatting (another thing the Caption Setup dialog box doesn't do). When that text frame touches any image frame, it will be populated by a dynamic caption tailored to your specific look.

You can also define a paragraph style to be used by all generated captions, send generated captions to a specific layer, and opt to group the image and caption frames. Once all options have been set, you need to click OK to exit the dialog, then right-click the image again and choose either Generate Live Caption or Generate Static Caption.

Live Captions vs. Static Captions

A live caption remains dynamically linked to the metadata in the image file. If the metadata is updated, the Links panel shows the image as modified, and updating the image also updates the caption. However, live captions are actually a new kind of text variable and have the same disadvantage as all text variables—they can't wrap, so they have to fit entirely on one line or the text is crushed together to fit (**Figure 85d**).

Figure 85d The text of a live caption can't wrap, so long captions will result in text that's jammed together onto a single line.

One way around the text-wrapping limitation is to instead choose Generate Static Caption which populates a text frame with a caption produced from the current metadata but breaks the dynamic association to that metadata from that point on. That text will wrap and behave like any normal text (**Figure 85e**), but the caption won't change if the metadata does.

The speckled sunlight filtering through the trees onto the sidewalk, ivy-covered facades and bright bicycle colors sum up the character of Amsterdam perfectly.

Figure 85e A static caption wraps properly but loses its dynamic link to the metadata.

#86 InDesign Tips for Easy Acrobat Forms

Forms present unique design challenges. Their function is to be filled out, so nothing about a form's design should impair that process. Most forms also need to fit into a finite amount of space, so they need to be arranged very efficiently. In addition, more and more forms are being completed digitally—as fillable PDF forms—so another challenge when designing forms is to make them as Acrobat-friendly as possible, so you don't have to do a lot of manual work in Acrobat Professional after you've exported them from InDesign.

Acrobat's Form Field Recognition feature (Advanced > Accessibility > Run Form Field Recognition) has improved dramatically over the last few versions, but it's still rather particular about what it recognizes, and how it determines what's a form field and what adjacent text is associated with that field. Just because something looks like a form in InDesign (**Figure 86a**) doesn't mean it will in Acrobat (**Figure 86b**).

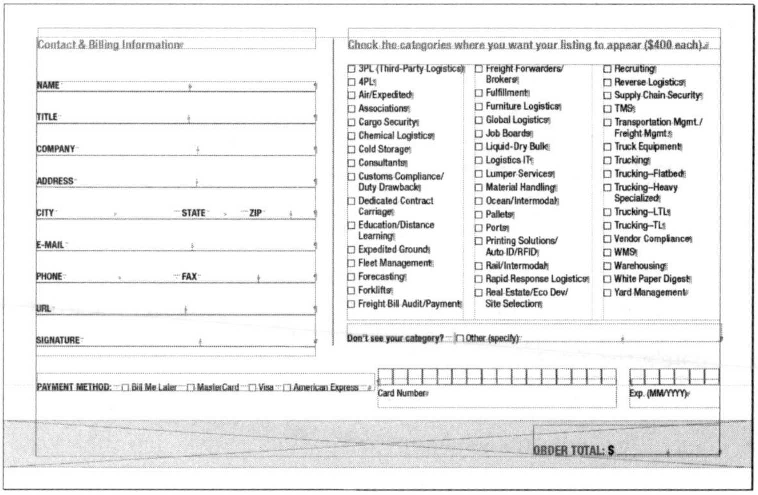

Figure 86a A form layout in InDesign. Fill-in lines are established using paragraph rules, check boxes are created using characters in a symbol font, and the credit card number and expiration date number comb fields are created with individual boxes.

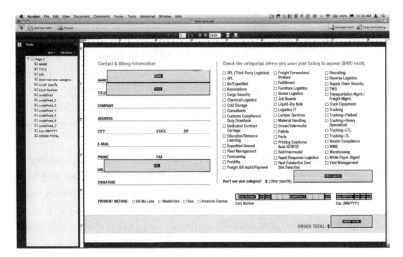

Figure 86b The form from Figure 86a in Acrobat Professional after running Form Field Recognition. Most of the fill-in lines were not recognized, nor were any of the check boxes. The credit card and expiration date comb fields were also interpreted incorrectly as multiple comb fields.

To avoid potential pitfalls, here are some best practices for form layout techniques that will produce Acrobat forms most reliably.

Fill-in Lines

Acrobat is best at recognizing lines that extend out from the end of the text related to them. The fastest, most flexible way to set up form lines is to:

- Create a character style with only one attribute: underlining. It's best to keep the underline offset set at zero.

- Build a GREP Style into your form-line paragraph style that applies the underline character style to any tab or right-align tab (**Figure 86c**). In GREP syntax, that's \t|~y.

- Set tab stops in the paragraph style where necessary for those parts of the form with many fill-in areas on one line (i.e., City, State, Zip).

- Use right-align tabs for any lines you want to extend fully across the width of the text frame. All other tab stops will be bypassed and the underline will extend all the way across the frame (**Figure 86d**).

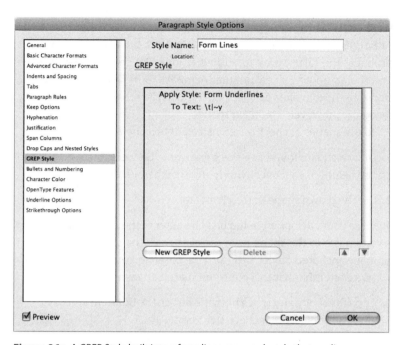

Figure 86c A GREP Style built into a form-lines paragraph style that applies underlining to the space occupied by any tab or right-align tab.

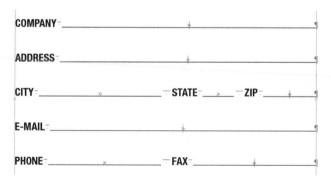

Figure 86d The styled form lines using the paragraph style shown in Figure 86c. Full-width lines (Company, Address, E-Mail) require a right-align tab (Shift-Tab). All others use a standard tab. The buffer spacing between the text and the lines is accomplished with em and en spaces.

280

(continued on next page)

Use GREP to Speed Up Check-Box Insertion

You can use Find/Change to quickly insert a shape copied to the clipboard into the start of multiple lines at once. Select all of your form's check-box text, then open Find/Change, go to the GREP tab, and, from the menu at the end of the Find What field, choose Beginning of Paragraph from the Location submenu. That inserts a caret (^), which represents the beginning of a line. Next, choose "Any Character" from the Wildcard submenu. That inserts a period (the GREP metacharacter meaning "any character"). Enclose that period in parentheses, which tell Find/Change to remember that found character so you can put it back later. The Find What field should look like this: ^(.).

Check Boxes

Although using a symbol font and InDesign's bulleted lists feature is probably the fastest way to add what look like check boxes to a layout, there's no way to ensure that Acrobat's form-field recognition will translate those bullets as check boxes. What Acrobat does consistently recognize, however, is a drawn shape.

To use shapes as check boxes instead of text characters:

1. Draw a square frame at a size somewhere between the x-height and cap height of your check-box item text, wherever looks best to you.

2. Cut the drawn shape to the clipboard.

3. Place your cursor before the first character of the first check-box item and paste in the shape from the clipboard. The shape goes in as an inline anchored object, sitting on the baseline. You may want to add a space after the shape to put some space between it and the text.

4. Copy the shape and space from the first check-box item and paste it in at the start of all other check-box items.

Radio Buttons

In electronic forms, you can check as many boxes as you like. For some options, however—like a credit card payment method—only one selection is permitted, regardless of the number of choices available. This either/or choice is controlled by radio buttons. Establishing a radio button choice that Acrobat will recognize is simply a matter of using circles instead of squares (**Figure 86e**).

PAYMENT METHOD: ○ Bill Me Later ○ MasterCard ○ Visa ○ American Express

Figure 86e A series of payment methods in a form using circles that Acrobat will interpret as radio buttons, allowing only one of the four to be chosen.

Here again, pasted-in shapes are more reliable than using symbol font characters. When you open an exported InDesign form in Acrobat Professional, the program considers all options to be associated with the text directly to the left of or above the first of the radio button choices. Acrobat will group and display these choices in its Fields panel (**Figure 86f**).

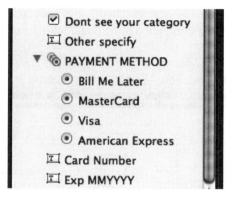

Figure 86f Radio button options shown in Acrobat Professional's Fields panel. Note that Acrobat correctly groups all four options under "Payment Method" and drops the trailing colon that was present in the original layout.

Next, go to the menu at the end of the Change To field and choose Clipboard Contents, Formatted from the Other submenu. Finally, you need to recall the first character defined by that "any character" metacharacter by typing in $1 or choosing Found Text 1 from the Found submenu. The Change To field should look like this: ~c$1.

Click Find, then Change All, and you're done.

Comb Fields

The easiest and most reliable way to establish a comb field—like that used for credit card number or expiration date entry—in InDesign is to create a table. For the credit card number, use a one-row, 16-column table. The expiration date is also one row, but only six columns (two for the month, and four for the year). We suggest using a border for the table cells that's a consistent weight with the form's other lines—such as fill-ins and check-box borders—and setting the top border to zero, so the table looks less like a row of cells and more like a comb (**Figure 86g**).

Figure 86g Tables are the most efficient, flexible way to set up Acrobat-friendly comb fields for credit card information.

If you follow the simple setup guidelines described in this tip, you'll get reliable and accurate form-field recognition in Acrobat Professional (**Figure 86h**).

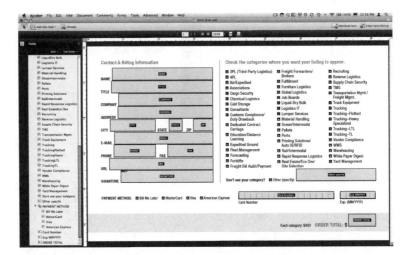

Figure 86h The exported form (created using all of the techniques in this tip) after running Form Field Recognition in Acrobat Professional. All fill lines and check boxes are recognized, and radio buttons and comb fields are properly set up. Note also Acrobat Professional labeled each field accurately based on the adjacent text in the layout.

#87 Sharing Color Swatches Between Illustrator, InDesign, and Photoshop

Does this ring a bell?

You're in the middle of an InDesign layout and you need to create some Photoshop or Illustrator artwork with the same color swatches you're using in InDesign. Or maybe you're in Photoshop or Illustrator creating artwork and want to use a matching palette in an InDesign layout. So you grab for a pen and a scrap of paper and start frantically scribbling down RGB or CMYK values…

Sound familiar? If so, you'll want to keep reading this tip.

Illustrator, InDesign, and Photoshop use a file format—Adobe Swatch Exchange (.ase)—for swatches (**Figure 87a**) that allows you to export the swatches from one application and load them into another.

Figure 87a The file icon for Adobe Swatch Exchange (.ase) files.

Exporting Swatches

Each application has a slightly different method for exporting. Here's how each works:

- In InDesign, select the desired swatches in the Swatches panel (note that gradient, mixed-ink, and tint swatch export are not supported), then choose Save Swatches from the panel menu and save the swatches with your desired name (.ase is automatically assigned as the extension and file format).

- In Illustrator, choose Save Swatch Library as ASE from the Swatches panel menu and save the .ase file. Although you can select a specific

ASE's No-Exchanges Policy

Photoshop, Illustrator, and InDesign don't discriminate as to which color space your swatches occupy. Any mix of RGB, CMYK, Lab, etc., is fine for the Adobe Swatch Exchange format. A few types of swatches, however, don't make the cut. From InDesign, you can't export gradient, mixed-ink, or tint swatches. If you select those types of swatches, you'll see a warning indicating this limitation. You can just click OK and continue exporting. InDesign will create an ASE file without the unsupported swatch types. In Illustrator, gradient, tint, and pattern swatches are not supported. Photoshop doesn't handle gradients, patterns, or mixed inks via the Swatches panel, so everything Photoshop *can* create a swatch from will successfully export to ASE.

(continued on next page)

range of swatches, Illustrator ignores what you've selected and instead exports all of the document's swatches except for gradients, tints, and patterns.

- In Photoshop, choose Save Swatches for Exchange from the Swatches panel menu and save the .ase file. Like Illustrator, Photoshop doesn't support selective export of a range of swatches. All swatches in the Swatches panel get exported.

Importing ASE Swatches

Despite their exporting differences, the three applications are similar when it comes to importing Adobe Swatch Exchange files.

- **InDesign and Photoshop:** Choose Load Swatches from the Swatches panel menu, then locate and select the desired .ase file.

- **Illustrator:** Choose Open Swatch Library > Other Library, then locate and select the desired .ase file.

Once loaded, your swatches will appear at the bottom of the Swatches panel in InDesign and Photoshop, and as a new swatch library panel in Illustrator. Your days of scribbling swatch values on scraps of paper are officially over.

#**88** Linking Photoshop Images to Dreamweaver with Smart Objects

In CS5, Dreamweaver and Photoshop build upon a round-tripping feature that was originally added in CS4, making it more seamless and bringing the kind of linked image behavior that InDesign uses to the suite's Web development and design application.

You can now maintain a dynamic link from a JPEG file in Dreamweaver to the layered, nonoptimized source Photoshop file. This allows you to modify the original Photoshop file and automatically have Dreamweaver generate a new optimized JPEG reflecting those changes. This dynamic updating will happen everywhere that image appears on your Web site.

Making this work requires inserting not an optimized GIF, JPEG, or PNG file, but instead the source Photoshop image itself, layers and all. When you do, Dreamweaver's Image Preview dialog box appears (**Figure 88a**). Here, you can optimize and resize the incoming Photoshop file prior to its insertion on the page.

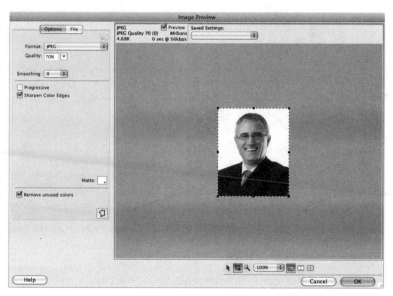

Figure 88a Dreamweaver's Image Preview dialog box allows you to optimize incoming Photoshop files with settings similar to that application's outgoing Save for Web & Devices dialog box.

Be Smart About Smart Object Source Files

Unless you save the original Photoshop file within your site, Dreamweaver considers the path to the original file as an absolute local file path and won't recognize the Photoshop file as part of the site. Saving the Photoshop file within the site establishes a site-relative path. This approach maintains the dynamic relationship between the JPEG and its source for anyone else with whom you share the site.

The dialog box previews the result of your settings so you know what the final optimized image will look like. Once you've decided upon the optimal settings and are happy with the preview, click OK and save the Web-optimized file in the appropriate folder for your site's assets. Once saved, you'll see the *optimized* image listed in Dreamweaver's Files panel, not the original Photoshop image.

In Dreamweaver's Design view, you'll notice a Smart Object icon on any image added to your site this way (**Figure 88b**), indicating that a dynamic link exists between the image in the Web layout and an external Photoshop file. When the two files are in sync, the two arrows in the icon are both green.

Figure 88b The Smart Object icon appears on all images optimized within Dreamweaver from an inserted Photoshop source file.

If you insert that optimized image anywhere else on your site (by dragging it from the Files panel to the Web-page layout), that instance will also have the Smart Object icon and the link to the source Photoshop document.

To modify the original Photoshop file, you can access it directly from Dreamweaver by right-clicking the image in Design view and choosing Edit With > Adobe Photoshop CS5 or by Command-double-clicking (Ctrl-double-clicking) the image to open the source file in Photoshop.

Once you've made your changes to and saved the original Photoshop image, you'll notice a change to the Smart Object icon when you return to any page where the optimized Smart Object is placed in Dreamweaver:

the bottom half of the Smart Object icon will be red instead of green (**Figure 88c**), indicating that the optimized image on the Web page no longer matches the most recently saved version of its source file.

Figure 88c An image displaying an out-of-date Smart Object icon with a red arrow at the bottom.

To bring the optimized image into sync with its source, right-click the image in Dreamweaver's Design view and choose Update From Original from the context menu. This updates not only the current image, but also every other optimized instance of it on your site that's linked to the modified Photoshop file. Dreamweaver reoptimizes the newer version of the Photoshop file using the settings that you chose the first time you inserted it.

Work with Images to Size

Although you can resize an incoming PSD file via the Image Preview dialog box, that's the one setting that's not honored when you update the Smart Object later on. If you've resized an image, then use the Update From Original option, your updated image will reflect the Photoshop file's current size, not the size you scaled it to when it was inserted. Be sure to factor in this limitation before inserting the image, especially if it's going to appear in many places on your site. Resizing every placed instance negates the benefit of maintaining a dynamic link between the PSD and the site. Instead, insert images that are already at their intended size.

#89 Taking Advantage of Photoshop and Illustrator Layers with InDesign

Using layers is the best way to manage the various components of your Illustrator and Photoshop artwork, and you can further capitalize on that layered structure in InDesign by selectively hiding and showing any layer in an Illustrator file, and any layer or layer comp in a Photoshop file. This is a great way to keep complex, composited images together in one AI or PSD file, rather than multiple files, and have the ability to pick and choose elements from those files to use in InDesign.

For example, you may have a photograph of a person against a background, but you need to silhouette the subject so that you can put text or some other elements between that subject and the background in the page layout. Once silhouetted, your Photoshop image would likely be composed of two layers: one with the full image of the person against the background (**Figure 89a**), and a duplicate of that layer with the background masked out (**Figures 89b**).

Figure 89a The full image on the Background layer of a Photoshop document.

Figure 89b The top layer of the Photoshop file with the figure silhouetted from the background.

When the file is placed in an InDesign layout, it appears with all active Photoshop layers showing by default (**Figure 89c**).

Figure 89c The image placed in InDesign as it was saved in Photoshop—with the background layer visible but the silhouetted layer hidden.

The goal in this magazine cover example is to have the subject's head overlap the magazine name. To do that, you can copy the frame

Choose Your Layers When You Place

If you know you're going to want only a specific layer, set of layers, or layer comp before you place your image, you can select those as you place the file by checking the Show Import Options check box in InDesign's Place dialog. The Image Import Options dialog box opens, showing you a preview of the incoming file and its entire layer structure. Choose what you want to see when the file is placed, then click OK. The image arrives in your InDesign layout with only your selected layers or layer comps visible.

containing the placed Photoshop image, then use the Paste in Place command—Shift-Command-Option-V (Shift-Ctrl-Alt-V)—to put an exact duplicate of the image on top of the original. That copy is then moved up in InDesign's Layers panel above the magazine headline type as well.

Next, right-click on the duplicate image and choose Object Layer Options from the context menu (**Figure 89d**). Alternatively, you could go to the Object menu and choose Object Layer Options.

Figure 89d Accessing InDesign's Object Layer Options from the context menu.

The Object Layer Options dialog box displays all layers and layer groups present in the source Photoshop document. Next to each is a visibility icon that toggles that layer on or off in the InDesign document (**Figure 89e**). This does not affect the original Photoshop document: whatever layers were visible or hidden when the PSD file was last saved remain as they were.

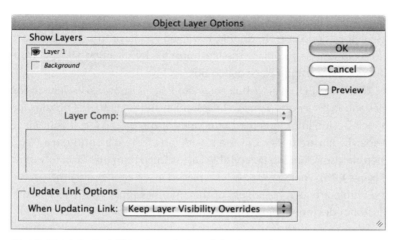

Figure 89e InDesign's Object Layer Options dialog box with an image's background layer turned off and its top layer visible.

Pick One Layer the Fast Way

If your placed file has a complex layer structure and you want to show only one of those layers in InDesign, don't waste time turning off many individual layers. Instead, Option-click (Alt-click) the layer that you want visible. All other layers will be automatically turned off.

When you've turned off the background layer and turned on the foreground (silhouette) layer, the same Photoshop file, placed twice in the InDesign layout, can appear differently in each instance (**Figure 89f**).

Figure 89f The top placement of the PSD file—with its background layer turned off using Object Layer Options—is placed above the magazine title, which appears on top of another instance of the same PSD that shows the whole image.

Photoshop files with Object Layer Options settings are always placed in a frame that's the full size of the Photoshop document's canvas, regardless of how little of the image you're revealing in InDesign.

Illustrator files, however, can automatically crop artwork to the extent of its vector boundaries. To do this, however, you have to set your Object Layer Options as you place the Illustrator file by selecting Show Import Options in InDesign's Place dialog box.

The Place PDF dialog box for incoming Illustrator files (Illustrator files and PDFs are the same to InDesign) includes additional options for how InDesign interprets the boundaries of the placed file. If you select a specific Illustrator layer in the Layers tab of the dialog (**Figure 89g**), then choose Bounding Box (Visible Layers Only) from the "Crop to" menu (**Figure 89h**), your artwork will be placed in a frame exactly the size of the visible artwork, regardless of the amount of hidden artwork in the Illustrator document or the size of that document's artboard.

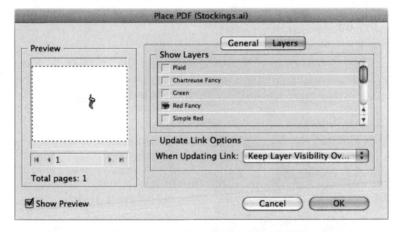

Figure 89g A single Illustrator layer selected in the Place PDF dialog box.

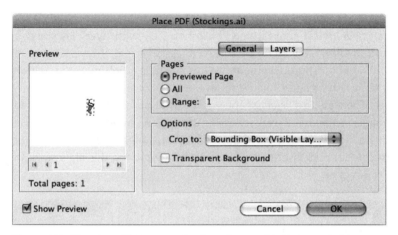

Figure 89h The selected layer cropped to Bounding Box (Visible Layers Only).

What Those Crop To Options Mean

The Place PDF dialog's "Crop to" menu provides several different cropping options for incoming Illustrator and PDF files.

- **Bounding Box (Visible Layers Only):** limits what's placed in the layout to the extent (the farthest top, left, right, and bottom edges) of the visible artwork on the Illustrator artboard; hidden artwork and layers are not included
- **Bounding Box (All Layers):** limits what's placed in the layout to the extent of all artwork on the Illustrator artboard, whether or not it's visible
- **Art:** limits what's placed in the layout to the extent of the boundaries of all artwork on the Illustrator artboard (hidden or visible) or all content on a PDF page
- **Crop:** places the file at the default artboard size (or to the size of any crop area you've specified in Illustrator), or the trim size of the PDF page
- **Trim:** places the file at the size of the Illustrator artboard without bleed
- **Bleed:** places the file at the size of the Illustrator artboard or PDF page with whatever bleed values have been built into that file
- **Media:** places the file at the size of the Illustrator artboard or PDF page defined by the document's geometry; in most cases, media and trim will produce the same result

#90 Preserving Photoshop Layers and Styles in Flash

If you've prototyped a Flash interface entirely in Photoshop, in CS5 you can now import your layered Photoshop file—with layers, layer styles, and editable text intact—into Flash Professional as Flash layers.

The Photoshop document in **Figure 90a** is a prototype for a Flash interface that's been built using several different layers and layer properties. There are text layers, shape layers, and layers containing pixel-based images. Some have layer styles like outer glows applied, and some use blend modes. All of these Photoshop layer features can be preserved (or discarded) on a layer-by-layer basis when you bring this file into Flash Professional.

A Few Exceptions

Flash Professional accepts and imports shape layers, text layers, and what it calls "image layers" (which would be any pixel-based Photoshop content). It does not, however, recognize Adjustment Layers, and while it will import a Clipping Mask layer—and that Clipping Mask layer will look as it should in the Import to Stage dialog's layer thumbnails—the actual masking relationship between that layer and the layer below it will be lost. It's best to merge the clipping mask layer and the layer it's associated with in Photoshop prior to importing to the Flash stage to preserve the desired effect.

Figure 90a   A Photoshop mockup for a Flash user interface (left) and the file's layer structure in the Photoshop Layers panel (right).

In Flash Professional, choose File > Import > Import to Stage, or press Command-R (Ctrl-R), then select the source Photoshop document and click Open. In the Import to Stage dialog box, the column on the left lists all the Photoshop file's layers (**Figure 90b**). You can check the layers you want to import and uncheck those you don't want to bring in.

Using Multiple Applications for Maximum Efficiency

Figure 90b The Flash Import to Stage dialog box reflecting the incoming PSD file's full layer structure on the left and layer-specific import options on the right.

You can also set specific options for how individual layers will be imported. The available options change depending on the type of content on any given layer. Type layers, for example, can be imported as vector outlines, as a flattened bitmap image, or as fully editable text. The latter choice is your best option for maximum flexibility. A shape layer with a Layer Style like a bevel, glow, or shadow can be imported either as a flattened bitmap image or as an editable path with a layer style. The latter is both more flexible and automatically converts the layer to a movie clip upon import.

Once you've set your import options for individual layers, there are a few remaining options to set. If your Photoshop file is a design prototype, you'll want to stick with the default of Convert Layers to Flash Layers. If your incoming Photoshop file is made up of a series of sequential images on individual layers, you might want the other choice, Keyframes.

Make Movie Clips as You Import

A movie clip is a master Flash library item that you can use many times in a Flash project, very much like a symbol in Illustrator. Automatic movie-clip creation occurs when you opt to bring any layer into Flash Professional as something other than a flattened bitmap image. When you choose Flattened Bitmap Image for any incoming layer, movie-clip conversion is optional. One reason you might want to make an incoming Photoshop layer into a movie clip is when you know you'll be using Action-script in your Flash project, because movie clips are best suited for this process.

Set Similar Import Options Simultaneously

If your incoming Photoshop file has ten text layers and you want them all to come in as editable text, you don't need to select each layer one-by-one to make that choice. For a continuous range of layers, click the first layer, then shift-click the last to select all in-between. For layers that are not arranged that way, you can Command-click (Ctrl-click) to make a discontinuous selection of multiple layers. With all of the similar layer types selected, choose how you want them imported and that choice will apply to all selected layers.

Finally, if your Flash stage hasn't been set up to the same size as your Photoshop document's canvas, you can have the incoming Photoshop document determine the Flash stage size by selecting the Set Stage Size to Same Size as Photoshop Canvas option. Then click OK, and your stage will be adjusted; your Photoshop file's content will be imported and placed on that stage; and the content will be distributed and organized as Flash layers, each with the same name it had in Photoshop (**Figure 90c**).

Figure 90c The imported Photoshop artwork on the Flash stage with all layering preserved as layers in the Timeline, and all imported artwork listed in the Library panel.

Photoshop is a far more flexible design and image-editing tool than Flash Professional, so it's great to be able to use Photoshop to handle prototyping yet still capitalize on your layering and organization efforts when it's time to take that prototype into Flash and make it a real interactive project.

CHAPTER TEN

Automating Routine Tasks in CS5

As instructors we're often amazed by how many people fail to take advantage of simple automation when using their computers. We're not talking advanced programming here, but simple keyboard shortcuts for daily things like Open, Save, Copy, or Paste.

If you prefer clicking on a menu rather than using shortcuts, this chapter probably isn't for you. As our friend Mordy Golding says, "Let's hope you're getting paid by the hour."

But if doing something faster rather than slower is your preference, you've come to the right place. Faster may not always be better than slower but, let's face it, there are many boring processes in Photoshop and Illustrator that are just as well handled by automation.

#91 Automating Illustrator and Photoshop with Actions

Actions are a series of recordable events that can be played back over one or many files. Not only do actions perform their tasks perfectly each time, but they also work much more quickly than you could. For example, an action could be created to open a folder of JPEG images, convert them from RGB to CMYK, and then save them into another folder as TIFFs.

Although actions can't automate Photoshop functions like painting, dodging, burning, and spot removal, actions can include steps that let you perform such tasks before continuing. Actions can also be programmed to stop and let you enter values in a dialog box, then continue. Photoshop actions can also be used to create *droplets*, which are applets that automatically process files that are dragged onto an icon.

As a safety net, we suggest working with a copy of your file until you're comfortable creating actions. At the start of your action—before you record other commands—be sure to direct the application to save a copy of the file. In Illustrator, you would record the File > Save A Copy command, and in Photoshop you'd record File > Save As and choose As A Copy. Another way to protect yourself in Photoshop is to click the New Snapshot button in the History panel before you record your action.

Recording a Basic Action

In the Actions panel, click the Create New Action button (**Figure 91a**). Enter an action name, select an action set, and set additional options.

Figure 91a Creating a New Action can be done either by clicking this button at the bottom of the Layers panel or by selecting Create New Action from the panel menu in the upper-right corner.

Name your action and choose any additional settings like Function Key shortcuts or Button Mode colors (**Figure 91b**).

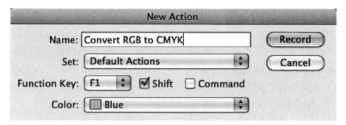

Figure 91b These settings can be easily accessed from the panel menu. When you click Record, the New Action dialog box will close and recording of your action will begin.

Click the Record button to start recording your action. The button will turn red, indicating your action is being recorded.

Unlike recording sound or video, recording an action records steps only when something happens. In other words, don't feel pressured to quickly perform your action. Photoshop doesn't care if you take two hours between steps; it only records the steps themselves.

To stop recording, click the Stop Playing/Recording button, choose Stop Recording from the Actions panel menu, or press the Esc key.

Figure 91c Click this button to stop recording the action. You can also choose Stop Recording from the Actions panel menu or tap the Esc key.

Playing Back Actions on Differently Sized Files

Some actions will play back differently depending on the size of the file. If your action will be played back on files of different sizes, use percentages as your unit of measurement instead of inches, picas, or pixels (Preferences > Units & Rulers > Units). By using percentages, the action will play back in the same relative position in all images.

Undoing a Photoshop Action

Because actions involve multiple steps, undoing an action means applying Undo (Edit > Undo) followed by consecutive Step Backward commands (Edit > Step Backward) until you have returned to the original state just prior to running the action.

To simplify undoing an action, start by taking a snapshot in the History panel before you play the action. From the panel menu choose New Snapshot, or click the Create New Snapshot icon at the base of the panel. When you decide to undo the action, just click to select the snapshot.

Playing Back an Action

Playing back an action executes the recorded commands in the active document. You can exclude specific commands from an action or play back only a single command. If the action includes a modal control, where the user must interact with the action via a dialog box, you can specify values in a dialog box when the action pauses.

To play back an entire action, select the action name and click the Play button in the Actions panel, or choose Play from the panel menu. If you assigned a key combination to the action, just press that combination. To play only part of an action, select the command from which you want to start playing, and click the Play button in the Actions panel, or choose Play from the panel menu. To play a single command, select the command, and then Command-click (Ctrl-click) the Play button in the Actions panel. You can also press Command (Ctrl) and double-click the command.

#92 Using the Image Processor in Photoshop or Adobe Bridge

Unlike the Batch command, the Image Processor in Adobe Bridge or Photoshop CS5 can convert, process, or batch process multiple files without requiring you to create an action first. To invoke the Image Processor in Photoshop, choose File > Scripts > Image Processor. To invoke the Image Processor in Bridge, choose Tools > Photoshop > Image Processor (**Figure 92a**).

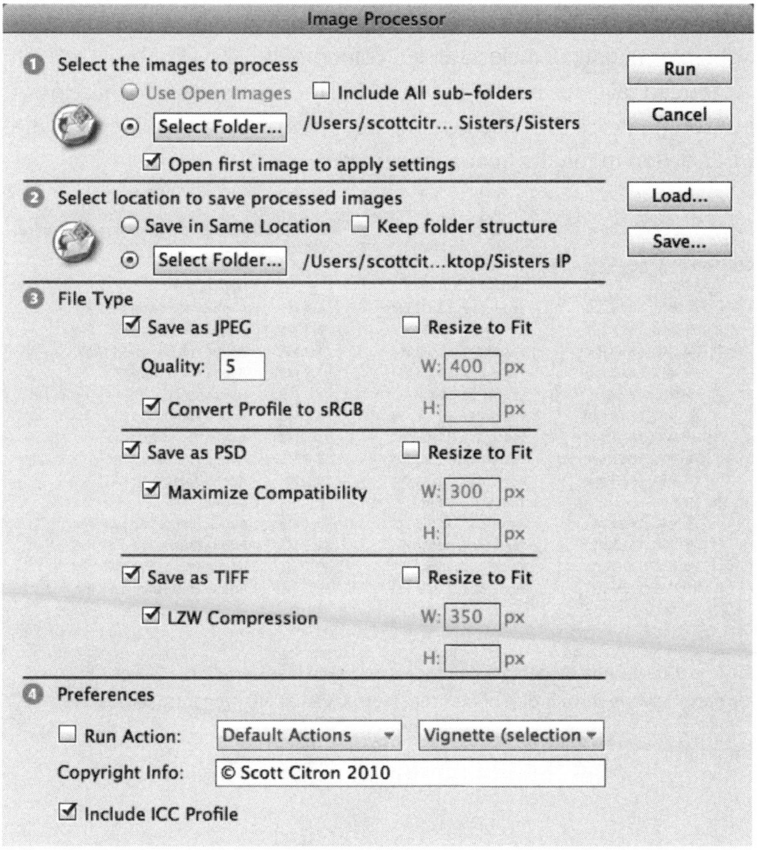

Figure 92a The beauty of the Image Processor dialog box lies in its simplicity. Here we see how its functions are divided into four discrete sections from top to bottom.

Starting at the top, Section 1 lets you select the images to be processed. The "Open first image to apply settings" option allows you to open the first image in Adobe Camera Raw so that its settings can be applied to all subsequent images.

Section 2 instructs Image Processor to return your processed images to their original folders or to a newly created folder upon completion.

Section 3 specifies which file format or formats (JPEG, PSD, or TIFF) to use when saving your files. Image Processor can also resize your files according to set dimensions.

Section 4 lets you run any custom actions you've saved, apply copyright information, or include an ICC color profile.

You can save these settings by clicking the Save button. To reuse previous settings, click the Load button, then navigate to a saved settings file.

Click Run to run the Image Processor.

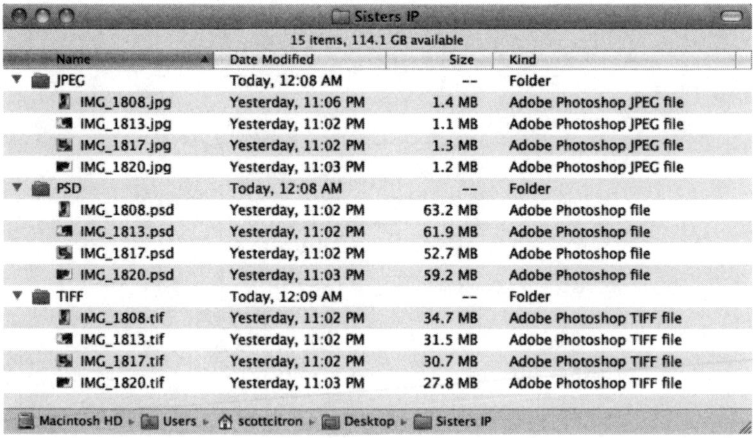

Name	Date Modified	Size	Kind
▼ 📁 JPEG	Today, 12:08 AM	--	Folder
IMG_1808.jpg	Yesterday, 11:06 PM	1.4 MB	Adobe Photoshop JPEG file
IMG_1813.jpg	Yesterday, 11:02 PM	1.1 MB	Adobe Photoshop JPEG file
IMG_1817.jpg	Yesterday, 11:02 PM	1.3 MB	Adobe Photoshop JPEG file
IMG_1820.jpg	Yesterday, 11:03 PM	1.2 MB	Adobe Photoshop JPEG file
▼ 📁 PSD	Today, 12:08 AM	--	Folder
IMG_1808.psd	Yesterday, 11:02 PM	63.2 MB	Adobe Photoshop file
IMG_1813.psd	Yesterday, 11:02 PM	61.9 MB	Adobe Photoshop file
IMG_1817.psd	Yesterday, 11:02 PM	52.7 MB	Adobe Photoshop file
IMG_1820.psd	Yesterday, 11:03 PM	59.2 MB	Adobe Photoshop file
▼ 📁 TIFF	Today, 12:09 AM	--	Folder
IMG_1808.tif	Yesterday, 11:02 PM	34.7 MB	Adobe Photoshop TIFF file
IMG_1813.tif	Yesterday, 11:02 PM	31.5 MB	Adobe Photoshop TIFF file
IMG_1817.tif	Yesterday, 11:02 PM	30.7 MB	Adobe Photoshop TIFF file
IMG_1820.tif	Yesterday, 11:03 PM	27.8 MB	Adobe Photoshop TIFF file

Macintosh HD ▸ 📁 Users ▸ 🏠 scottcitron ▸ 📁 Desktop ▸ 📁 Sisters IP

Figure 92b Image Processor can process and save files into JPEG, PSD, or TIFF formats. Here we see a group of files that were saved as all three formats.

#93 Taking Advantage of InDesign Scripts

One of InDesign's lesser-known strengths is found in the Scripts panel (Window > Utilities > Scripts). Despite the number of weighty volumes devoted to the art of writing scripts, using scripts couldn't be simpler.

Start by familiarizing yourself with InDesign's default scripts. When you open the Scripts panel you'll find two folders. Mac OS users have a choice of AppleScripts or JavaScripts. Windows users can choose from VBScripts or JavaScripts. All the scripts are identical, regardless of format. We tend to favor the JavaScripts because of their cross-platform compatibility, but in truth they all function the same. Inside the JavaScript folder are 20 default scripts that come preinstalled with InDesign CS5 (**Figure 93a**).

Figure 93a InDesign CS5 comes with these 20 scripts preinstalled.

Got More Scripts?

If the 20 default scripts that ship with InDesign aren't enough, you'll be happy to know that the Internet is your scripts oyster. Even better, there are tons of free scripts, too. Here are just a few of our favorite resources:

http://bit.ly/9nu4RA

http://bit.ly/dy4lav

http://bit.ly/d0MNsh

http://bit.ly/depyAQ (this is a tutorial by Anne-Marie Concepción of *InDesign Secrets.com* on how to install scripts).

To run a script, start by selecting something on your page. For example, **Figure 93b** shows a page of eight business cards. Before this file can go to the printer, the business cards must have individual crop marks applied. InDesign can produce crop marks per page, but not per item. Fortunately, there's a wonderful script to handle this chore.

After selecting the eight objects, double-click the Make Crop Marks script. In the dialog box that appears you can set preferences like the length of the crops, their distance from the object, line weight (in points), and more. Once everything is as you like it, click OK.

Not only will the script instantly draw the crop marks you specified, but it will create a new layer (myCropMarks) and assign the crops to that layer.

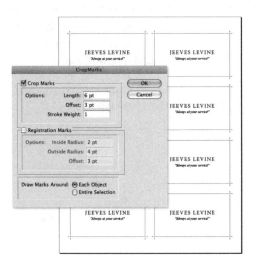

Figure 93b The CropMarks script dialog box allows you to set various attributes for your crops.

Using Keyboard Shortcuts to Trigger Scripts

If you find yourself using certain scripts frequently, you should consider assigning keyboard shortcuts to those scripts. (Fact is, if you find yourself doing *anything* frequently in InDesign, keyboard shortcuts are the way to go.) To create a keyboard shortcut, follow these steps:

1. From the Edit menu, choose Keyboard Shortcuts.

2. Click the New Set button and create and name your shortcut set, based on the Default set.

3. Choose Product Area > Scripts.

4. Click to highlight the script you wish to trigger. Make sure you select the proper script format, because the list will include both AppleScript and JavaScript (Mac OS) or VBScript and JavaScript (Windows) choices.

5. Type the key combination for the script shortcut into the New Shortcut field. Check to make sure the shortcut is Unassigned, which means you're free to use it. If the shortcut is previously assigned to another function, you can either continue to use the shortcut (thereby overwriting its previous assignment), or simply try using another key combination (**Figure 93c**).

Figure 93c Start at the top of the Keyboard Shortcuts dialog box by creating a New Set. From there, select the Product Area where the command normally lives. In this case, Scripts are found on the sixth line from the bottom of the drop-down menu. Click in the New Shortcut field and type the keystrokes you'd like to use to trigger the script. Click the Assign button. If the key combination you type has not been previously assigned to another shortcut, click the OK button to confirm your choice.

6. Leave Context selected to Default, and click the Assign button, which will move the shortcut into the Current Shortcuts area.

7. Click OK to exit the dialog box.

Now you're free to close the Scripts panel. Select an object on your page and give your keyboard shortcut a try. If the Script panel appears, you're in business. If it doesn't, reopen the Keyboard Shortcuts dialog box and try to figure out where you went wrong. Most often, users tend to forget to click the Assign button before clicking OK.

#94 Using Custom Stamps to Sign Forms in Acrobat Professional

Among the most significant inventions of the last 50 years, the Adobe Acrobat Electronic Form must surely rank. Gone are the days of squinting, hunchbacked, over tiny lines and boxes, trying to fill out complicated tax or credit applications, frozen with fear that one careless goof might ruin an otherwise perfect job.

Today, thanks to computers and the ubiquity of a strange file format called PDF, humankind can relax when filling out forms, confident in the knowledge that messy paperwork is a thing of the past.

But what about adding that final, all-important signature that graces your form before it's sent on its merry way? If you're like us, you hate having to print out a form, hand-sign it, jam it into a crummy envelope, find a stamp, and then snail-mail it to some town named Young America, Minnesota. Isn't there a better way?

Fortunately, there is. And once you learn this valuable tip, your life, like ours, will never be the same. We promise.

Create Your Own Acrobat Stamp

Start by digitizing your signature. Use a black pen on white paper, then either scan the signature or photograph it with a digital camera. If you have a pressure-sensitive tablet, even better. Once you've created an image file with your signature in it, open it in Photoshop. Use Adjustments > Threshold to make your blacks black and your whites white.

The next objective is to put your John Hancock on a transparent layer. If your signature is on a layer named Background, it's flat and lacks transparency. To convert it, hold down Option (Alt) and double-click the signature layer thumbnail. Your Background layer will now be named Layer 0, which means it can now support transparency.

Next, we need to delete the white background. Use the Magic Wand or Color Range command (Select > Color Range) to select all the white tones. Make sure to get inside letters that trap white, like a capital A, for example. After making an initial selection, use Select > Similar. This should pick up any other whites that were not originally selected. Press Delete or Backspace to remove white, leaving only the black signature. Photoshop's gray-and-white checkerboard should be visible behind your signature, indicating transparency.

Next, we'll check the size of your image. Too big is a pain to work with and too small is no good, either. Go to Image > Image Size. Make the file about three inches in width. 300 pixels per inch is the best, but don't fret if your file has a lower ppi. Click OK.

Now it's time to save your work. Don't forget to straighten and crop your signature. Acrobat Stamps can be almost any file format, but we want to choose one that will maintain the transparent background. We suggest saving the file as a TIFF and preserving transparency by selecting the Save Transparency check box (**Figure 94a**).

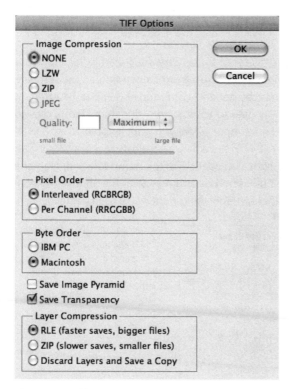

Figure 94a Although we chose to save our file as a TIFF, custom stamps can use almost any format. When saving as TIFF, make sure to check the Preserve Transparency box.

Back in Acrobat, choose Tools > Comment & Markup > Stamps > Create Custom Stamp. Choose a Category and name your Stamp. Also, select the "Down sample stamp to reduce file size" check box (**Figure 94b**). Click OK to close the Create Custom Stamp dialog box.

Figure 94b Clearly identify and categorize your stamp so that it's easy to find when you need it.

Now you're ready to give your stamp a try. You'll start by locating your custom signature stamp within Acrobat Pro. Depending on the software version you have, Stamps can generally be found under Tools > Comment & Markup > Stamps. Navigate to your custom signature stamp, click to select it, and then click once more where you want it applied.

Have a look at **Figure 94c** to see where we used it. Once you apply your stamp you can also resize it, if needed. With the stamp selected, grab one of the handles on the bounding box and drag with the Shift key to constrain its proportions. If everything works right, you'll be in digital heaven.

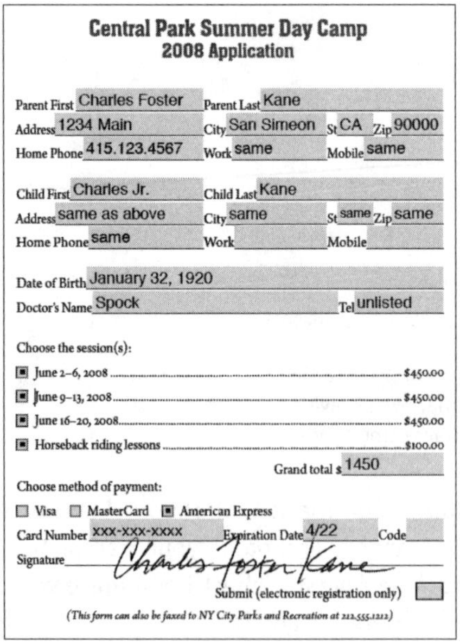

Central Park Summer Day Camp
2008 Application

Parent First Charles Foster   Parent Last Kane
Address 1234 Main   City San Simeon   St CA   Zip 90000
Home Phone 415.123.4567   Work same   Mobile same

Child First Charles Jr.   Child Last Kane
Address same as above   City same   St same   Zip same
Home Phone same   Work   Mobile

Date of Birth January 32, 1920
Doctor's Name Spock   Tel unlisted

Choose the session(s):

☒ June 2–6, 2008 .... $450.00
☒ June 9–13, 2008 .... $450.00
☒ June 16–20, 2008 .... $450.00
☒ Horseback riding lessons $100.00

Grand total $ 1450

Choose method of payment:

☐ Visa   ☐ MasterCard   ☒ American Express
Card Number XXX-XXX-XXXX   Expiration Date 4/22   Code
Signature _____   Submit (electronic registration only) ☐

(This form can also be faxed to NY City Parks and Recreation at 212.555.1212.)

Figure 94c If signing forms by hand has annoyed you for years, be prepared for the joy afforded by this simple addition to your toolbox.

#95 Creating Flash Web Galleries in Bridge

On the Adobe Bridge list of greatest feats is its ability to create Web galleries that use Flash technology. Once the sole province of Photoshop (or Flash itself), Bridge has taken over this handy task so that those owning any CS5 product can now produce professional Web galleries by choosing from among a number of built-in choices.

To begin, open Bridge and go to Window > Workspace > Output, or click the Output button at the top of the main application window. In the top row of the Output drawer, click the Web Gallery button. Click Template > Lightroom Flash Gallery and Style > Flash gallery (default) (**Figure 95a**).

Figure 95a The Output drawer is the first stop on your way to your very own Flash Web gallery.

Use the Folders drawer in the far-left column to navigate to the folder of images you want to use for your gallery. The images in the folder you select will populate the Content drawer at the bottom of the Bridge window. Click to select any or all of the images in this drawer for your Web gallery. The images you select will be displayed above in the Preview drawer (**Figure 95b**).

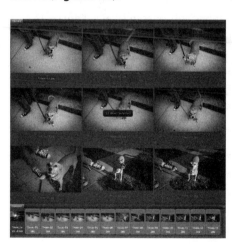

Figure 95b The images selected in the Content drawer will be displayed temporarily in the Preview drawer. Clicking Refresh Preview in the Output drawer replaces the thumbnails with a preview of your Flash gallery.

Pick a File, Almost Any File

One of our favorite features of Web galleries is the way Bridge automatically converts any file for use on the Web. Not that you couldn't do a better job manually, but here's the deal.

All popular graphics formats are okay. This includes TIFF, PSD, EPS, PDF, AI, and PICT. Bridge can even convert DNG and other major raw formats. Convert to what, you ask? Oh, this is where the "you could probably do a better job manually" part comes in. That's because all files, regardless of their content, are converted to simple JPEGs by Bridge. This means that images with large, flat areas of color that would typically be optimized best as GIFs become JPEGs. Likewise, files with transparency that would best be converted manually to PNGs or GIFs are also turned into JPEGs.

In other words, if high-quality Web optimization is essential to your galleries, you'll need to roll up your sleeves and optimize your images manually. If you're looking for quick (and a touch dirty) Web galleries, though, and can overlook a less-than-pixel-perfect job, you've come to the right place.

The Site drawer provides fields for adding text to your gallery. These mostly self-explanatory fields can be filled out or not, as you wish. To see how and where this information is used, click the Refresh Preview button in the Output drawer, which generates a new drawer, named Output Preview (**Figure 95c**).

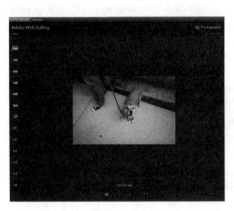

Figure 95c Clicking the Refresh Preview button in the Output drawer displays your Web gallery in the Output Preview drawer.

The Color Palette Drawer and Beyond

Beneath the Site drawer is the Color Palette drawer. This drawer is where you specify colors for things like your text, your background, and your controls. Clicking the small color swatch displays the Colors dialog box (Mac OS) or the Color palette (Windows). Here you specify the colors you'd like applied to these various components of your Web gallery page. You can click either the Refresh Preview [Refresh Preview] or Preview in Browser [Preview in Browser] buttons to see your color choices.

Beneath the Color Palette drawer is the Appearance drawer. This drawer is where you set the pixel size for slideshow images, gallery images, and thumbnails, and choose their respective image quality and layout (**Figure 95d**).

Figure 95d Use the Appearance drawer to set how and where your gallery images and thumbnails display.

The last stop on the Web gallery tour is the Create Gallery drawer. This is where you tell Bridge how and where to save your gallery. Galleries can be saved locally on your computer or automatically uploaded to an appointed Web server for immediate Internet display. Settings files can be saved by clicking the Save Preset Name button found to the right of the Upload Location > Custom drop-down menu. To save your Web gallery or to upload it to a server, click the Save or Upload buttons at the very bottom of the Save Location drawer (**Figure 95e**).

Figure 95e The Create Gallery drawer is your last stop before saving or uploading your Flash Web gallery.

Saving Your Gallery Style

Once you go to the trouble of customizing the style of your Web gallery, you'll want to save its many settings for future use. To do so, click the Save Style icon in the Output drawer. Clicking this button will invoke the New Style dialog box, where you can give your custom-gallery style settings a descriptive name.

#96 Creating PDF Contact Sheets with Bridge

The Trouble with Folders

Much to our chagrin, folders and their contents are completely removed from Bridge's PDF Contact Sheet feature. That's because the software has no way to look inside folders or subfolders of images and include them among other images in your document.

This means that if your PDF contact sheet needs to include images in lower-level folders or subfolders, you'll need to either move them to the same level as other upper-level images, or build separate contact sheets for each folder or subfolder.

If we had a dollar for every time we've been asked, "What happened to the Create InDesign Contact Sheet command in Bridge?" we'd be rich. Granted, ditching this feature seems like a goof to many, but at least Adobe had the decency not to ditch it completely. In the wake of its demise, Adobe generously left users with the next best thing: a Create PDF Contact Sheet command in Bridge. Sadly, most users are ignorant of its existence. As a public service to contact sheet aficionados everywhere, we offer this tip.

Start by clicking the PDF button in the Output drawer of the Output workspace. After highlighting the images you wish to use, click the Template drop-down menu to select from among the two available contact sheet configurations: 4 x 5 or 5 x 8. A word of explanation is in order here. The dimensions 4 x 5 and 5 x 8 refer to the number of vertical columns by the number of horizontal rows on your contact sheet. They do *not* refer to the size of the paper you'll be printing to, as seen here in the Document drawer (**Figure 96a**).

Figure 96a The Document drawer is used to tell Bridge how to configure the basics of your contact sheet.

Once you've conquered the Document drawer, you'll need to open and address the remaining six drawers found below. Those drawers are (in order displayed by default): Layout, Overlays, Header, Footer, Playback, and Watermark (**Figure 96b**).

Figure 96b Fear not the remaining six drawers seen here. Most of the fields are easy to fill out without mussing your do.

Navigating these drawers is mostly self-explanatory. If there's something you don't understand, our advice is to give it your best shot, and then check it against either the PDF Preview or your final PDF document.

Before you know it you'll have reached the final Save button and its corresponding View PDF After Save check box (**Figure 96c**). We think you'll know what to do when you arrive here.

Figure 96c The end of the road when it comes to creating PDF contact sheets in Bridge CS5. Have a cold one on us.

One last word of advice. Like with the Web galleries, if you've spent precious time customizing your PDF contact sheet template, it behooves you to create a preset of your settings to come back to in the future. To do this, click the tiny Save Template icon on the right side of the Output drawer.

CHAPTER ELEVEN

Using the CS Live Services

When you buy a new car, the moment you drive it off the dealer's lot, it begins to depreciate in value. Computer software and cars are quite different, of course, but technology changes quickly. By the time a new version of the Creative Suite is mastered to discs, reproduced, packaged, and shipped, it can be argued that what was the best possible version when the engineers did their final testing and the product was deemed "final" might not meet a need that arose between the software's ship date and the time you upgrade. Online updates have made keeping software current much easier and more immediate, but there are several things that the Web and cloud-based computing can do that software installed on your computer can't. These capabilities simply can't be packaged in a shrink-wrapped box. Web-based services complement, extend, and complete an already powerful software package.

Adobe's online services include Acrobat.com for file sharing and online meetings, Buzzword for collaborative online word processing, BrowserLab for cross-platform Web-site testing, CS Review for integrated remote document review and commenting, SiteCatalyst NetAverages for Web analytics, and more. Collectively, these services are referred to as CS Live, and they're yours to use free for one year from the time you register your copy of CS5 Design Premium. All you need is an Adobe ID (See Tip #5, "Setting Up an Adobe ID").

#97 Placing Buzzword Documents in InDesign

If you've never heard of Buzzword, don't despair. Years ago when free word processors were first making their way to the Web, a small group of Boston developers decided to build a Flash-based solution. Fast and elegant, the online software was named Buzzword. It wasn't long before Buzzword caught the eye of Adobe Systems, which bought the product for inclusion in its Acrobat.com Web site.

Among Buzzwords' strengths is its ability to allow multiple authors to collaborate on the same document. Buzzword also handles graphics well, making it a good candidate for simple office newsletters or flyers.

Today, Buzzword documents can also be placed with ease into InDesign CS5. To start, go to the File menu in InDesign CS5 and choose Place from Buzzword. After logging in to Acrobat.com with your Adobe ID, you'll be presented with the Place Buzzword Documents dialog box (**Figure 97a**).

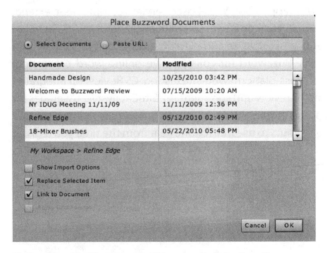

Figure 97a The Place Buzzword Documents dialog box allows you to select from a variety of options, including placing multiple documents based on their Web location.

After choosing a document and its options, click OK. The document will quickly download from the Buzzword server to your InDesign document in the form of the typical Place Cursor. Click once more to place your text as you would normally.

Selecting the Show Import Options check box invokes a dialog box that looks like the Microsoft Word Import Options dialog box that InDesign has used for years (**Figure 97b**). Among the many features of this voluntary stopover is the ability to map incoming paragraph and character styles to those already resident in your InDesign document.

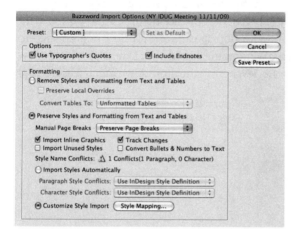

Figure 97b Although daunting at first glance, the Buzzword Import Options dialog box is surprisingly understandable provided you stare at it long enough.

#98 Creating an Online Review

If you've grown weary of waiting on design clients to slog through the old respond-and-review dance, the new CS Review service might be your salvation. Working in real time, this CS Live component allows you to upload your latest masterpiece to a shared Adobe server, where you and your client can both chat (that is, type) about its pros and cons. Other files can even be added to the review to support your discussion.

When you're ready to begin, start by clicking the CS Live button in the upper-right corner of Photoshop, Illustrator, InDesign, or Premiere Pro. You could also open the Window menu and go to Extensions > CS Review. Select the Create New Review item in the drop-down menu (**Figure 98a**).

Figure 98a To initiate an online review, click Create New Review in the CS Live drop-down menu.

Clicking the Create New Review button will open the Create New Review dialog box. Here you name your review and tell it whether or not to use the currently active document (**Figure 98b**).

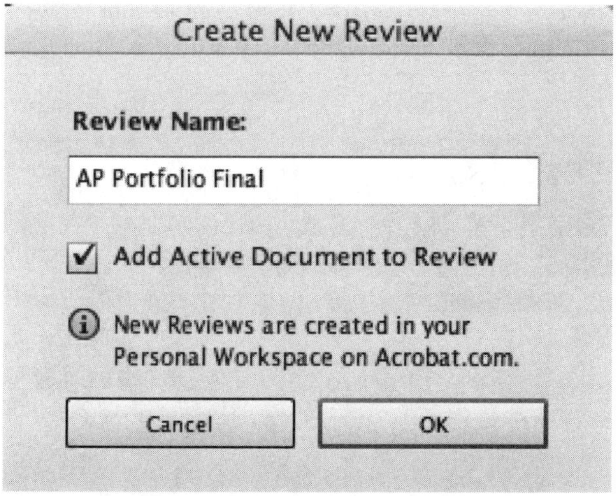

Figure 98b Use the Create New Review dialog box to name your review and to indicate if it uses the active document.

The next screen to appear is the Upload Settings dialog box (**Figure 98c**). Use this dialog box to indicate the specific pages (or parts) of your document you'd like to review, and whether the quality of the page snapshots should be Low, Medium, or High. The Intent menu lets you choose between Web or Print.

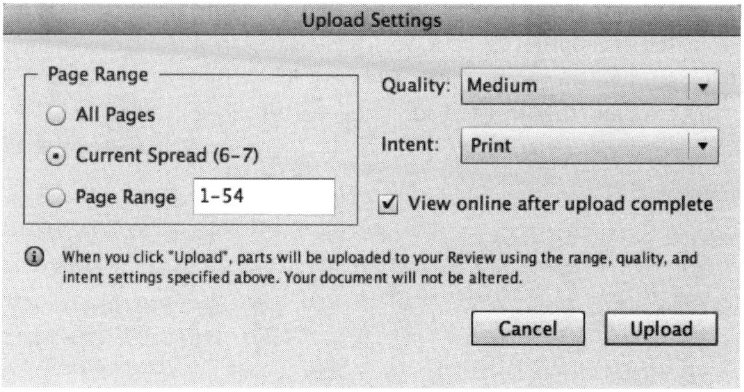

Figure 98c The Upload Settings dialog box is where you tell the software which pages to upload, what quality to use, and what their intent is.

Who's In? Who's Out?

To initiate a CS Review, you must subscribe to Adobe's CS Live services. CS Live services are available on a complimentary basis by registering your CS5 product or by signing up online by April 30, 2011. For more information about these services, log on to Acrobat.com. To participate or respond to an online review, you need only a free Acrobat.com account.

Once your review pages are uploaded, they open in your browser on Acrobat.com (**Figure 98d**). It's from this window that comments are added.

Figure 98d You conduct your review in the main window on Acrobat.com.

The next step is to invite your client or clients to participate in the review. Clicking the Share File button at the bottom left of the screen invokes the Share dialog box (**Figure 98e**). Note that participants can be invited as coauthors or reviewers. Reviewers can add and delete their own comments; coauthors can add and delete their own and others' comments, and they can add additional parts to the overall review.

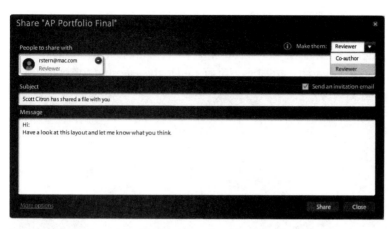

Figure 98e The Share dialog box is where you go to send e-mail invites to those you'd like to participate in the review. Clicking the Options button allows you to extend sharing to others.

To add comments to a review, click on the green Add Comment button in the navigation bar of the main window, or select it from the Review menu. Comments can apply to the entire layout or to specific areas for review. In **Figure 98f** we've highlighted the inset photo and written a query about its page position.

Figure 98f The Add a Comment cursor highlights a specific area, seen here as a red rectangle, for discussion.

To make reviewing even more intuitive, each reviewer's comment has a Jump To and Reply button at the bottom (**Figure 98g**). Clicking Reply produces a small window for entering your comment reply. Clicking Jump To takes you to the area being discussed in the snapshot and enlarges it.

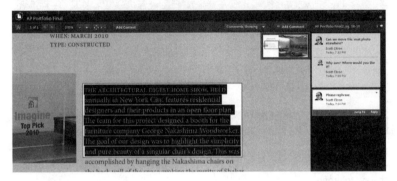

Figure 98g Here we can see how clicking Jump To enlarges the area being discussed, and highlights its text.

Meanwhile, back in InDesign CS5, the CS Review panel maintains a real-time connection with what's happening remotely on Acrobat.com. As pages are viewed and comments added, the panel keeps a running account of the activity for each review (**Figure 98h**). The icons (left to right) indicate the number of persons the review is shared with and the number of persons currently engaged in the review, the number of times the Review has been viewed, and the number of comments made.

Figure 98h The CS Review panel does an excellent job of keeping the designer apprised of the activity on the review. Here the top review is highlighted, indicating it's currently active.

#99 Screen Sharing via Adobe ConnectNow

Sending a PDF to your clients is a great way to show them a color version of a project in progress—but once it's been sent off via e-mail, follow-up is often complicated. It invariably involves another e-mail or a phone call in which your customers describe the PDF and discuss desired changes or bring up questions. A face-to-face conversation would be ideal, but it isn't always practical or possible. However, with the Share My Screen feature built into most of the CS5 applications, you can quickly share your screen with clients or colleagues so they can see exactly what you see, and vice-versa (**Figure 99a**).

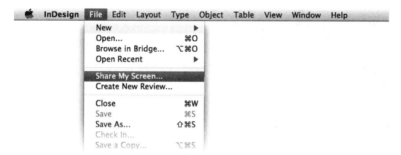

Figure 99a The Share My Screen feature is available from the File menu in InDesign, Photoshop, Illustrator, Dreamweaver, and Flash Professional. In Acrobat 9 Pro, it's also under the File menu, but within the Collaborate submenu.

Share My Screen launches your browser and connects you to Adobe's ConnectNow screen-sharing service that allows you to create online meeting rooms where you can host meetings, share your screen, or control another meeting attendee's screen. A plug-in is required to enable screen sharing. Once you've logged in with your Adobe ID, you'll be prompted to install the plug-in, if you haven't already. The installation is quick and seamless.

Once you've logged in to ConnectNow, your meeting room is assigned a default (but customizable) URL that your clients and colleagues use to join you for an online meeting. ConnectNow will also send an e-mail invitation to everyone you invite to the meeting, including a link to the meeting room URL. The people attending your meeting won't need an Adobe ID—they can simply log in as guests—but they're required to install the ConnectNow plug-in.

CS Review vs. ConnectNow

While CS Review offers a remote commenting and review process with the benefit of full integration into applications like InDesign, the process is not "live." Files are available on Acrobat.com for client and colleagues to review at a convenient time, but there's no immediacy. A ConnectNow meeting allows the kind of dynamic, impromptu brainstorming and feedback many of us are used to in a face-to-face meeting.

Alternate Point of Entry

Depending on whether you already have an Adobe ID, and sometimes whether you're currently logged in via the CS Live panel, you may not go directly to the ConnectNow Web page. Instead, you'll be redirected into Acrobat.com. In that case, click the Meetings option in the top of the window, then click the Go to My Meeting button. Sharing requires setting up a meeting between yourself and at least one other person.

Seating Is Limited

The free screen sharing available from the ConnectNow service is limited to three people per meeting room—that's you and two others. If you need more than that, you can sign up for a paid Acrobat.com account and host online meetings with up to 15 attendees at a time.

When you activate screen sharing—which you can limit to just document windows or a specific application, or expand to everything going on your computer screen—the ConnectNow interface "falls away" on your end except for a floating panel in which you can see some of the "pods" that support the meeting (**Figure 99b**). These include an Attendees pod, where you can see who's in the meeting with you, a Chat pod where you can type messages to all attendees or a specific person, and a Webcam pod where you can allow ConnectNow access to your Webcam and add audio/video conferencing capability to the meeting.

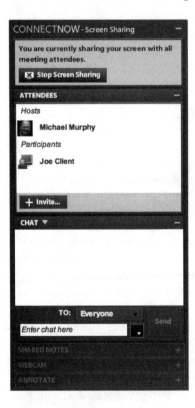

Figure 99b The ConnectNow panel floats atop all other windows on the host's computer during a ConnectNow meeting.

The people attending your meeting view the interface in their browser, with the majority of the window taken up by what's on your screen. Surrounding that are the Chat, Webcam, and other pods, consolidated in a single window (**Figure 99c**).

Figure 99c An InDesign document shared via ConnectNow, as seen in a meeting attendee's browser.

At any point, you can also annotate what's on the screen with highlights, text callouts, and drawn shapes (**Figure 99d**) by clicking Start in the Annotate pod. This freezes the screen to its current display and opens up the Annotation toolbar, from which you choose the tools you need to mark up the snapshot of the screen being displayed. You can click the toolbar's Save icon to save a screen shot of the marked-up image to document the notes and changes. Click Stop to exit Annotation mode and return to live screen sharing.

Figure 99d An annotated screen image with highlighted changes in ConnectNow.

Open Door Policy

As attendees enter your meeting, you'll be given the option to accept or decline their entry. If they log in with an Adobe ID, you can also opt to accept them every time they log in, so they can always enter your meetings in the future.

Hide the Gray Box

As a meeting host, you see your screen normally with the compact ConnectNow panel floating over everything. That panel may be unobtrusive to you, but what your attendees see is just a patterned gray rectangle where that panel appears on your screen. This might be distracting or confusing to your guests, so consider minimizing the panel while you're sharing your on-screen activity. If a chat message, note, or other information gets added to any of the pods in the panel while it's minimized, you'll get a visual cue—like a bouncing icon in the Mac OS's dock—that the panel needs your attention.

#100 Tracking Web and Mobile Trends with SiteCatalyst NetAverages

Although a word like *analytics* doesn't play into a designer's typical vocabulary, the rapid migration of content from the printed page to the Web and mobile platforms is likely to bring it more into our project discussions at the planning stage—just as we all had up-front discussions about paper stock, trim size, and number of Inks when print stood alone in the publishing landscape. As the final tip in this book, it's fitting that we look at Web analytics, which will greatly influence our project planning and impact our design decisions in the coming years.

In the past, there was greater control over the deliverable—a newspaper ad ran in a specific newspaper at a given size, *on paper*; a catalog went out in the mail to a defined list of recipients who browsed through it page by page *on the paper we printed it on*. Now, of course, a newspaper or catalog can be distributed on the Web. But that's not a simple change in distribution media because there isn't an equivalent for a standard paper stock when you're publishing content via the Web. The "paper" is a browser, and we don't get to pick which one displays our content—the reader does.

To further complicate things, mobile device use has exploded, and smartphones and tablets are poised to become people's primary and preferred way to access online content. There are already several competing front-runners in the mobile device arena and there are different platforms and different standards. The effect is like asking a designer to design a newspaper or catalog that must be deliverable on any paper stock, at any physical size, and look great in both portrait and landscape orientations.

That's a pretty tall order, and what designers need before they can take on these new challenges is a frame of reference as to which browsers, operating systems, and devices have enough market share to warrant influence on how they optimize and structure their online and mobile designs. SiteCatalyst NetAverages—part of the CS Live online services—provides fast, up-to-date access to that kind of data.

When you first use your Adobe ID to log in to SiteCatalyst NetAverages—by either clicking on that option in the CS Live menu or choosing Window > Extensions > Access CS Live—you're presented with a snapshot of the top yearly desktop trends (**Figure 100a**). The trends include the largest increased or decreased prevalence of operating systems, browser versions, Flash Player installations, and so on, over the past year. You can switch to a monthly view for more recent trends, and you can click the Mobile button in the site's top menu bar to view the yearly and monthly trends for mobile devices.

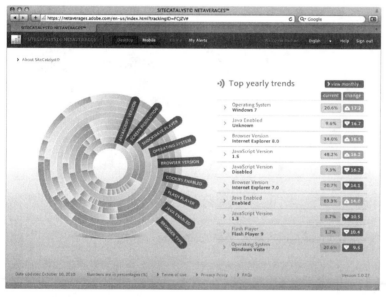

Figure 100a SiteCatalyst NetAverages' Top Yearly Trends overview screen for desktop browsers indicating the percentage change for each over the year.

For more granular-level information, SiteCatalyst NetAverages uses a Flash-based, visual display of data when you want to drill down into specifics. Simply click on the appropriate radiating labels such as Browser Version (**Figure 100b**) or switch to the Mobile tab and choose Operating System (**Figure 100c**) to view statistics for that subset of data.

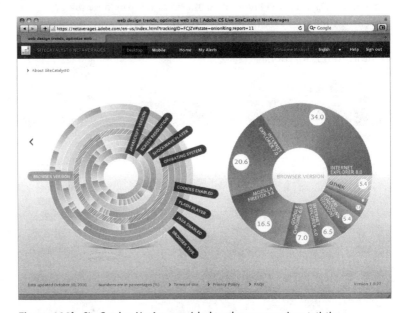

Figure 100b SiteCatalyst NetAverages' desktop browser version statistics.

Figure 100c SiteCatalyst NetAverages' mobile operating system statistics with a detail pop-up showing percentage changes from the previous month and year.

Click on a specific piece of data in that graph (a specific mobile device operating system's percentage of use, for example), and you drill further down into specifics showing changes since the previous month or year (**Figure 100d**).

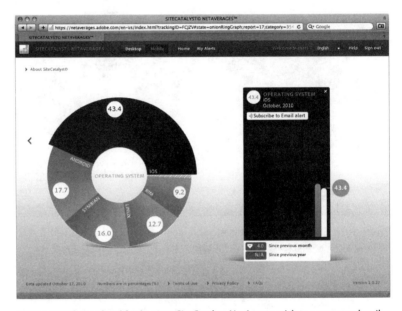

Figure 100d One level further into SiteCatalyst NetAverages' data, you can subscribe to e-mail alerts for changes in a specific trend.

At this point you can subscribe to an e-mail alert about this particular piece of data by targeting a percentage that's meaningful to you (**Figure 100e**). For example, you may want to know when the Apple iPhone/iPad's iOS mobile operating system reaches 50 percent of the market, or when Google's Android OS reaches 25 percent. These may be strategic game-changers for the resources and level of support you throw behind devices with these operating systems, and you'll want to know as soon as data reflects that they've hit your target.

•)) My alerts

	current	target
Operating System iOS	43.4%	⚠ 50.0%
Operating System Android	17.8%	⚠ 25.0%

Figure 100e SiteCatalyst NetAverages' list of requested e-mail alerts comparing current trends to the targeted percentages you specify. When a data point reaches your target, you'll be notified at the e-mail address used for your Adobe ID.

Your purchase of CS5 Design Premium includes free access for one year to this real-time data on the current state of Web usage, browser types, operating systems, mobile device profiles, and screen resolution. This data helps inform your content-creation choices and reduces guesswork early in the creative process. With it, you can quickly determine the levels of browser and device support that will best serve your audience or your client's needs in the ever-changing media landscape.

Index

Dreamweaver *(continued)*
WebKit layout engine, 186
Widget Browser, 188–193
workspace button in, 10
droplets, defined, 298
DTBook format, using with
EPUB, 166

E

easing styles
Bounce, 241
Elastic, 241
Linear, 241
Power, 241
Sine, 241
using with transitions, 241
eBooks. *See* EPUB
effects, repeating in Flash
Catalyst, 242
Elastic easing style, 241
email addresses, using as
watermarks, 30
encoding for Flash Catalyst, 230
envelope master pages,
creating in InDesign, 131
EPUB
adding metadata, 164
CSS files, 163, 166
DTBook format, 166
export options, 164–167
exporting for, 163–167
handling covers, 163
inserting pages, 163
organizing sections, 166
preparing documents for,
163–164
setting JPEG options, 165
specifying InDesign
styles, 163
splitting documents, 163
table of contents, 164

TOC style, 166–167
XHTML format, 166
Exchange, 12
for Dreamweaver, 13
for Flash, 13
for Illustrator, 13
for InDesign, 13
for Photoshop, 13
widgets on, 189
exporting. *See also*
importing
to FLA from InDesign, 158
HTML files from
InDesign, 157
interactive PDF with video,
159–162
to SWF from InDesign,
156–157
extensions, downloading, 12–13
Eyedropper tool, changing
behavior of, 121

F

Fidelity options
Blend, 223
Filters, 222
Gradients, 223
Text, 222
files, opening, 25. *See also*
linked files
Fill dialog box, opening in
Photoshop, 37–38
fills
adding in Illustrator, 120
as appearances, 118
filters. *See also* Photoshop
filters; Smart Filters
Chalk & Charcoal, 62
Lens Correction, 75–76
final render process, using
with Photoshop filters, 69

fireplace illustration, 98, 100
FLA files
ActionScript in, 158
exporting to FLA, 158
interactive features in, 158
Flash Catalyst. *See also* Design
workspace
adding sound, 230–232
adding transition
effects, 238
adding video, 230–232
Align to Pixel Grid, 221
On Application Start
interaction, 237
button interaction,
236–237
Code workspace, 218
components, 215, 233
converting wireframes to
components, 235
creating components,
233–235
creating interactions,
236–237
creating scrollbar, 233–234
Design workspace,
216–217
drag-and-drop
components, 214
easing styles for
transitions, 241
editing components in, 234
editing vector images,
227–228
Edit-in-Place mode, 234
features of, 214–215
Fidelity options for
Illustrator, 222
font embedding, 243
Illustrator Import options,
222–224
pages, 215

INDEX

RGB working space, changing to, 3

Rollover appearance, adding to buttons, 148

rotating objects in perspective, 96

rotation cursor, using in InDesign, 138

rounded corners, defining, 205–207. *See also* Corner effects

round-trip editing
in Illustrator CS5, 227–228
in Photoshop CS5, 228–229
preserving fidelity in, 228–229
using in Flash Catalyst, 227–229

S

scaling with Transform tool, 83

scratch disks, setting up, 6

screen sharing, 323–325

screen shots
delaying in BrowserLab, 182
saving in BrowserLab, 182

scripts
CropMarks, 304
triggering, 304–305
using in InDesign, 303–305

selecting versus targeting, 119

selections
loading images as, 37
making in Photoshop, 48–51

servers, adding for Web sites, 170–172. *See also* test server

shadows, defining, 205–207

Shape Builder tool
Color Swatch Preview, 106
vs. Live Paint, 105
vs. Pathfinder, 105, 107
using in Illustrator, 105–107

Shape tool, using in Illustrator, 106

Shockwave-Flash (SWF) format, 268
ActionScript in, 158
exporting to, 156–157

silhouettes. *See* Refine Edge tool

Sine easing style, 241

SiteCatalyst NetAverages service, 17, 326–331

sites. *See also* Web sites
adding servers for, 170–172
column layouts of, 174

sky, decreasing color noise in, 72

Slice Selection tool, using in Illustrator, 126

slide shows, creating in InDesign, 146–150

Smart Filters, applying, 73. *See also* filters

Smart Guides
using with artboards, 116
using with perspective grids, 92

Smart Objects
converting video to, 68
source files, 286
using in Photoshop, 70–74
using to link images, 285–287

Smooth Transition Options panel, 239–240

social networking sites, exporting to, 26

Sorenson Spark codec, 230

Span/Split columns, setting up in InDesign, 134–136

Spot Healing Brush tool, using with Content-Aware Fill, 39

Spry accordion code, 186

sRGB default color space, 3

St. Peter's Basilica, 46–47

stamps, using with forms, 306–308

starter layouts
HTML5, 202–203
using in Dreamweaver, 173–175

stationery packages, creating in InDesign, 131

strokes
adding arrowheads to, 103–104
adding in Illustrator, 120
as appearances, 118
dashed, 101–102
distribution in Illustrator, 124

swatches. *See* color swatches

SWF (Shockwave-Flash) format, 268
ActionScript in, 158
exporting to, 156–157

symbols
adding animations to, 260–262
saving artwork as, 123
using on perspective grid, 95–96
using with Flash Catalyst, 222–223

T

tablet.css file, 211–212
targeting appearances, 119
templates
downloading, 175
using in InDesign, 131
test server, setting up for
Dreamweaver, 194. *See also*
servers
text, modifying on perspective
grids, 95
text frames, animating in
InDesign, 154
"Thirsty" animation, 152,
154–155
TIFFs
opening in Camera
Raw, 34
processing in Camera
Raw, 24–25
Timeline panel, using in Flash
Catalyst, 238
Timing panel, using with
animations, 155
TLF (Text Layout Format),
using in Flash Professional,
252–253
TLF text, threading, 253
Tour state, using with button
interaction, 236–237
Transform tool, scaling
with, 83
transition effects, adding with
Timeline panel, 238
transitions
adjusting duration
of, 241
adjusting timing of, 242

easing styles, 241
establishing in Flash
Catalyst, 239–242
repeating effects, 242
trends, tracking on Web,
326–331
type
enhancing in Flash
Professional, 252–253
improved composition
options, 254
type layer, copying, 64

U

updates, keeping up with,
19–20

V

vanishing point
for 3D mock-up, 82–85
moving in perspective
grids, 91
vector images, editing in Flash
Catalyst, 227–228
video. *See also* PDF with video
applying Photoshop filters
to, 67–69
applying texture to, 68–69
converting to Smart
Object, 68
encoding for Flash
Catalyst, 230
importing into Flash
Catalyst, 231
in interactive PDFS, 160
playing in Flash
Professional, 265–267

setting properties for Flash
Catalyst, 232
Video Import Wizard, 266

W

watermarks
adding in Bridge, 30
adding in Photoshop, 30
using email addresses
as, 30
Web
browsing with
Dreamweaver, 186–187
creating artwork for,
123–124
Web analytics, 326–331
Web animation, creating in
InDesign, 151–155
Web designs, 164, 183–185
Web galleries, creating in
Bridge, 309–311
Web graphics, scalable,
125–126
Web sites. *See also* sites
Acrobat.com CS Live
service, 17
Adobe Developer
Connection, 174
Adobe Labs, 13
Adobe Marketplace &
Exchange, 12–13
Adobe TV, 16
Kuler support for
Dreamweaver, 16
scripts, 303
templates, 175
testing servers, 194
WordPress, 194

WATCH
READ
CREATE

Meet Creative Edge.

A new resource of unlimited books, videos and tutorials for creatives from the world's leading experts.

Creative Edge is your one stop for inspiration, answers to technical questions and ways to stay at the top of your game so you can focus on what you do best—being creative.

All for only $24.99 per month for access—any day any time you need it.

creative
edge

peachpit.com/creativeedge